IMAGINE A NEW YOU IN 30 DAYS!

JUSTIN SACHS

Motivational PRESS®
LEADERS IN GLOBAL PUBLISHING

Published by Motivational Press, Inc.
1777 Aurora Road
Melbourne, Florida, 32935

www.MotivationalPress.com

Manufactured in the United States of America.

ISBN: 978-1-62865-264-2

CONTENTS

SUCCESS

SELF HELP

HEALTH

RELATIONSHIPS

IMAGINE...

Lew Bayer

Einstein said that the most important decision you'll ever make is whether you live in a friendly universe or a hostile universe--in a positive or negative universe. **Imagine for a minute...What would happen if each of us woke up tomorrow and made the decision that we live in a friendly, positive universe?**

Would we be kinder? Happier? More generous? More polite? I think definitely "YES" to all of these. Unfortunately we can't control what everyone else thinks or feels, but what if we start with ourselves and personally make this decision. Right now, before you read any further, make the decision that you live in friendly universe. Write down, or say aloud, *"I live in a friendly universe".* Repeat this statement a few times with surety and emotion. And then expand on this thought, say, *"I live in a friendly universe, I am surrounded by friendly people, I am positive and friendly", "There is kindness all around me", I live in a friendly universe".* Commit to making these statements your personal mantra or add them to your daily affirmations. I promise you'll be amazed and encouraged by what happens next.

As a civility expert for the past 18 years, I have frequently found myself in very uncivil or hostile environments. A side effect of this is I often focused on searching out positivity and civility so as not to get mired down in the messy, sometimes dark aspects of the human condition. I'm actively seek for ways to change this and make the world a better place. Over the years I've lectured and published books on respect, social competence and etiquette. I've devised civility training materials, assessed toxicity, counselled others as to how to be respectful, and co-developed civility initiatives and anti-bullying campaigns etc. Absolutely some of these strategies work. But time and time again I have seen how making positive change doesn't have to be a complicated, expensive or time-consuming endeavor. And you don't have to take intensive training to be a change-maker. Change starts with the individual. It is actually simple and costs very little. Each of us need only choose to believe that we live in a friendly universe. It's really that easy.

If you consciously make this decision and choose to believe that the universe is friendly, your personal experience will change in immeasurable ways. I've highlighted a few of these here.

» **You will begin to assume the best of people and as a result give more of your own best self.**

If you come into every situation and conversation assuming that people are basically friendly, your demeanor changes. Rather than being protective and defensive, you'll be open and this will show in your body language, your tone of voice, and your overall approach. And when you are positive, happy, and friendly, people will usually respond to you in the same way. It's not that you should not be cautious or careful- it's true that not everyone has good intentions and of course you want to be safe. But when you are in a generally safe environment, let's say at home or a friend's house or a workplace, try to always look for the best in people. As an example, when people are rude or behave in ways that don't meet your expectations, try not to immediately assume that they are intending to disrespect you. Instead, consider the other person before yourself. If your co-worker Bob is late for your meeting, don't assume he's trying to make you angry or that he doesn't care about your time. Tell yourself that Bob is generally a decent person. Assume that he has a good reason for being late, and give him the benefit of the doubt. Greet

Bob warmly and give him an opportunity to apologize or explain. Don't make the whole encounter be about you and your feelings, focus on the desired outcome of the meeting. Do what you can to ease the experience for Bob. In doing so you bring your better self to the situation. You will present yourself as kinder, more restrained, understanding, and other-focused; these are the qualities that will help you achieve success in that situation. Berating Bob or sulking because you didn't get an apology will not facilitate cooperation or positive outcome. Remind yourself of the times you were late, and recall how rarely it was your intention to cause distress to others. If you would forgive yourself, surely you can forgive Bob. This approach can be applied to almost every perceived rudeness or social faux pas that you may encounter.

» **You will be less fearful and as a result be more present**

If you believe the universe is kind, you tend to be more positive and anticipate positive, happy experiences. In this way, rather than worry about all the terrible things that could happen, you instead imagine all the incredible things that could happen. It's not that you barge into dangerous situations blindly. And it's not that you assume nothing difficult or challenging will ever happen to you. Of course you still take precautions, e.g., get the necessary immunizations before you travel to a foreign country, keep a spare tire and tire jack in your car, bring along an Epi-pen if you have severe allergies, etc. But, when difficult or scary things do happen, you don't see these occurrences as insurmountable barriers. And you don't see them as the universe picking on you or some test you have to pass. Instead you approach these situations as opportunities to learn. Take the opportunity to use and build on your current knowledge and strengths. And you take stock of all the positive that potentially arises out of what seemed a negative, fear-filled experience.

One of the most profound examples of this concept in practice is the story of Immaculee Ilibagiza. Immaculee wrote a book called *Left to Tell: Discovering God Amidst the Rwandan Holocaust* (2006). The book is an autobiographical work detailing how Immaculee survived the Rwandan Genocide by hiding for 91 days with seven other Tutsi women in a small bathroom, no larger than 3 feet (0.91 m) long and 4 feet (1.2 m) wide with an area of 12 feet. The bathroom was concealed in a room behind a wardrobe in the home of a Hutu pastor. During the genocide, most of Ilibagiza's family was killed by Hutu Interahamwe soldiers: her mother, her father, and her two brothers. Besides herself, the only other survivor was her brother Aimable, who was studying out of the country in Senegal and did not know the war was going on. In *Left to Tell*, Ilibagiza shares how her faith guided her through her terrible ordeal, and describes her eventual forgiveness and compassion toward her family's killers. With respect to choosing opportunity over fear, Immaculee, even under daily threat of death, had the presence of mind to focus – not on her fear- but instead on the French/English dictionary (the only material possession she had) to learn English. Every day she silently memorized and repeated the words – and she taught herself to speak English. By believing that the universe intended that she should live, Immaculee chose to spend the precious time she had learning, rather than focusing on the fear she most certainly was experiencing. With recognition (and hope) that you never have to endure the same hardship Immaculee did, challenge yourself to determine that the universe is a friendly place and try to see the challenges you face as gifts of sorts. When you accept these experiences as opportunities to learn, and when you anticipate and seek out a silver lining, you are present in the moment and live more fully.

» **You will judge yourself and others less harshly and experience more love**

When you believe that most people are basically kind, thoughtful, and generous, it's easier acknowledge that you too are basically a friendly, positive, and good person. You're a good person, who is learning and occasionally makes mistakes. Making mistakes doesn't make you a bad person and this is the first step to forgiving yourself for poor choices you've made, to let go of grudges you've felt. It's necessary to forgive yourself before you can forgive others. Once you change your thinking patterns and your habits of mind, you will see that the things you look at will change. For example, if your habit is to see yourself as someone with no control, you will likely continue to give control to others. But if you change your story and see yourself as someone who has control, accept that in the past when you relinquished control you were doing the best with the knowledge and resources and skills that you had at that time. Forgive yourself and let go of that personal story. Remind yourself that you are different now, and that with your current knowledge, skills, and circumstances, you can take back control. Love and accept yourself as you are. This shift can start small, maybe you take control of what you eat or change the way you speak to yourself. An inspiring story that captures this is from self-development author and speaker Dr. Wayne Dyer. Dr. Dyer spoke often in his lectures about how his father had abandoned him when he was a baby. Left alone to care for three boys under the age of four, his 22 year old mother had the boys put in foster homes. As a result Wayne grew up with a deep hatred for his father.

In 1974, Dr. Dyer found out his father had been dead for ten years from cirrhosis of the liver from alcoholism. He decided to visit his father's grave in Biloxi, Mississippi and upon arriving, stood there for three hours. He stood at the grave and was filled with anger. But something came over him and just as he was about to end his visit, he said to his father: "From this moment on I send you love, and I forgive you for everything that you have done." He said that, while he couldn't understand why his father did what he did, he (Wayne) accepted that his father did the best he knew how to do with the skills and resources he (his father) had at that time. When Wayne walked away from his father's grave that day, he said everything in his life started to change. This strategy can work for you too. Forgive yourself and forgive others. Let go of judgment and choose to find the good- no matter how small, in yourself and others. Doing this will open you up to love yourself more, and receive love from others.

» **You will begin to recognize abundance and as a result feel more gratitude**

When you look at the world around you as friendliness and positivity, you suddenly start to see kindness– big and small- everywhere you look. You begin to focus on the happy and positive in your life. When your heart is open, you see blessings and understand that the universe is vast and abundant. You feel grateful and see that the possibilities for abundance are limitless. I remember my father saying to me "What gets watered grows" and I find this to be true. What you pay attention to, where you put your energy naturally expands your life. If you put your attention on, and energy into things that are positive you tend to experience more positivity. When you acknowledge that you have much to be grateful for, more abundance comes your way. This is the basis for the Law of Attraction. One way to start shifting to an attitude of gratitude is to make thankfulness a part of your everyday life. A few ways you can do this:

» Make it a habit to send at least one heartfelt, hand-written thank you cards out every week

» Before you go to bed at night, make a list of ten things you are thankful for

» Say a silent prayer, or statement of thanks for your food at mealtime

» Give something away every day; a compliment, a dollar to a stranger in need, 10 minutes of your full attention, something you don't need that someone else can use etc.

» Keep a log of all the unexpected gifts you receive from the universe and/or the world around you every day; a great parking spot, the last strawberry Danish, a smile from a stranger etc.

» **You will be able to give with no expectation of return and as a result experience more peace**

When you see the world as abundant, people as kind, and the universe as friendly, you worry less about what comes next. You start to feel a quiet confidence that the universe will provide. You know that you will be taken care of and that you will have enough of whatever you need. When you experience this peace, philanthropy and generosity become imbedded in everything you do. The more you feel comfort, and kindness, civility and grace, the more you are able to give these things. And because you get back what you give three-fold, you always have more to give. With practice you will be able to:

1. **Give with no expectation of return**: Give without knowing you might not be rewarded or acknowledged, and give knowing you may never recoup the time, money, or energy that you gave.
2. **Give what you value most**: For example, my current most prized commodity is time, so squeezing even 20 minutes extra out of a day for me is a huge challenge and sometimes very hard to give. But I have learned that the biggest return comes with the gifts that are hardest to relinquish.
3. **Give without being asked to**: It's hard to ask for help and for a range of reasons, people will often say no- even when they really need it. So, I find it is sometimes best just to take action. Help, support, jump in, and give however you can rather than spend a lot of time talking about what you could do and waiting for an invitation to do it.
4. **Give without measuring the gesture**: I often hear people say they only have a few dollars or 15 minutes isn't enough, or they can't commit to all 6 meetings. I'm of the opinion that something is usually better than nothing and often even the smallest gesture, a tiny kindness, or a few focused moments of attention, can have big impact.
5. **Give often**: Like any other behavior, giving- whether it's a kind word, a few minutes of your complete attention, a few dollars, etc., can become a habit. When exhibited consistently giving becomes part of your character.

6. **Give without judgment:** Don't be concerned about what anyone else is giving, and don't compare or assess why someone else gives - each gift has value. You don't always have to understand the gift, but do try to acknowledge the giver and appreciate the giving.

> *Lew Bayer is President & CEO of Civility Experts Worldwide and recognized as the leading expert on civility in the workplace. Lew believes that civility is its own reward and that we each have the power to choose civility. With this one choice, one kind word, one polite gesture, one minute of paying attention, we can ease the experience of others and make the world a better place.*

Grilled Shrimp and Corn Salad

Serves 4

Ingredients

For the salad:

1 pound of large shrimp, peeled and deveined

1 tablespoon extra virgin olive oil

2 heads Romaine lettuce, chopped

2 cups red cabbage, shredded

1/2 English cucumber, thinly sliced into half moons

4 ears sweet corn, husked, silks removed, scrubbed clean and kernels sliced off the cob

1 bunch scallions, cleaned and thinly sliced

2 large carrots, cleaned and thinly sliced

1/4 cup cilantro, thick stems discarded, roughly chopped

Coarse sea salt and freshly ground black pepper to taste

For the dressing:

1/4 cup aged Sherry vinegar

1 tablespoon Dijon mustard

1/2 teaspoon each kosher salt and freshly ground black pepper

1/2 cup extra virgin olive oil

Instructions

Place all of the salad ingredients in a large salad bowl.

In a blender add the Sherry vinegar, Dijon mustard, salt and pepper. Whir to blend. With the motor running slowly drizzle the olive oil into the blender jar and whir until emulsified.

Just before served pour the dressing over the salad and toss well to coat all of the ingredients. Serve immediately.

BUSINESS

MASTERING THE ART OF OPTIMAL TIME USE = BREAKTHROUGH BUSINESS SUCCESS

Terri Levine

If you are a typical business owner you may feel burnout from daily interruptions and constantly putting out fires in your business. You may not be accomplishing your business goals and getting frustrated. You have to spend a lot of time making it rain to find more customers yet at the same time you also have to handle the day-to-day operations of running your business. It might feel at times like a juggling act suspended above a tightrope.

There are a few critical ideas that can make all the difference to your business success and can alleviate the stress you may feel from your business. Once learned these simple tips will make a real difference to your bottom line, too!

The first tip has to do with your mindset. You always have a choice of how to react in any given moment. Reacting is actually something that can be learned. Your reaction can either create more time for you or it can take time from you and take away from your ability to find more customers. Answer this question honestly. Are you proactive or reactive? By proactive I mean that you have systems in place and you delegate appropriately and have written 10 year, 5 year, and 1 year business and personal goals. You have a marketing plan you follow and adhere to daily as well. By reactive I mean you are constantly putting out fires and doing damage control, you never leverage yourself. You spend your time being interrupted by people and activities. You lack systems, lack a team or have the wrong team. In other words you don't have your marketing planned out.

Which mode do you operate the most from? If you are like most business owners that I have coached, you will most likely notice that you operate reactively. If you learn to be more proactive and master a few skills to manage your time better so that you can improve your business. Now let's talk about how else we waste time.

We know the purpose of every business is to have customers and without selling products or services to customers we would not be in business. A lot of the business owners I work with spend too much of their time with customers who take up too much of their time and aren't top customers. Think about grading your customers using a system like this: customers who are "awesome" assign the letter "A". "A" means they refer others to you, they pay on time, they are courteous to you and your team and they appreciate your products/services. Continue grading your customers from there rating them all the way down to the letter "D" with "D" being "draining". "D" is a customer who takes up too much of your time or your staff's time, complains, doesn't pay on time, never refers others to you and takes up valuable resources.

Many business owners spend far too much time with "C" and "D" customers. You must free up your time so you have more time to dedicate to your "A" and "B" customers. Once you change your focus to "A" level customers they will spend more, return more frequently, refer more and ultimately will allow you to make more money with less effort.

So far we've given you more time for marketing and helped you focus. Now let's also create a bit more control of your time with a secret calendar system I have developed. I have all of my consulting clients us a time template. A time template is a customized outline of how you want your week to be organized. For example:

1. Block off the number of hours to see clients or patients (group them together) per day
2. Block off time to do paper work (group them together) per day
3. Block off phone time (some AM hours some afternoon)
4. Block off morning huddle time
5. Block off marketing time

I tell all my clients the first couple of weeks or months of shifting to a time template you will not be perfect. We are not looking for perfection. Do your best and know you are moving towards a calendar that allows focused, uninterrupted time to produce your most leveraged and optimized work.

In my experience, the biggest obstacle that interrupts a time template are phone calls. It is important you create a phone screening tool. Either have an administrative assistant screen your calls or create a web-tool or another form of automation to serve as such for you. You cannot speak to every prospective customer and must have a way of knowing who the right prospects you need to talk to. Be certain you handle telephone interruptions as well.

The other interrupters are people. People who walk into your office, for anything other than a true emergency, take you out of the flow of your work and interrupt your focus. To keep in flow and to accomplish your goals you want to educate your team about the advantages of uninterrupted time and the boundaries you need in place to be most productive.

One strategy I use and share with my clients is to work productively for 50 minutes of each hour and then to give myself a break 10 minutes as a reward for keeping focused and accomplishing my goals. During my productive work time my door is closed and my team knows I am not to be interrupted when it is shut. My phone is turned off, my email program, Skype, Facetime and anything else that could possibly interrupt my attention are closed down. I keep my commitment to be productive and use a timer to get my urgent tasks done in 50 minute blocks of time. Then I emerge having accomplished my goal and take a 10 minute break knowing I am moving towards my goals each hour of every day.

Another system I have integrated into my business that has made a big difference in reaching my goals and maintain my focus. I've also shared this system with clients and they thank me for instilling it and love the simplicity of it as well. I end every week with one quiet hour reflecting on the things I accomplished in the prior week and determine the most important goal or project I want to accomplish. I then decide what are the most important physical actions needed to move that project forward during the next week.

I'll spend this quiet time on a Friday afternoon planning the next week and reflecting on the past week. I will prioritize the upcoming week by first reviewing my mission and goals and decide what I need to accomplish the next week. I determine what actions will further my 1 year goals that I can accomplish this coming week by taking a look at the actions I've written down and asking myself "will these actions really help me reach my goals?". And if the answer is "yes" then I decide if I am the one who needs to take those actions or if they can be delegated to another member of my team. I must use my time, energy and skills doing what I can and delegate all other tasks and oversee them in order to dramatically increase revenue while actually reducing workload.

During this weekly check in I plan my calendar for the upcoming week to be certain I am using my time effectively. I check to see if all of my scheduled activities support my goals and my vision for my company. Just by stopping and taking the time to do this review I have dramatically improved my business.

I also re-check my vision every single week. Am I still inspired by my vision? Am I excited and eager to take actions to bring my business closer to achieving my goals? If our vision doesn't compel and excite us then it's time to change our visions. We have to resonate and be aligned with our visions so they magnetically pull us into action. We don't want to have to force ourselves to accomplish "to-do" tasks. Instead we want to feel passion and enthusiasm for doing what we love and moving towards our dreams.

Being excited about your vision and knowing what will help you achieve that vision makes it easy to determine your priorities. Anything that moves you towards your vision is a priority. Anything that blocks you from your vision is no longer important.

I suggest you sit down and look at your calendar for the past 30 days. Where have you been spending your time, energy, money and resources? You get what you focus on. Whatever you have been achieving, whatever you do and don't have, is a direct result of where you have or have not been focusing. By being aware of how you spend your time and your energy and resources, you can now consciously allocate calendar items that will match your vision with your newly established priorities.

Before adding another meeting to your calendar or a phone call to your list or an email to your "to do" list, stop to think how these things fit with your how they move you towards or away from your goals. You may notice, as most of my clients have, that a lot of your time is spent doing non-productive things that don't move you towards your real goals. By pre-planning your week you will finally stop those endless "to do" lists which are never really done until you are being put in the grave! Instead, have daily priorities that move you towards your goals - nothing more. And don't forget you are delegating those things that don't need your attention so that you do less. In fact you are turbo-charging your time by the clarity you have with your vision and your new focus on achieving your goals by taking the actions necessary to reach them. You are mastering the art of optimal use of time to produce results.

When I mentor a business I always share my top list of strategies to quickly help them feel like they are gaining control of their time. Clients quickly tell me they feel like they are getting their lives back and I know they have more time to focus on their business so they can make more revenue and profits for long-term success. Here are my mentoring time tips:

Mentor Terri's Time Tips:

1. Schedule all tasks on your calendar
2. Close your door when doing tasks
3. Turn off phones and email and other sound notifications when doing scheduled tasks
4. Do scheduled tasks during uninterrupted time
5. During uninterrupted time - NOTHING and NO ONE interrupts you - no phone calls, no texts, no visitors, no emails, etc.
6. One focus; one goal - this means no multi-tasking - when you multitask you are actually less productive and make more errors
7. Work on difficult tasks first thing in the morning - we are more productive first thing
8. 50 minutes on - 10 minutes off - work for 50 minutes continuously then take a 10 minute break stretching, getting water, taking a walk, making a personal call, meditating or anything that takes you away from work - productivity increases and so does creativity when you work this way.

Whenever a client asks me the "secret" to building a seven figure business and having a great life, I tell them this, "Spend your time focused on your vision. Do the things that move you closer to your vision every day. By doing those things over and over and over again you will achieve your goals." I think people are hoping I am going to give them some magic pill or formula. I am giving them something simple. Do the right things over and over again. The truth is many people spend their time, energy and money focused on doing the wrong things. They make mistakes with their marketing and how they invest their time and they spend hours speaking to the wrong prospects. They talk with the wrong customers, attend the wrong networking events, they hire the wrong mentors and invest in the wrong market. Learn from your mistakes quickly and move on so you can cut your losses and get your focus back on your vision. If you get off course go back and take the right actions that align with your goals. By taking the right physical actions over and over and over again consistently, I have been very successful in achieving a seven figure income and have maximized the use of my time so that I have been able to create the lifestyle I desire as well.

It's not about spending hours of your time in business. It's about finding the time to make it rain so you can get more customers which makes you more money. It's about having a vision. It's about taking focused actions. It's not about chasing shiny objects and trying every strategy under the sun. It is about being consistent and sustaining your effort, energy and intensity. It is about creating, planning and delegating time so you can properly execute actions to be successful long-term.

Your business success is not going to be magic and it is certainly not going to be luck. It is going to happen by design. The good news is that, unlike me, you don't have to go through all the trial-and-error I had to go through. I have given systems I created that already work for me and my clients. I wish that I had known this when I was struggling in my business. You can take these ideas to build your business that are proven to work in hundreds of other people's businesses. You will be relieved to know that your business can become more hands-free than you might have ever dreamed possible. You are on the verge of bigger profitability, more free time, less stress and more enjoyment from your business.

Are you ready? We've covered a lot so let me remind you of critical points. Get clear on your vision and realize YOU are responsible for making your vision a reality. How you choose to spend your time on tasks and people will determine your results. The actions you take will result in the outcomes you get. The strategies I shared with you can change your business today if you put them into action. Don't forget that you must do the right actions over and over again consistently and work your powerful action plan to get the results you desire.

What I have shared in this chapter is a goldmine of business mentoring advice. If you put these ideas to work today, I have no doubt you'll begin to see more success tomorrow. What I've shared with you is just the tip of the iceberg. There are hundreds of shortcuts, secrets, little-known tips, tools, strategies and tactics I'd love to teach you so you can get incredible growth and profits for the business of your dreams and have a great lifestyle, too.

Best-selling author, ***Dr. Terri Levine*** *was named one of the top ten coaching gurus in the world and the top female coach in the world and assists businesses worldwide with creating the right inner mindset and outer actions for business growth. Terri is a keynote speaker, popular TV personality and host of The Terri Levine Show: Business Advice You Can Take to The Bank.*

THE MOVIE-STAR METHOD FOR WRITING A BOOK: FROM BLANK PAGE TO PUBLISHED AUTHOR IN 6 WEEKS OR LESS

Travis Cody

Every business or entrepreneur today needs a book. Yet, in many ways it's more critical than ever and here's why: It used to be that people with the most authority and credibility had a PhD, an MD, or some other advanced education. Yet that's no longer the case.

We are now more likely to listen to a celebrity than a scientist. For instance, imagine a PhD from MIT is having a debate with Tom Cruise about global warming. If the doctor is dreadfully boring, dry, and speaks in a monotone voice- while Tom Cruise is very animated and passionate- chances are you will remember more of Tom Cruise's comments. And even though you may agree with the scientist's viewpoint, if he is totally boring, you will probably tune out what he says as you go watch Funny Cat videos.

The great news is that today it's easier than ever for you to create near-instant credibility, authority and celebrity in your marketplace so people will want to hear what you have to say. And the way to do that is with a book.

Having your own bestselling book is the ultimate unfair advantage in today's business world. You'll have easier access to speaking engagements, media interviews and more importantly customers.

I promise you... creating a book is much easier than you think. And I am going to show you how to do it. Notice that I didn't say I will show you how to write a book. There are ways to share your voice, your experience, your expertise and your knowledge that require very little writing from you personally.

Ways that don't involve hiring expensive ghostwriters either. If you:

» Have a hobby that you love

» Have been at your job for two years or more

» Are a parent

» Have a special skill or talent

» Are an Entrepreneur

» Own your own business

» Have read more than three books on one topic

Then you have a book inside you that is just waiting to be written and published.

THE SECRET TO GOING FROM BLANK PAGE TO PUBLISHED AUTHOR IN 6 WEEKS OR LESS

Yes, it really is possible to write your book in six weeks or less. I know... six weeks sounds pretty ludicrous. Yet I have a client who actually created his last book in a single day. (Many clients finish in less than 4 weeks).

When we start the process many of my clients are skeptical to be sure. They feel it's going to be too hard and too laborious. Or they think they're not a good writer and it's going to suck. And perhaps this is what's going through your mind right now as well.

The great news for you is that there are much more effective ways to get your expertise out of your noggin' and onto the page other than just pecking away at the keyboard one key at a time. The most sure-fire way is the "movie star method" of writing books.

I am sure that as a successful entrepreneur, parent, or hobbyist you may be thinking: "There's no way I have enough time to write a book." However, my clients who have gone through this process are able to finish the first draft of their book in less than two weeks. And they are able to do that without investing more than 10 hours of their personal time during the entire process.

Yet have you ever wondered how someone who is always on set making a movie finds the time to write and publish a book? Or someone who runs a country? (After all, if they're running a country... when do they have time to write?).

The reason is simple. They have knowledge, interesting stories and experience in what they're doing. They want to share their unique perspective about the world in a way that will outlive them. But, how do they do it?

Here's the secret: rather than sitting down in front of a blank computer screen and typing, they simply hire someone to interview them. The process works like this:

Step 1: "Author" is interviewed.

Step 2: Interviews are transcribed.

Step 3: Transcriptions sent to an editor who cleans them up.

Step 4: The edited manuscript is organized and outlined into a logical flow.

Step 5: 2nd edit for grammar.

Step 6: Manuscript is sent out to graphic designer to be laid out.

Step 7: Cover is created.

Step 8: Publish.

In a nutshell, that's how the majority of famous people get their books written.

And it doesn't take much. A Three-to-four hour interview will yield a 150-200-page book.

Now that you know how it works all you have to do is follow the process. And to make it even easier, I'm going to share with you a variation that I feel is the #1 way for creating your own book fast.

MY METHOD

If you deal with clients directly, then I'm sure you get asked questions all the time. And many of them are probably the same question over and over again. There's even a term for it: frequently asked questions.

Yet, ask yourself, how much time do you waste answering these same questions again and again? What if there was a way you could answer all those frequently asked questions just ONCE... so that you can get right to the business of serving you customer? Luckily for you, there is.

Step 1: Set a timer for 20 minutes.

Step 2: Turn off all distractions. Shut down your Internet browsers, turn off your Facebook messenger and put your phone on silent so it's not pinging you.

Step 3: Start the timer and for 20 minutes write down all of the most frequenlty asked questions that you get asked in your business. Don't edit and don't censor yourself. Just write down as many as you can think of in 20 minutes.

Step 4: At the end of 20 minutes STOP. Get up and walk around for 5-10 minutes, get a drink of water, etc. After your short break come back, set the timer for another 20 minutes and then repeat the process again.

Repeat this process for as many times as you can until you just can't think of any more questions to write down. At first you may only have 30 questions. However, the more you times you do this, the more you are going to come up with. I've had clients that have gotten as many as 200 questions in a matter of a couple of writing sessions.

Another thing you can also do is to take your list and show it to your staff. Ask them, "are there any questions that our customers ask you that aren't on this list?" Have them write down their questions and then add them to your list.

Once you're finished, you'll repeat the exercise only this time you're going to write down all of the "should ask" questions. These are all of those things that your customer doesn't know that they don't know.

If you're a Real Estate Agent and you're dealing with a first time homebuyer they may ask you all of the standard questions they found online about square footage, year built, cost of utilities, etc. Yet what they should be asking you are detailed questions about the types of materials used to build the house, if the house ever had any water damage, or how old the roof is. So write them all down.

Now that you have your two lists, go through and organize the questions into groups that relate to one another. For example, if you're a Real Estate Agent then you may have a dozen or more questions that are just about financing a home; or how to sell a house quickly; or things that new home buyers should look out for. By organizing similar questions together you are forming a basic outline for your book.

NOW THE FUN PART: THE INTERVIEW.

The easiest way to do the interview is to get a voice recorder or to use the recorder on your phone and start answering the questions that you just wrote down. Just imagine that you are having a conversation with a close friend and he or she is asking the questions.

If it seems awkward or strange for you to talk to yourself, (oddly, I seem to have no problem with this) have someone else interview you. You can have your spouse, a friend, a co-worker or even an employee do the interview. Do what is most comfortable for you and that will give you the best chance of getting it done. You may even want to treat this like a radio interview, which is good practice for all the ones you will do once your book comes out!

If you have yet to do any media appearances... here's a little secret. They almost always ask you the questions you give them. Yep... on Radio and TV the people being interviewed are simply being asked questions that they already know the answer to... because they wrote them. That's why when you see an expert on TV they seem so polished and knowledgeable.

My last book, When a Book Is a Gold Mine: The Entrepreneurs Shortcut to Market Domination, was completed while driving in my car. I had a business appointment that was a two-hour drive each way. I turned my voice recorder on and then imagined that there was a good friend on the ride with me. We had a very lovely conversation during which I revealed all my secrets to him.

When I sit down and ask my clients to tell me the story of how they got into the business they're in, we end up having an hour-long conversation. That conversation alone is 30 pages of a book and that's just from us talking about how they got into business. If I then ask about the things they really enjoy about their work, that's another 30-45 minute conversation; another 15-20 pages of a book.

So let me get you started with a few questions you can answer about YOUR business or service.

- How did you get into the business you're in?
- What do you enjoy about your job?
- What are the most exciting advances in your industry right now?
- What changes have you seen over the last few years?

» Based on your experience where do you think your industry will go next?
» What are some of the best experiences you've had with clients in your business?
» What has been some of the results that your clients have had?
» How have your clients lives been changed by the service that you offer?

Answer those and your introduction is already done. Answer your FAQ/SAQ's and you're practically finished.

See How Easy That Was? Now that you know the secret, just repeat the process to create multiple books and before you know it you'll be the dominant force in your industry.

Tim Ferriss was totally unknown until he released The 4-Hour Workweek. He leveraged a single book to create a mini-empire all his own. Makayla Léone and Pamela Donnelly - two of my coaching clients - followed this exact process for their first book. (Both of which went on to become #1 Bestsellers.) They then leveraged those books to build thriving businesses.

I'll leave you with one last insider tip: When you create your first book you don't need to share 100% of everything you know. Break up your knowledge into multiple books. For instance, going back to our Real Estate Agent from earlier: You can have a single book on "How to Finance Your Dream Home; The Top 25 Things to Look for When Buying a House or even Insider Secrets to Selling Your House Fast."

The Movie-Star Method for Writing a Book is just one of several ways to create your own bestselling book quickly. If you'd like to learn more about the others, as well as get more information on my "Guaranteed Best-Seller" Marketing Service, visit my website at www.TravisCody.com/6FigureAuthor.

Travis Cody invented the Amazon best-seller strategy for building your brand. A four-time #1 bestselling author himself, he has helped dozens of people become bestselling authors, including nine who became number-one bestsellers. He is also a top advertising copywriter and has helped individuals and businesses bring in huge sums of money with the written word.

Butternut Squash Soup

Serves 4

Ingredients

1 pound peeled butternut squash cubes

2 cups low sodium chicken stock, hot

4 slices thick cut bacon cut into 1/2-inch lardons

1 teaspoon canola oil

1 large sweet onions such as Vidalia or Maui, peeled, cut in half and thinly sliced

1/2 cup frozen sweet peas, defrosted

kosher salt and freshly ground black pepper

4 scallions, cleaned and thinly sliced

1 tablespoon flat Italian parsley leaves, chopped

1 teaspoon fresh thyme leaves, chopped

Instructions

Place the butternut squash cubes in a microwavable bowl with a tablespoon of water and cover with a damp paper towel. Place in microwave and cook on high power for 5 minutes, or until soft. Transfer to a blender or food processor and add the hot chicken stock. Purée until smooth and transfer to a medium saucepan.

In a large heavy sauté pan heat the canola oil over medium heat until shimmering. Add the bacon to the pan and cook until the bacon pieces are crisp and brown. Remove bacon, keeping the oil and rendered bacon fat in the pan. Place on paper towels and reserve. Add the onion to the pan, season with salt and pepper, and cook over medium heat until caramelized, about 10 minutes. Add the peas to the pan to heat through.

Warm the soup in the saucepan over medium heat until piping hot. Divide the onions and peas among 4 soup bowls. Pour over the hot soup and garnish with the bacon, scallions and herbs. Serve immediately.

THE POWER OF TRANSPARENCY

Tracy Spears

Have you noticed that transparency is getting a lot of lip service these days? It has found its way into a lot of mission statements and corporate credos. The big question is: Are leaders being more transparent or are they just talking about it in an attempt to gain trust from their teams?

Transparency is often referred to as a "character trait" because both the commitment to it, and the lack of it is a reflection of the character of the leader. Historically, leaders and managers have used calculated transparency to grow their own power. The decision to share or not share certain kinds of information is one of the key differentiators between leaders and coaches.

To answer this question, we need to start with the basics. What is transparency? You will probably never find another "strategy" that is simpler to explain. In a team context, transparency is just telling the truth to more people than you normally would. More staffers, more customers, more stakeholders... transparency means more truth to more people.

Transparency is aspirational. Leaders and organizations that value it will be constantly challenged with just how much transparency is actually good for their teams. We have worked with companies who deeply valued transparency as part of their corporate culture. They were overt in the discussion and debate of key strategic decisions. We have seen how this commitment to transparency has been very positive and conversely, negative in different situations.

The following two studies are real clients of ours, and reported exactly as they happened. We have left the names of the leaders and organizations out to protect their privacy.

CASE STUDY #1

One company in the petrochemical industry leveraged their commitment to transparency to great effect during a recent commodity-pricing crisis. The global value of their refined product had dropped so drastically that they were shutting down certain operations and initiating a staged furlough program for important workers in these locations. Their company was in the news and experts in their industry were not certain they would even survive the pricing crisis.

We were in the room when the CEO addressed the team at their company headquarters. He walked to the front of the room and without any hesitation began to address the situation at hand to the many executives in attendance. He had a calm demeanor and explained the plans for what would have to happen if the prices continued to drop. He discussed which personnel would have to be released and why, and what the company was trying to do to remain solvent through the crisis. Next, he discussed how the company would ramp back up again once the pricing pressures were relieved and what that would mean for the people who had been let go. He understood what great crisis leaders all understand: the absence of information creates a vacuum, and what fills that vacuum is angst and fear. Presenting a tough truth, even when it is uncomfortable for everyone involved is almost always better that letting people's imaginations fill in the blanks.

CASE STUDY #2

Let's look at a situation where transparency did not exist, where the leader did not think it was her job to make sure the team knew the situation they were in. The company was a mid-sized aerospace equipment company that had grown quickly to around fifty employees. Most of the fifty were fabricators in a large machine shop where the aluminum parts were milled and finished for shipment to their aerospace customers.

We were hired as consultants because the owner/president of the company was very concerned about the morale. She had reported that the atmosphere had become negative and was taking its toll on the employees and the overall productivity of the organization. Absenteeism and tardiness were way up and none of the good-natured camaraderie that had characterized the shop previously seemed to be there anymore... or at least when she was around. Business was slow but everyone was still getting paid, she said. She had even confessed that she and her husband (also on the payroll) had each gone without pay for the previous several months because the orders had dropped so dramatically.

We scheduled a series of one-on-one meetings with the employees. It was explained that their opinions would be considered confidential, so they could share their feelings safely. When we began the interviews we quickly found exactly what the owner had reported- these people were in a nasty mood. They had nothing but negative feedback on the business, the working conditions, the owner, the owner's husband... you name it. When we started asking for specifics we got a laundry list of slights and negative changes perpetrated by the owner. Here is the partial list:

» No more coffee service in the shop

» No more overtime pay for Saturday shifts

- No more free Friday lunches ordered in
- Two vending machines in shop have been broken for months
- Shop employees being asked to wash their own uniforms (no laundry service)
- Company was no longer sponsoring the softball team
- No holiday bonus
- And a few more general grievances

Now it was time to meet with the owner behind closed doors to review our findings. We were prepared to review the list and discuss how the accumulation of these complaints and grievances was affecting the overall morale and energy level of her business. We went through the entire list, being careful to mention when a particular complaint was mentioned more than once. We asked the owner not to react to any individual items on the list, saying she should instead focus on the spirit of the complaints and how they may be affecting the working environment.

When we were done with the review the owner was silent for a while and then she explained what was actually happening at her company. She said that one of her first priorities when she started the business was to provide stable employment for good people. In an industry with a lot of ups and downs, she felt that being able to provide stable and consistent work would be a great way to attract and keep a great team. This is especially true in the fabrication shop where the really skilled people worked.

She went on to say that every one of the comprises that had been made: the coffee, the lack of overtime on Saturday shafts, not repairing the vending machines, the unpaid holiday bonus, etc., were decision made to keep from having to lay anyone off. She added that she had not, in fact, laid a single person off during this entire down cycle in her business and that competitors were aggressively laying people off.

We asked why she had never shared this information with the staff, especially when the morale had gotten so low. She said that she did not want people to worry about their jobs or the company, because that was her job.

We scheduled a meeting the next day for all of the shop workers, the office staff, and the owner. We talked through what we had learned from both sides. The meeting ended with some tears, lots of hugs, and most importantly, understanding. The bottom line was that this was a bad situation that could have been completely avoided with simple transparency. The workers had not given the owner the trust that she was working in their best interest, and the owner had not believed that the workers could grasp the business situation they were in. Both sides were wrong.

A FINAL WORD ON TRANSPARENCY

In some organizations the video does not match the audio. The leaders talk about the value of transparency and their commitment to it, but the team rarely sees it. This kind of false transparency does not engender trust or appreciation. Rather, the product of this lip-service kind of transparency is cynicism and distrust.

Developed leaders and coaches understand that it is better to err on the side of too much transparency, rather than too little. When you offer too little transparency in decisions and direction, you are risking your credibility. When a leader seems to be offering too much transparency, they open themselves to some criticism, but their credibility is not at risk.

Remember, transparency is just telling the truth to more people than you normally would. More staffers, more customers, more stakeholders... transparency means more truth to more people. It is a decision you are making about your organization's character. Making a habit of demonstrating real transparency in your role will make you a better leader and create more loyalty from your team.

Tracy Spears has been a national business consultant for over 25 years. She specializes in developing leaders, inspiring teamwork, and working with high performing teams. In addition to her workshops, Tracy is a highly sought after keynote speaker.

She is a graduate of the University of Oklahoma and an accomplished athlete who played in Japan as a member of the U.S. National Softball Team. Tracy is the Co-Founder of the Exceptional Leaders Lab, a community of progressive business and organizational leaders and an active member of the National Speakers Association.

THE LEAN BUSINESS PLAN

James Klobasa

How did business planning get a bad name?

Almost every business owner I've ever known would often spend odd times – while in the shower, when driving alone, walking, waiting in line – thinking about business. Priorities, next steps, problems, they roll around in your head. And thinking about the business leads to decisions, and management. It's a good thing.

On the other hand, say the phrase "business plan" and most business owners shudder. Palms get sweaty. They react with all the enthusiasm they'd show if it were an invitation to do a master's thesis, or that term paper we all hated in high school.

I think what happened is the myth of the big business plan. Somewhere along the line, what should have been just planning a business became something bigger, harder, more specialized, and probably a lot less useful. When you read the phrase "business plan," do you assume it's a carefully compiled masterpiece document, beginning with a finely crafted executive summary, and flowing beautifully through a detailed market analysis, with lots of descriptive texts, careful formatting, and elaborate financial projections? Most people do. Do you assume it's just for startups, not real businesses? Most people do and that's a shame.

The shift in business planning has been happening over the last 10 or 20 years, as startups, angel investment, and entrepreneurship caught the public eye. Because business plans are a natural part of the process of startups getting investment, that particular variety became what people think of as a business plan. As the mystique of the business plan grew, so too did the requirements. Where once what mattered was knowing a market, and making decisions, over time it became a need for market research and market analysis, not just making decisions but proving the existence of market potential, for outsiders. What used to be a matter of setting priorities and steps to follow became a matter of selling business ideas to outside investors considering writing checks. Don't sweat the big business plan.

Forget the myth. Use business planning not to create some big formal document, but to help you get what you want from your business.

Skip the descriptions and explanations. Just to a lean business plan. It will help you get where you are going without bogging you down. It's a fast, easy, and efficient way to get what you want from your business.

Who doesn't like planning a vacation? When I was a kid, we'd get together before our big backpacking trips and plan routes, food, and what to pack. As an adult, I'd join my wife planning our family vacations. Planning is part of the fun.

And planning your own business? That can be fun too. Set your strategy, and the tactics to execute it. Figure out pricing, marketing, and product. It's dreaming and telling stories, and then adding what it takes to make them come true. It's making things happen. It's going from a vague, daunting, hard-to-manage uncertainty to specific educated guesses, to being linked together, so you can deal with them. Get things done.

The term lean in business means focusing on what adds value and avoiding waste. It's also about taking small steps and evaluating results often. So just do lean planning instead.

Who cares about planning? Who cares about business plans, lean or otherwise? Planning isn't the point; the point is to get what you want from your business, to work smarter, not harder. It's about better business and getting what you want out of your business.

Strategy is focus. Don't do everything – you can't – but do the most important things. Don't try to please everybody – you can't – so please the people who matter most, depending on what you want from the business.

Develop and execute tactics to make strategy real. Make sure what you're doing matches what you think is most important. Figure out optimal pricing, channel marketing, and product (or service) developments.

Make sure you are actually executing your tactics by boiling them down to specific milestones and performance measurements. Track results and compare them to expectations. Develop accountability.

Manage your money. Figure out what you expect to sell, use that to figure out what to spend, and make sure you never run out of cash.

Lean business planning isn't about planning. It's about business. And getting things done. Run your business to make your life better. Don't run your life to make your business better.

It comes from the idea of lean, as in lean manufacturing and lean startups. Lean is a management technique, and a way of thinking. It focuses on taking small steps and reviewing results, and often revising plans. The lean manufacturing wave started 70 years ago, and established the idea of PDCA, for "plan-do-check-adjust." The idea of lean startups began just a few years ago, with the publication of the book "The Lean Startup" by Eric Ries in 2009. They changed PDCA to "build-measure-learn." They introduced the idea of the minimum viable product (MVP), which is what the lean startups do first.

It starts with a lean business plan. Lean business planning adopts the ideas of small steps, constant tracking, and frequent course corrections to planning. It includes doing only what adds value, without waste. It starts with a core business plan for internal use only, just big enough for optimizing the business.

This lean plan is clearly not the "elaborate business plan" that lean startup experts reject. Unlike the elaborate plan, the lean plan doesn't include carefully worded summaries or detailed business information for outsiders. It is not even a document. It's a collection of lists, tables, and bullet points.

A LEAN BUSINESS PLAN HAS FOUR MAIN PARTS

1. Set simple business strategy

A good lean business plan starts with a page or two of bullet points defining strategy. Doing today what will seem obvious tomorrow, is genius. I say the best strategies seem obvious as soon as you understand them. Furthermore, it seems to me that if they don't seem obvious after the fact, they didn't work.

Strategy is what you're not doing. My favorite metaphor is the sculptor with a block of marble – the art is what he chips off the block, not what he leaves in. Michelangelo started with a big chunk of marble and chipped pieces off of it until it was his David. Strategy is focus.

Strategy has to be easy to define. I've also worked in depth with several competing strategy frameworks, and every one of them works well if it's applied correctly and executed. In fact, I say you can also define strategy with a story, or a small collection of stories.

And let's be clear about this: Methods don't matter. I use what I call my IMO method, which focuses on your unique identity, your target market, and your business offering. But you could also just use stories, or some other method. What matters is focus, what you do and don't do, and whether it works.

And strategy will change over time. It's planning, not just a plan.

2. Tactics to execute strategy

Strategy needs tactics for execution. In practical terms, this is your marketing plan, your product or service plan, and other tactical plans. Aim for strategic alignment and match your tactics to your strategy. You should be able to think of your business as a pyramid, with strategy at the top, tactics in the middle, and concrete specifics at the base.

These include marketing tactics. Marketing, in its essence, is getting your customers to know, like, and trust you. To do that, you must understand your customers: know how and where to find them, how to help them find you, and how to present your business to best match your strategy and business offering. You have to make choices for pricing, messaging, distribution channels, social media, sales activities, and so forth. For your lean plan, these are mainly bullet points. They are defining the tactical decisions that you make. In the lean plan they are for internal use only.

They also include tactics for the business offering. Product or service tactics are the decisions you make about pricing, packaging, service specifications, new products or services, product launches, sourcing, manufacturing, software development, technology procurement, trade secrets, bundling, and so forth. Your lean plan contains the decisions you make on these items as bullet points. You know your tactics by heart, so just list them briefly in your lean business plan.

Some plans have other tactics too. Financial tactics, recruiting tactics, and so forth.

Remember, the lean plan is for you, to help you manage. Don't worry about explaining things to outsiders. Use it to keep track of what you want to do.

3. Concrete specifics: dates, deadlines, etc.

» The review schedule: The most important single component of any real business plan – lean plan, traditional plan, etc. – is a review schedule. This sets the plan into the context of management. It makes it clear to everybody involved (even if that's just you) that the plan is going to be reviewed and revised regularly. All the people charged with executing a business plan have to know when the plan will be reviewed, and by whom. This makes it clear that the plan will be a live management tool, not something to be put away on a shelf and forgotten.

» List of assumptions: Listing assumptions is extremely important for getting real business benefits from your business planning. Planning is about managing change, and in today's world, change happens very fast. Assumptions solve the dilemma about managing consistency over time, without banging your head against a brick wall.

» Milestones are what you use to manage responsibilities, track results, and review and revise. Without tracking and review, there is no management, and no accountability. Milestones are what's supposed to happen, and when, for ongoing tactics related to products, services, marketing, administration, and finance. They include launch dates, review dates, prototype availabilities, advertising, social media, website development, programs to generate leads and traffic. The milestones set the plan tactics into practical, concrete terms, with real budgets, deadlines, and management responsibilities. They are the building blocks of strategy and tactics. And they are essential to your ongoing plan-vs.-actual management and analysis, which is what turns your planning into management.

» Performance metrics: Ask yourself how you'll know whether you are on track or not. Tracking results is an important part of your regular planning process. They are numbers people can see and compare. Make them explicit as part of your lean plan. Management often boils down to setting clear expectations and then following up on results. Those expectations are the metrics. And with good lean planning, you can look for metrics throughout the business, aside from what shows up in the financial reports.

For example, marketing is traditionally accountable for levels of expenses in the financials, but also generates metrics on websites, social media, emails, conversions, visits, leads, etc. Sales is traditionally responsible for the sales reports in the financials, but there are also calls, visits, presentations, proposals, store traffic, price promotions, and so on. Customer service has calls, problems resolved, and other measures. Finance and accounting have metrics including collection days, payment days, and inventory turnover. Business is full of numbers to manage and track performance. When metrics are built into a plan, and shared with the management team, they generate more accountability and more management.

4. Essential business projections

Every well-run business has a sales forecast, spending budget, and cash plan. Hard as it may be to forecast sales and expenses, it's harder still to run a business without forecasting them. You need to break things down into meaningful chunks, make some educated guesses, and then follow up with regular plan vs. actual review and revisions.

The math is pretty simple. Lay out a spreadsheet with months along the top and items on the left. Break it down into meaningful categories, and where possible use assumptions like units percent of sales too.

It's a lot easier to do when you realize it's not supposed to be correct, just reasonable, and trackable. Your sales forecast and spending budgets won't accurately predict the future. We know that from the start. What you want is to understand the sales drivers and interdependencies, to connect the dots, so that as you review plan vs. actual results every month you can easily make course corrections. Keep it Live and use it well.

Just like lean manufacturing and startups, lean business planning is a process of continuous improvement. It takes small steps, analyzing results, and making corrections. I've revised the classic PDCA cycle to make a lean planning version that I now call PRRR, for plan-run-review-revise. So, lean business planning is more than just the lean plan itself, it's the plan plus regular review and revisions. It's never finished. Every latest version will need revision within a few weeks.

A good lean business plan includes the review schedule as part of the concrete specifics. The idea is to set a specific day, such as the third Thursday of the month, to review results of the plan, track progress, and make course corrections. So the plan is never out of date.

The review meetings use the assumptions list to check unexpected results against their initial assumptions. If the assumptions are still valid and the results surprising, then it's time to correct problems in execution, or – better still – shift resources to take advantages of good surprises, better results than expected.

There will always be an inherent question in the results review: Do we change the plan or stick to it? That's one of the key questions the business owner has to manage, as things are constantly changing. Add more only as needed.

As much as the lean startup experts complain about what they call the elaborate business plan, real businesses do occasionally need to present a business plan to outsiders. They have what I call business plan events, when a business plan is required.

But times have changed. You don't need the big plan. Do your lean plan and keep it up to date with regular review and revisions. And when somebody asks for a traditional business plan (if they do), then add the extra ingredients you need. That might be a market analysis, an exit strategy, a detailed description of product or a marketing plan. Do them as summaries, presentations, or appendices. Don't do it for the plan ... do it for the results.

Lean business planning is all about getting what you want from your business. The point isn't the plan, but using the planning process to set goals, track progress, review results, and manage better. It's supposed to make running a business easier, not harder. Don't do anything that doesn't make your business better, and your life easier.

YOUR OFFLINE BUSINESS AND THE FIRST 90 DAYS ONLINE.

Launch a New or Existing Offline Business Online, By Leveraging the Power of the Internet to Reap Massive Rewards Quickly, Cheaply and Easily ... No Rocket Science Required...!

In this chapter, I'll show you just how easy it is to build and promote your offline business using online launch strategies. We'll go inside one of my new business launch successes to reveal the exact tactics and strategies you can use to deliver your own success.

The Goal: Add $22,000 per month income to a new offline business in 90 days or less on a budget of $300/month.

THE SPECIFICS:

- Launch a new service based business
- Has to deliver its services in the same way offline businesses have been running for decades, with real products and services, delivered by real people.
- Launch it using only online methods - no magazines, no newspapers, no radio, television or Yellow Pages.
- The business must be seen by a national audience and recognised as a leader in its field.
- It must be rolled out on a small business budget, $300 per month.
- Profit must be made from day one to service business growth into the future.

In this chapter, you may notice how your current business could be grown with the ideas offered, whether starting from scratch or expanding an existing business. Included are the steps in the exact order implemented. You can follow along and use this as a blueprint to build or start your own business.

IT'S YOUR TURN FOR SUCCESS

The figures achieved and used within this case study are proof, not of my ability, but of how following a system and using specific tactics and tools can produce amazing results. And the best part is you can do it yourself, not just once, but over and over again.

Success ... it's a funny word. Most people only measure this word by the monetary result, but I don't want to have this confused with being successful in taking the steps required to produce a result. For me, the first 90 days of building this business was a massive success, and after that, bigger challenges called and they will for you too.

Yes, it did produce a nice monetary result, but it was the roll out – the perfect design and execution, the viral growth, the positive customer feedback and the brand being recognised nationally as a leader – that made this a very successful project.

It checked the boxes I set out for it. Only measuring success by the money you generate clouds your more important goal of serving your customers.

LAUNCH BASICS REVEALED

In this chapter we'll be talking about launching a business, but in essence this is Product Launch Strategy 101. Consider your business as a single product for a moment.

Product launches help a business quickly build large lists of raving fans/customers via the creation of an event or sequence of events leading to an anticipated conclusion. Much like Hollywood releases movie trailers leading into a big movie launch, you can do the same to promote a new service your business offers.

Huge cash reserves are often a by-product of creating raving fans. These fans regularly deliver unique market information that allow the development of new products and services. Once delivered, these new options create more raving fans and more profits.

Why create raving fans? Because, they will continue to buy from you time and time again, become your best advertising sources and build your business for you.

KEY LAUNCH TOPICS

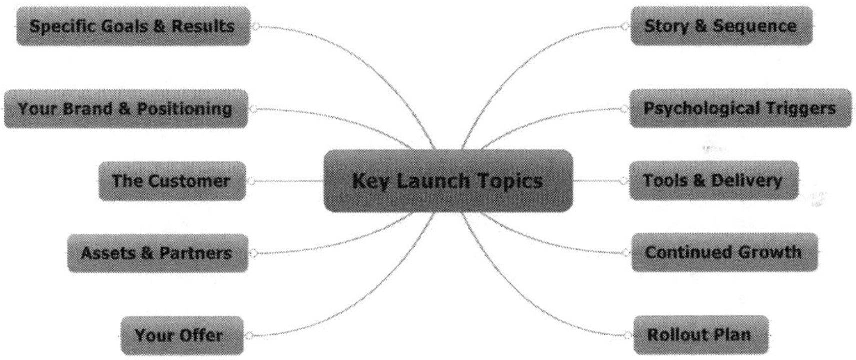

This chapter and the above diagram is your working model - we'll go into depth on each topic. There will be checklist steps, specific tasks and easy to implement strategies that will give you a great foundation to launch any business or product. Let's dive right in!

WHY LAUNCH

Having a clear understanding of ***'Why'*** gives you the drive for those tough days.

Specific Goals and Results- Knowing your result in advance gives you items to measure success by and the direction to achieve them.

For the project outlined above, clear and specific goals around the monetary results were part of the plan. This had a lot to do with the drive, determination and the actual results that were produced.

But, aside from the end dollar figure, you may also have other reasons for launching. You may wish to attract new partners, develop a new list of prospects or customers, and even research new products your clients are in need of. The end goal doesn't always have to be money, but when done right, it is usually the end result.

Setting these goals will give you measurable targets to gauge your success or failure by. Many people get caught up in these, making them dream numbers instead of just basic and achievable targets.

Yes, the results achieved in the above case do seem high but in fact, given the market, the service delivered and the time frames, were all very realistic. Doing this will keep you and your team focused on the tasks at hand to achieve the results.

Demanding results that are unachievable will kill off any enthusiasm for the work needed to achieve them. They must challenge and inspire you, not scare you.

Simple steps, and effective strategies combined with direct action produce results.

Complete the tasks below each section. Later in the chapter you'll use this to develop your own launch roll-out plan.

Task #1: What are the specific goals and results you desire for your business or product?

____

____

____

YOUR BRAND AND POSITIONING- THINK BIG, START SMALL.

As mentioned, the project aimed to have a national audience and be recognised as a leader. The two are tied together and gaining the authority to complete this was the key.

We began very small, never speaking of our greater vision. The call just kept being answered at the highest standard with a consistent message, feel and look. Starting out, we targeted local clients and got their feedback. This allowed us to adapt our response to suit the vision and our much larger audience that awaited- this was a crucial step.

This was kept very simple. There's no need for 'big noting' or being extravagant around this area. There is a fine line between cheap and just plain simple. However, we made sure the brand would be easily associated with the service provided and not be limited to an area, a size or a dollar value.

In essence, we allowed our clients to determine for themselves what the brand meant to them. By not limiting it, the client' perceptions took over. When seeing the brand, the clients immediately had their own vision of the quality they would receive, the price they would have to pay, and whether we were a 'next door business' or a 'multi-national'.

We allowed our clients to talk the brand up and tell us what they expected from the company.

Our client feedback gave us a direction to fulfil and positioned us as a leader in our field, and over time, our clients actually determined for themselves what they would pay for the services we sold. They gladly paid top dollar. They said we were a national company and they told us to only deal with the biggest names and work on specific projects. Who were we not to listen?

In reality, we controlled the show throughout. We hand fed our customers bite sized pieces of information about what we did and how we operated and gauged their response to those bites of information.

We simply listened and adapted by giving them what they asked.

Task #2: Is your branding limiting you to an area, size or value? What is your customer saying about you? What do they expect from you? Where do they think your company is positioned in the market? Are you listening and adapting?

THE CUSTOMER- KNOW YOUR CUSTOMER WELL.

This is one of the most important steps any business can take. You must know the intimate details of your customers and create an 'avatar' or a 'client description' that describes them in detail. Everything from their needs, wants, lifestyle and values will ensure that you are servicing the needs of your customer.

Meeting their needs on a personal level is an important key for success. This makes the creation of an irresistible offer easy. They will be happy to part with their hard earned cash and thank you for it if you meet their needs exactly.

Our customers were our greatest asset and you should cherish yours. Know them...and know them well.

It's easy to get your customer wrong. For example, a new business selling PVC pipe glue, may think a local plumbing contractor is their customer- and this is true to a point. But when it comes to being a successful business, is it really true? How many plumbers are you able to sell to if you're the maker of the best PVC pipe glue in just one area, say Bondi, Sydney?

Well, you'll have the local plumbers, maybe a few extra from the next suburb and a few blow-in contractors that take your product back home with them. But this is where the average business fails, by staying a small business. They haven't outlined their perfect customer.

Who's the perfect customer in this case? The local plumbing store and ideally a big chain store that wholesales to all the plumbers in the city, with stores across the nation, if not the world.

Going deeper, and knowing their sales goals and targets is part of knowing your customer. Knowing whether they're making budget is important. Knowing the key-purchasing officer is important. Knowing how you can solve their most pressing concern around how to make more money selling 'PVC pipe glue' would be vitally important.

It may take detailing who that key person is and outlining every last detail of their life so you know how best to present your product as the answer to their needs.

It may seem like a lot of work, but it's much easier to sell one million pots of glue to one person than 100 pots to 100 people!

Task #3: Describe your ideal customer ... What age are they? What sex? What is their lifestyle like? How much do they spend on products and services in your area of expertise? What are their hot points for buying? How can you describe them in as much detail as possible to understand why they buy? How can your product solve their most pressing concern ...?

WHAT MAKES IT WORK

This is assuming you do know 'something' about the market you're entering. You can't chop wood without a saw of some description.

Assets and Partners- Align yourself with the best; you can't do it alone.

Both to begin and to grow, the assets of the project were detailed. These included everything from suppliers and machinery to the skills required to deliver the services.

This was very simple to outline. We listed what was in our favour and for who we wanted to work.

We didn't want to spend all our time building random relationships. Instead we had a clear idea of the ones we wanted and knew they had to be effective in key areas in order to produce profitable and measurable results.

Aligning yourself with key partners allows leverage. The key here is outlining all the items that make your business/product more valuable to another's business.

If you are able to create strategic alliances with key players in your market- helping their business grow and in turn having them help your business grow- you are creating leverage.

The bit that takes a little time is knowing who is worth creating that leverage with; you must research your partners to make sure your goals are aligned. It does you no good having another business promote your services to an area you don't service.

Your assets are critical in launching also. Knowing what you have to work with is a must. These may be skills in certain tasks, teaching materials or specialised staff. For this case study, the assets needed were specialised machinery, and occupational health and safety manuals.

These assets, allowing entry to a larger and much more lucrative market, were sourced and created before even registering the business name. Risky...no. From day one, we knew we were going to be profitable.

Task #4: Who are the people in your market that you'd like to work with? What could you add to their business? Are they a good match for your future goals?

What special skills or requirements are needed in the market you're entering? Do you have them? Can you source them? Also, list everything in your favour for entering your market.

YOUR OFFER- AN IRRESISTIBLE OFFER IS THE GOLDEN GOOSE.

Regarded as the single most important factor in any sale, creating an irresistible offer crafted to meet the exact needs of your exact customer at the exact time they wish to buy will make the sale an absolute no-brainer.

Creating need is also important and can be a route to market, but meeting the needs of others is the quicker way to profit. Keeping your eyes and ears open will have you recognise opportunity before a market is flooded.

In this project, we entered the market in the early stages of its growth within a certain industry. Essentially, seeing and acting on this was one of the factors that guaranteed our success. We knew what the irresistible offer would be.

The creation of an irresistible offer will keep your customer coming back to you over and over again. They will become your raving fans and that is your best form of advertising, the type money can't buy.

The golden goose delivers the golden eggs and the delivery of your clients' exact wants, which fill the gap between where they are and where they want to be, is your single most important task.

You must provide a complete solution to their needs. If you can't supply a complete solution to 'all' of their needs, you must be specific and supply them with a complete solution to a specific area of their needs.

When my project began, we serviced a local area. Occasionally, we'd have requests for services from the other side of the country. The way we provided the irresistible offer in this situation was to partner with someone. We'd have them deliver the exact service we promised in the same way we would in our local area, even wearing our branded clothing. The simple act of doing this gave our client the view we were a national company able to deliver what and when they wanted. They also perceived it as being on their terms. This created 'Big Brownie Points' for our company going forward.

This one action built our reputation as a 'big brand' in the industry. Our customers started telling others (raving fans) which put our services in greater demand in these areas. As our demand grew, so did the ability to create scarcity around our services and in time, raise our pricing.

Our irresistible offer was really created by the customer: they told us what they wanted, we delivered and they grew our business for us.

Careful attention must be taken in this process. Delivering quality and exactly what the client needs is essential. You must over deliver at every stage.

The irresistible offer is not defined by price; it is defined by what the customer wants, when they want it and how they want it. It must give them the result they are looking for. It's really nothing to do with you being the 'best at what you do'.

Task #5: What can you do to provide for your customer in the exact way they want and need? How can you differentiate your business offer from your competitors?

____

____

____

STORY AND SEQUENCE- IT COMES DOWN TO THE RIGHT THING AT THE RIGHT TIME.

Getting these factors right can be tricky, but if you've done your homework and know your customer- their wants, fears, frustrations and desires- you'll know what to act on and the story you need to tell your customer to gain the result you desire.

There are also many sequences that add to your roll out. The time before or leading into your launch (pre-launch), the actual launch period, the post launch and re-launch periods. Extra factors that can be considered are partner launch time frames and even automated launch sequences.

Turning your business or offering a story with a beginning, middle and end will have your customer go through your buying funnel in a deliberate and effective manner. (See diagram.)

From the opening phone call, we started delivering the unique result we guaranteed they would receive if using our service. We would then take them through their concerns, making them feel comfortable and even confident of the service we provided.

We would build on this and establish how we could best meet their needs by adapting our delivery of services to better suit their particular time frame or specific situation. Then they would ask, 'When can you help us...?'

All throughout this process, clients were told the story of the brand, its beginnings, its people, its development and processes. To tell you the truth, I don't believe we ever had to ask for the sale when using this story and sequence technique. It works so well that the customer ends up believing you are their best option, the authority in the market and is left almost begging to purchase from your business.

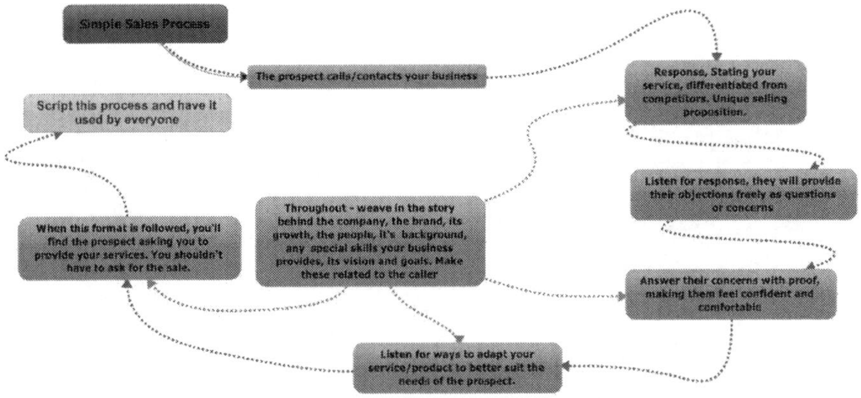

HOW IS THIS DONE

Psychological Triggers- Influencing is not manipulation when done with integrity.

Getting into their head ... There are time old mental triggers that will affect buying patterns. If you can identify these within your target market, you can repeat a buyer experience, their buying cycle and even control the amounts that they buy.

The mental states of excitement, anticipation, authority, proof, surprise, controversy, the common enemy, scarcity and reciprocity are like your secret weapons. Influencing your customers by using these triggers at various times creates customers that are responsive to your actions, your offers, your story and most of all you.

In dealing with phone calls, I'd often answer as though I was under time pressure or with huge excitement, giving the customer the impression of being busy or in demand. What does this do in your customer's mind?

It leads them to believe that your company is in demand, automatically creating scarcity or urgency in their mind. Being a company in demand must mean you're good at what you do, which increases your authority and your ability to charge more.

Once in the conversation and after qualifying the prospect, I'd move quickly to slowing down the conversation, taking time with the customer, answering all of their questions and concerns, and giving freely the knowledge or information in the form of video or pdf material that make them feel listened too.

This creates respect and reciprocity. In the end they feel as though you have just stopped your whole world for them and they want to repay the favour and purchase your services.

While I've listed some triggers above, there are many more. I have included resources at the end of this chapter that will help you become skilled in the art of influencing your prospects and creating customers.

These tactics are massively powerful and should only be used for good! I'm certainly not condoning the use of these psychological triggers to manipulate. It's about being able to influence your prospect, take them on a journey, of sorts, until they reach their desired destination.

TOOLS & DELIVERY- FINDING THE RIGHT RESOURCES AND OUTSOURCING IS EASIER THAN YOU THINK.

All that it took was $300 per month and some time to grow a very profitable business through the right promotional avenues and using the right strategies. You don't have to go back to university, although you may want to hire the kid next door.

I am not going to go into how I used all of the tools in detail here, although I am going to provide you with all the links and a description of how they were used plus other resources at the end of this chapter. Remember, they will be in the order that you will need them for the rollout of your launch. The reality of it was once I had the site designed and setup (outsourced for $250 - one-time fee), fifty articles were written and submitted to the directories (outsourced for $200 – initial fee, and became a cost of $30 per month).

All I had to do was spend just a few hours each week, monitoring my ads (the setup of this was outsourced for a one-time fee of $150 and later became fully monitored and managed by others for under $50 per month), checking traffic stats and making small improvements.

For the first eighteen months the whole advertising system and website ran on autopilot for $300 per month while we provided the services of the business.

WHAT IF IT ALL GOES WRONG?

Don't panic ... there's no need. If you've come this far, chances are you've built a great name for yourself in your market, and even the most dire of economic climates can be triumphed.

So nothing can really stop you from succeeding if you follow the key topics listed here.

CONTINUED GROWTH- EDUCATE AND OVER DELIVER TO RETAIN.

The Stick Plan- Once a prospect becomes a customer never ever lose them. Getting new customers these days is hard work and can be costly, so you should always be nurturing them and coaching them into staying with you.

The easy way to do this is just train them; train them that your business is the best provider of what they need, when they need it and how they need it. It can be done very simply and quickly. So, you've found a new customer and they've used or purchased your goods/services. In order to build on growth, follow up with a phone call or an email and ask them some basic questions.

» Did you feel you received the level of service we promised we would provide?

» Did you feel it was worth the cost?

» Is there anything we could have done that could have improved the result for you?

» Is there any other added service we can offer you to help you improve your results?

The list could be endless, but there are a few important items to note. Ask in a way that's perceived as an opportunity for them to make a contribution towards improvement. Most of all, offer something in return for the answers. This could be a discount on the next purchase, a free trial period on a service or a partner discount. Make sure they feel like they are receiving more than they're giving and repeat this process.

Once initial follow-ups are completed, it's the perfect time to offer more services/products to a customer. Continue to teach them about your business, its staff, the methods used and special training or skills available. This should be done through audio, video, and pdf material.

Ask, listen, and educate to build stronger connectedness with your customers.

Task#7: What are the important questions you could ask your new customers to have them help improve your service? What could you offer as a gift for helping you? How could you educate them on your business?

____

____

____

Rollout Plan- 'Give away, help others and it will be returned to you in a greater way, like a drop of water from your glass ... picked by the sun and rained back in your backyard...'

Here's where we tie all this work together. The diagram below gives a specific rollout plan for a product, but the same can be applied to a business rollout. It includes some of the mental trigger points you should be trying to hit along the way.

If you have done your homework from above you will be able to add all the elements to the plan in order. You will be able to see how they all link together forming a very strategic formula, one that you can follow over and over again.

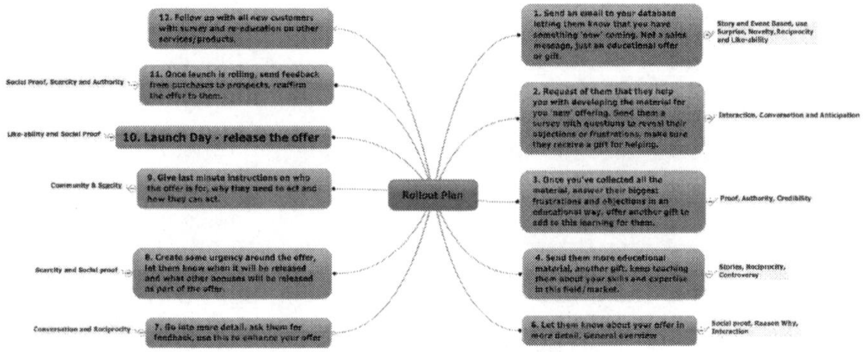

In closing, I guess you'd like to know the final results of my challenge.

The project did make it to $22,000 by the third month then went on to $42,000 in the fourth month and continued to fluctuate from there. So yes, for a $300 per month investment, the business brought in $42,000 per month within four months ... not a bad return on investment!

How do I know you can do this? Because I know I'm no different to you. After leaving high school and completing my trade, I quickly began following my dreams of travelling and sports. I spent thirteen summers travelling as a professional water-skier and have had over a dozen different jobs; this isn't rocket science.

What am I up to now?

I'm currently mentoring clients across the globe.

Where to next?

I'll continue to build businesses and help clients while travelling the globe. It's what I love and do best.

What I do know?

Using these launch strategies work in any market at any time. Give one a go, you won't be sorry! You may just become hooked!

Thanks for your time in reading this chapter and all the best in your future endeavours.

> *James Klobasa*
>
> *The Experts Mentor*
>
> *www.JamesKlobasa.com*
>
> *'The greater danger for most of us is not that our aim is too high and we miss it, but that it is too low and we reach it.' Michelangelo*
>
> *Recommended Reading*
>
> *Dan Ariely – Predictably Irrational*
>
> *Robert B. Cialdini– Influence: The Psychology of Persuasion*

> *Tom Hopkins – How To Master The Art Of Selling*
>
> *Jeff Walker - Launch*
>
> *Napoleon Hill – Think & Grow Rich*

RELEASE & EMBRACE: SUCCESS IN WORK

Sarah-Jane VandenBerg

"Choose life" is attributed to chapter 30, verse 19 of a book in the Bible known as Deuteronomy. Ultimately, choosing life is what you will be doing when you assess your career life now, release yourself from unreasonable and unfulfilled expectations and embrace that which moves you closer to what you want in your world of work.

According to Howard Figler & Richard Nelson Bolles in The Career Counselor's Handbook, an "annual career check-up communicates that everyone inhabits a career and it's worth a look every twelve months to see if the career engine is running on all cylinders. This assessment allows an individual to take a step back and examine their career as a whole.

Three areas to assess include: satisfaction, skills, and job search. Satisfaction with your career examines your level of satisfaction with the use of your strengths, your career direction and your income. Assessing your skills means reviewing your weaknesses and negotiating skills. If you are already looking for other work, determining where you are at with your job search skills to see what needs to be addressed. For each area, there are key questions to ask yourself.

In looking at satisfaction with work, you might begin with asking yourself: "On a scale of one to ten, with one being not satisfied and ten being completely satisfied, how satisfied am I?" If the answer is not a ten, whatever the number, ask yourself, "What would need to happen for it to be a" and indicate the next highest number. For example, if your satisfaction is a five, ask yourself, "What would it take for my satisfaction with work to be a six?" Listen to your response. Perhaps, write it down. Consider the answer and decide, "What do I need to do to make that happen?"

The next question to consider is "On a scale of one to ten, with one being having no energy and ten being fully energized, how energized am I?" If the answer is not a ten, whatever the number, ask yourself, "What would need to happen for it to be a" and indicate the next highest number. For example, if your energy level with work is a seven, ask yourself, "What would it take for my energy level with work to be an eight?" Listen to your response. Perhaps, write it down. Consider the answer and decide, "What do I need to do to make that happen?" Are there new fields of work you've heard about that you would like to explore? How can you get the best information about them? If you aren't sure where to get information about careers, consider how to research any topic and use those same strategies.

Another area involved with satisfaction is around your use of your strengths. So, ask yourself, "What are my strengths?" If you aren't sure, Marcus Buckingham, in Go Put Your Strengths To Work: 6 Powerful Steps to Achieve Outstanding Performance, suggests that you look at three things: 1. When you are so involved in what you are doing that you lose track of the time?, 2. What are you doing when you feel an emotional high?, and 3. What are you doing when you feel invigorated? Notice and record these moments. If you are still having difficulty identifying your strengths, you might want to look at Strengthsfinder 2.0 by Tom Rath or by Marcus Buckingham Now, Discover Your Strengths, StandOut 2.0, and, for women, Find Your Strongest Life.

In asking yourself about your general satisfaction with work and in determining your strengths, did you identify some skills that you could add to your repertoire? For example: are there areas of "weakness" that are preventing you from advancing the way you would like in your chosen field? Do you need to learn how to negotiate with your employer regarding your strengths, the activities that energize you and how to get the most rewards for your services? The next question to ask yourself is: How can you begin remedying these deficiencies now?

If you don't think you can use all of your strengths at work, consider a number of opportunities that have developed over the last five years. According to dictionary.com, "portfolio career" is defined as "a tapestry of a variety of eclectic employment experiences; employment in a series of short-contract or part-time positions" and the Cambridge English Business Dictionary defines it as "several part-time jobs at once, rather than one full-time job". Some individuals combine seasonal work: gardening in the spring and summer and fall months and operating a ski lift or working in a kitchen in the winter. One individual I know, combines cooking at a camp in the summer and organizing customized vacations to Jamaica (see www.carribeanconceirge.ca).

Another opportunity that has come to light given the temporary nature of much of the labour market, is that of "careerpreneur", a term, JibberJobber takes credit for in an online post dated March 31, 2010. The post suggests that "professionals need to manage their own careers... they need to manage their careers like an entrepreneur manages his business [with] flexibility, vision, and discipline, etc." JibberJobber further identifies that the word is derived from: "Career-oriented + entrepreneur = careerpreneur"

At www.careerprocanada.ca, on January 2nd, 2014, the actions to become a careerpreneur are defined. If part of your satisfaction with work means that you may need to work in more than one area, you may want to consider how well you embrace:

Becoming an independent agent working towards your own career success

Scripting your own path versus waiting for someone else to tell you what it is

Keeping an eye out for new opportunities and

Proactively taking advantage of career development initiatives.

Howard Figler suggests that today's career success may carry many business cards and "be serious about them all" (page 246). He acknowledges that individuals "may not have grown up wanting to be entrepreneurs but they'll do it rather than be victims of this change-a-minute economy". Having numerous business cards may mean that an individual may be contracting their services to two or three different employers, have a part-time business that supports them when they are between jobs or contracts, have a business they have developed to supplement their regular income, and a source of income they're building for their retirement days. Many successful individuals talk about building multiple streams of income including Mark Victor Hansen and Robert G. Allen in The One Minute Millionaire.

These work opportunities may be in various stages of development and T. Harv Eker, author of The Millionaire Mind advises in one of his Peak Performance CDs, that it is best to focus and develop one stream of income at a time. Be assured that many business ideas can coexist and your can allocate your time according to what the market wants and what utilizes your strengths. These opportunities can all be clustered in a single field or industry or they can represent fields that are worlds apart as demonstrated by the example of cooking and concierging.

You may have decided through all this assessment that you need to make some changes. As Annie Johnson put it in 1903: "I looked up the road I was going and back the way I come, and since I wasn't satisfied, I decided to step off the road and cut me a new path."

Now you ready to job search, seek or develop new business opportunities or both.

When considering your job search questions to ask yourself include:

Am I having difficulty mobilizing my job search? If yes, what do you need to do to get it moving?

What strategies am I using to identify work opportunities? Are these strategies effective? If not, what other strategies could I use or where could I learn about other strategies?

Are my job search tools, my resume and online profile, up-to-date?

What are my interview skills like? Do I need assistance to prepare for interviews?

Do I know how to effectively follow up each stage at each stage of the job search?

Once you have assessed your satisfaction and skills if you aren't where you want to be, accept yourself. Release your unfulfilled expectations and begin to decide what you want to do next. Consider that, according to JibberJobber, if you are a careerpreneur, that you:

believe that you are the CEO of Me, Inc.

know that your ability to provide income, or income security, which replaces job security comes from the strategy and tactics you employ in your career management.

know that change is inevitable and you constantly position yourself to survive/win.

network because you have learned to love it and do it right, not because you are in a pinch and need to lean on others.

are FREE, not burdened down wondering when you might lose your job.

Embrace where you are and then embrace a plan. Understand that "You will be at your most inquisitive in your areas of strength. You will be most optimistic, most courageous & most ambitious when playing to an area of strength" (Page 55 Go Put Your Strengths To Work). Embrace the benefits of strong moments which are:

efficiency – you'll save a lot of your time, you'll eliminate activities in which you do not feel strong and magnificent

you'll free yourself from manic perfectionism – by focussing on creating a few specific moments in each aspect of your life, you are freed from trying in vain to do everything well

you'll feel more purposeful, you are now targeting something specific, rather than being yanked around by everyone else's demands

you'll wind up being able to do more for others as you will generate strength in yourself to handle everyone else in your life.

Embrace the numerous advantages (page 247, The Career Counselor's Handbook)of the numerous business card approach to life:

greater degrees of freedom

more flexibility in the marketplace

more income

a variety of spice in one's life and

the ability to replace any of the cards when the time seems right.

Embrace the challenges and opportunities you are facing now and determine the one action you can take that will most affect you current goals and provide the highest payoff. Jack Canfield, in The Success Principles, suggests that you be willing to take the risks required to create the something better you want. Embrace that you have control over the thoughts you think, the images you visualize and the actions you take.

Your plan might include:

- » taking responsibility to identify own strengths and weaknesses
- » discovering your strengths by looking a the moments in your regular week that make you feel strong and magnificent
- » taking a stand for your strengths with is consistent with Stephen M. R. Covey's book The Speed of Trust which suggests demonstrating integrity, being congruent, and having the courage to stand up for what we believe

- encouraging people at work to acknowledge and recognize your strengths
- show others at work where you will be at your most productive, where you will come up with your best ideas, where you will spontaneously set challenging goals, where your inquisitiveness will stay sparked, and where you will reach down willingly for that extra ounce of effort when things don't go your way
- changing the thoughts you think
- changing the images you visualize
- changing the actions you take.

By embracing an action plan is the day your life will begin to get better. If you want something different you have to DO something different.

The Road Not Taken

By Robert Frost

Two roads diverged in a yellow wood,
And sorry I could not travel both
And be one traveler, long I stood
And looked down one as far as I could
To where it bent in the undergrowth;

Then took the other, as just as fair,
And having perhaps the better claim,
Because it was grassy and wanted wear;
Though as for that the passing there
Had worn them really about the same,

And both that morning equally lay
In leaves no step had trodden black.
Oh, I kept the first for another day!
Yet knowing how way leads on to way,
I doubted if I should ever come back.

I shall be telling this with a sigh
Somewhere ages and ages hence:
Two roads diverged in a wood, and I—
I took the one less traveled by,
And that has made all the difference.

Sarah-Jane VandenBerg has been working with individuals in career transition for over 25 years. Her passion is to use her creativity and enthusiasm to motivate others to live their life's purpose and passion in connection with spirit.

LEADERSHIP

21ST CENTURY LEADERSHIP

Brittney Kara

We often think a leader as someone in the spotlight. Someone who exemplifies qualities of courage, dignity, integrity, and communicates effectively. You often hear the phrase, "A Natural Born Leader." When you hear this, you may think leadership is just something you are not cut out for, especially if you don't feel like you were "born with it." While I do believe that people are born with different natural talents and abilities, I also believe that leadership is a skill that can be developed and cultivated. Everyone can become a good leader if they focus on cultivating the qualities necessary for a leadership role. While a person might be born with God-given abilities, one must learn to become a leader. There are many amazing leaders that are inspiring, uplifting, and helping those around them, which is what good leaders do. Leadership is a skill that we can all develop regardless of upbringing, genetic makeup, or life circumstance. Leadership is an energy. Leadership starts with a choice.

Never before in history have we had such an opportunity to become leaders as we do now. Because of the advancements in technology and social media, it makes leadership and the ability to reach others easier than ever before. I believe the 21st Century will see a rise in leadership throughout all walks of life and careers. We are already seeing this to be true. People are stepping up and out by designing their lives and businesses with their own rules and terms. We will continue to see this growth of leadership as our global human consciousness continues to expand. Conscious shifts are taking place all around the world, where people are waking up to their own individual powers and will launch the world of leadership to a whole other level. The world is in desperate need of true leadership at this time, and that is why it is up to us to make that a reality.

I want you to think about your life right now and remember a time when you felt like you stepped into a leadership role. How did you feel? Were you scared or unsure of yourself? Or did you feel empowered and exhilarated? Whatever the sensation was, that feeling is a key point to consider if you are looking to develop your leadership skills further. If you felt a bit stressed, all that means is that you need to do that action more often so that you can reprogram your brain to be comfortable in that state. Leadership is a state of mind. It is not a thing. It is a presence that somebody has around them. At some point in your life you either learned how to harness it or dismantle it. And by knowing the latter you can begin to rebuild or add to what you already have within you. True leadership comes from a place of peace, not power. By identifying how you felt the last time you were in a leadership position will serve as a great starting point for you to gauge what you need to work on, or if you have some limiting beliefs that need to be changed.

Leadership starts from the inside out. To be a true leader means you are able to effectively lead yourself in your own life and by doing so you inspire other people to do the same in their lives. Good leadership is not about force, control, domination, or recognition. It's about contribution and service. Leadership is not about gaining a huge following, although many leaders do by default. Leadership is about showing up, being the best version of yourself, and always being open to learn from your mistakes. Too much importance is put on the title of leadership and this is something I work to dismantle in my own organization. In my network marketing business, I lead a team of over 2,000 people. Within that organization, I work with approximately 25-30 leaders at any given time that also want to grow large organizations. There are many people that step comfortably into the leadership role right away, and there are others that require more time, love, support, and confidence-building first. Instead of people focusing on their titles and the responsibly that comes with leadership, I encourage them to focus on the vibrational feeling they are experiencing. The energy they bring into or leave with a room is what a person should focus on. Many times people get bogged down in the politics of leadership and may think that one must be bossy, aggressive, and demanding to be a true leader. This could not be further from the truth. A true leader inspires others to find leadership skills within themselves, and then cultivates that strength in a loving manner. Not being aggressive does not mean that you are a weak leader. Power comes from peace rather than force. Coercion is not cooperation, and many leaders have fallen into the aggressive category throughout history spreading fear instead of love. This is a dictator not a leader, and if you are building a business or organization you do not want to fall into the dictator category. People may stay by you only because they are scared of you—and what is the good in that? You want people to want to be around you and support you because they genuinely like you and what you stand for, not because they are scared to leave you.

If you have difficulty getting people to follow along with your ideas or stay by your side, that is a clear indication that you must first balance something internally to be able to move past that. It could be an event from childhood, negative thought patterns, or even poor self-care that is blocking your true potential to shine through. But do not worry, because every great leader has had their own struggles that they worked through, just like you and I. I love the phrase, "every master was once a disaster," because it is so true when stepping into leadership. You will make plenty of mistakes,, but the key is to not let those mistakes define you and stop you. Instead, use the experience as a tool to help you build up your leadership skills as you go.

The unique thing that I see consistently when helping develop other leaders, is the difference in mindset of people who instinctively excel in leadership abilities vs. those who struggle. Those that are more comfortable with leadership out the gate are those that have a stronger self-image, use positive words with themselves and others, and have a can do attitude. Their success in leadership doesn't have as much to do with their "life skills set" per say as it does with the thoughts that they think in their head. As I mentioned before, leadership first starts in your mind. You must believe you are good enough. Many people wait to be good enough before they think they can become a leader, and that is completely backwards. You must first believe something to be true, then act on it, and you will change your own reality. This is the key step to leadership that I think a lot of people leave on the table. Skills are important, don't get me wrong, but your mindset will make or break you.

Once you have the mindset of a leader, it is much easier to start developing the skills necessary to be an effective one. But if your mindset is negative, then most likely your leadership skills will be as well. Just think about it for a moment—if you don't want to be around yourself, why would others want to be around you? To be an effective leader, you must first learn to love yourself unconditionally. There are no exceptions to that rule.

Through years of studying, I have come to the realization that there are 10 key qualities/attitudes that great leaders should have. Use this as your guide to see where you might need to tweak some areas, or in some cases start from scratch to help develop your leadership skills.

10 KEY QUALITIES/ATTITUDES LEADERS HAVE

1. **LEADERS ARE READERS AND RESEARCHERS-** If you desire to be good in any field you will need to continue to educate yourself. Leadership takes education, discipline, and the initiative to seek out answers. Great leaders continuously learn throughout

their lives. Great leaders are voracious readers and life-long learners. Make the decision to be one.

2. **LEADERS HAVE A HEART OF SERVICE-** A good leader always leads from the heart rather than the head. The head is the ego and will usually steer us in the wrong direction, while the heart is God-centered and functions in perfect harmony with the world. Whenever you are in a position of doubt, get out of your egocentric mind and into your heart. You will be amazed at how the answers will appear.
3. **LEADERS CREATE A PLAN AND STICK TO IT-** You cannot master something if you are always chasing something new. Great leaders have a strong sense of purpose and urgency to get the job done, but they are always aware of the big-picture. They stick to their plan and don't fall off course. They might make minor adjustments, but the plan remains the same. Leaders adapt and overcome any challenges that may come up. Most importantly, they never give up!
4. **LEADERS ASK FOR ADVICE AND TAKE RESPONSIBILITY** - Just because you decided to become a leader does not mean you know everything or should act that way. One of the most important qualities of good leadership is the ability to humble yourself and admit you need help. The best leaders always surround themselves with people who are even better than themselves, so that they can always challenge themselves and grow. If you are not growing, you are dying, so it is important to always be focused on continued growth.
5. **LEADERS SURROUND THEMSELVES WITH PEOPLE WHO ARE BETTER THAN THEMSELVES** - Some might think that the idea of leadership means that you are the king of the hill. However, all great leaders have mentors and role models. Great leaders know their weaknesses and surround themselves with

people who are better at the things they are. Leadership is not about being perfect, it's about being resourceful with what you have, and creating a team of support around you. You will only be as good as the team of people you surround yourself with. Leadership is not a solo job, rather it is a group effort.

6. **LEADERS SAY NO**- Saying no is an art and one that can be very challenging for people who over-obligate themselves, or are guilt-ridden. You cannot hold a position of leadership for long if you function out of guilt. Guilt is one of the lowest vibrational frequencies that a person can function from, so if you are feeling guilty, you won't be able to lead yourself or others effectively. Learn to release guilt by meditation, NLP, yoga, massage, and affirmations. When you live guilt-free, you can easily say no when it is needed. Great leaders know intuitively when to say no and when to say yes. The more you take on the leadership role, the more other people will ask for your assistance. You cannot help everyone. This is when you must learn to flex your "no" muscle. If it doesn't feel right just say "no!" Flexing your "no" muscle is one of the first steps to becoming a strong leader.
7. **LEADERS LOOK FOR SOLUTIONS RATHER THAN FOCUS ON PROBLEMS** - Challenges will inevitably be a part of leadership. The key is how to handle the challenges that may come your way. This goes back to cultivating a positive mindset and mastering one's emotions. If you are stuck in the problem, you won't ever see your way out of it. If you are solution focused, you can adapt and overcome anything that is thrown your way. Great leaders learn to do this daily. There is always a solution to every problem.
8. **LEADERS ARE LOYAL-** Great leaders know that relationship building is one of the most essential parts of success. If people don't like or trust you, they most certainly are not going to follow

you. Being loyal to the people you surround yourself with, on your team and in your life, is important. Your relationships are a direct reflection of you. Your mindset along with your personal and spiritual growth, will determine the quality of the relationships you allow in your life—both business and personal. Your, "vibe attracts your tribe," as the saying goes.

9. **LEADERS SEARCH FOR STRENGTHS INSTEAD OF WEAKNESSES -** When you are around great leaders, you will walk away from them feeling more empowered. This is because good leadership has the ability to transmute from one person to another. Because thoughts and actions are just energy, so is leadership. Instead of focusing on the negative qualities of others, or yourself, focus on the positive attributes and watch how things begin to shift!
10. **LEADERS ARE INTUITIVE-** Intuition is something we all have. It is our DIVINE Muscle, as I call it. It is no different than any other muscle in our body. It must be worked out and stretched daily so it can be strong. If your intuition is not in-tune, it is only because you are not flexing it and using it daily. The more you use it, the stronger it will become.

If you desire to be a 21st Century Leader, know that you absolutely can. The key is to make the commitment to never stop growing and take consistent daily action to develop and hone your skills. You can be a leader in many ways. You can be a leader in your home, at work, and just in your daily life. If you have ever stood up for something you believe in, you are a leader. If you ever were of service to another human being, you were a leader. If you ever stepped up and did something you didn't want to do, you were a leader. If you ever did something you wanted to do, you were a leader. You are constantly using leadership skills, but you just might have not ever defined it as that. We are all destined for greatness if we so choose to and commit to becoming and staying a leader; you will automatically start to attract great experiences, people, and results in your life. The world is awaiting your voice! Go for your dreams like never before and know that you were made to be healthy, happy, and free.

> *Brittney Kara is an Author, Success Coach, Network Marketing Professional, Speaker, Activist, and Mother. Her mission is to inspire people to take control of their health, live life with passion, and discover the greatness within them. Learn more about Brittney and her work at www.brittneykara.com*

Brussels Sprouts with Caramelized Onions

Serves 4

Ingredients

3 cups Brussels Sprouts, root end trimmed, cut in half

2 tablespoons extra virgin olive oil

1 tablespoon unsalted butter

1 large sweet onion such as Vidalia or Maui, peeled, cut in half and sliced thin

kosher salt and freshly ground black pepper

Instructions

Place the Brussels Sprouts in a microwave safe bowl and add 1 tablespoon of water. Cover with a damp paper towel and microwave on high power for 5 minutes, until soft.

Meanwhile, heat the olive oil and butter in a large skillet over medium heat until shimmering. Add the onions and season with salt and pepper. Sauté until caramelized, about 10 minutes. Add the Brussels Sprouts to the skillet and cook until the Brussels Sprouts have browned, about 5 minutes. Season with salt and pepper. Serve immediately.

50 SHADES OF LEADERSHIP

Bob Vanourek

Warning: Contains explicit content for adult leaders only

50 Shades of Grey was an erotic novel written by British author E.L. James in 2011. This rather poorly written book topped best-seller lists and was then made into a poorly reviewed movie. The plot involves bondage, dominance, submission, and sadism/masochism (BDSM) - a rather apt metaphor for the state of leadership today.

I'm a leadership junkie and have been for most of my life. I have had the honor to lead five companies as a CEO and co-authored an award-winning book on leadership with my son., I've been searching for a better way to lead for decades and have learned a lot in the process. My mentors have been wonderful work colleagues as well as the leadership experts I've met or read along the way.

Leadership seems to be in a sorry state today. Greed, ego, lies, manipulation, and malfeasance abound. Partisan factions barrel-bomb one another. Everybody points their fingers at one another. Leadership and the working lives of too many people involve bondage to a job they hate, dominance by narcissistic egomaniacs, and submission to mindless rules and regulations that sadistically suck their souls dry, like bad books made into B movies. It's depressing.

But there's good news too. I am convinced that a new paradigm of leadership is slowly emerging. It's not the breaking-news story of the day, but I see it in the faces of the students and adult learners I teach every day. I read about it in the growing list of titles and content of cutting-edge leadership books. I hear about it in the evolving rating systems of what constitutes a great company and great leadership. I'm realistic about where we are but I'm also optimistic about our future.

Our leadership world is slowly evolving mostly because people realize that what we've been doing isn't working. People hunger for more meaning and joy in their working lives. They fervently wish to be treated fairly, respected, and allowed to express their unique ideas and contributions. They are more than willing to tell the boss to shove it and move on to something more soul-satisfying.

So, change is coming. Not overnight and not in every sector. The old paradigms will not exit without kicking and screaming, and we can't change human nature. There will always be some evil souls and greedy Gordon Gekko's of Wall Street, who love to play the system. But we can change human behavior, and that's what leadership is all about. It's not fear-based controlling, exploiting, or submission to the system, where you degrade yourself and others in the process. It's about sincerely caring for people, helping them get to a better place, and achieving a shared vision together while enjoying the journey, hardships and all, in the process. Leadership has been discussed and analyzed for thousands of years and is still a puzzling subject with many paradoxes, nuances, and shades of grey.

In the spirit of this new paradigm of leadership, I've pooled my experience, the wisdom of the ages, and the emerging trends around us today. The result is not another leadership tome, but 50 practical leadership tips that will take you out of the BDSM-Paradigm. I call this new model the Triple-E-Paradigm because it will build an excellent, ethical, and enduring organization. Excellent means achieving significant results. Ethical means leading with integrity. And enduring means acting sustainably for the world, the employees, and using sustainable financial practices (not weird contortions to meet the quarterly targets of Wall Street).

If you're a leader searching like I was for a better way to lead, these tips are for you. If you're a worker-bee stuck in a mind-numbing, soul-sucking job, then it's time to speak up or find a way to escape to a better workplace. That takes courage and the willingness to lead yourself first.

I've phrased my 50 leadership tips in common-sense comments, contrasting the BDSM-Paradigm with what I see as the evolving Triple-E-Paradigm.

BDSM-Paradigm	**Triple-E-Paradigm**

Leading Yourself

1. *"Expertise is all important"* — *"Character is all important"*
   » Expertise and skills can be learned but your character, your moral compass, will determine if people follow you and if you can sleep with a clean conscience.
2. *"Hold back"* — *"All-in"*
   » Leadership hinges on committing yourself and gaining heartfelt commitments from others.
3. *"Alone"* — *"Together"*
   » Lone Ranger leaders fail. Leaders rely on relationships with others, even a higher power, whatever they believe that power to be.
4. *"I'm a different person at work"* — *"I bring my whole self to work"*
   » Good leaders have integrity, a quality of oneness that brings the whole person, body, mind, and soul, into every situation.
5. *"Self-serving"* — *"Serving others"*
   » People will only willingly follow you if they believe you are serving them not yourself.

6. *"I judge others"* *"I assess others"*
    » Good leaders must make risk-assessed judgments about people and actions, but they aren't self-righteously judgmental about people.
7. *"Look at all my toys"* *"My success is in my relationships"*
    » Good leaders measure their success through their relationships with people, rather than materialistic parameters. Good leadership is all about relationships.
8. *"The results I achieve are my legacy"* *"The organization I build is my legacy"*
    » The legacy of a good leader is their results, how they were achieved, and the quality of the people in the organization they have built.
9. *"I'm busy, busy but need to go faster"* *"I have places of sanctuary"*
    » Harried leaders make mistakes. Good leaders take care of themselves and have places of sanctuary to refresh and renew.

Leading Others

10. *"I make my numbers"* *"I make my numbers ethically"*
    » It's not about making your numbers any way you can, even cutting corners. Good leaders achieve their results ethically.
11. "I'll do this for you if you do that for me" "Let's do this together"
    » Transactional relationships are necessary but insufficient. Relationships that transform people endure. Good leaders transform people and organizations.
12. *"Delivering quantity"* *"Delivering quality"*
    » Growth has limits and can't continue forever. Good leaders deliver enduring value to all their stakeholders.

13. *"It's all about me"* *"It's all about you"*
    - » Your ego is your biggest risk as a leader. Good leaders focus on others and humbly tame their egos in the process.
14. *"Only the paranoid survive"* *"Let's grow the pie for everyone"*
    - » Living in a constant state of paranoia is debilitating for people, regardless of Andy Grove's (Intel's former CEO) oft quoted remark. Good leaders are realistic but they also paint a positive vision that draws people into a noble quest.
15. *"If it's not broke, don't fix it"* *"If we don't change, we're toast"*
    - » Leaders embrace change, encouraging people, and even pushing them at times to leave their comfort zones to journey to a better place.
16. *"It's their fault"* *"I screwed up"*
    - » Poor leaders blame others. Good leaders admit what others already know – that leaders are human and make mistakes.
17. *"I know"* *"I don't know"*
    - » Leaders can't possibly have all the answers, so they need to be humble, vulnerable, and ask for help.
18. *"Why are you ragging on me?"* *"I can live with the heat"*
    - » Good leaders accept that criticism comes with the territory of leadership. They have thick skins while listening to the critics to learn.
19. *"I don't need any more opinions"* *"I'm open to your thoughts"*
    - » Good leaders are good listeners and lifelong learners, constantly seeking inputs.
20. *"People need the fear of failure"* *"Let's encourage our people"*
    - » Fear-mongering freezes people into inaction or begrudging compliance. Good leaders engage people optimistically.

21. *"I can't deal with this"* *"I'm scared, but I'll act"*
    - Personal fear builds internal pressure, but good leaders proceed courageously anyway, facing down their fears.
22. *"I need to control these people"* *"Control is an illusion"*
    - No one wants to be controlled. We can barely control ourselves, let alone others. Good leaders liberate people to soar.
23. *"I'll just keep my head down"* *"I'll make ripples"*
    - Avoidance is an abdication of leadership. Good leaders make ripples; great leaders make waves.
24. *"People are lazy and stupid"* *"I believe in you"*
    - Most people have incredible latent abilities within them. Good leaders unleash those potentials.
25. *"I am who I am"* *"I can flex my style"*
    - Good leaders are not stuck in their natural leadership style, they are flexible with their leadership style and adapt depending on the situation.
26. *"Let's get more information"* *"Let's roll"*
    - Good leaders don't equivocate, procrastinate, or constantly ask for more data. They act decisively when the situation requires it.
27. *"We need to eliminate politics here"* *"I'll bridge these groups"*
    - No organization is immune from sub-groups that form with common interests. Good leaders find the overlapping ground between natural factions to encourage people to work together and move ahead.
28. *"Trust only a few"* *"Extend trust smartly"*
    - Where trust is absent, people hold back and don't perform to their potential. Good leaders go first in extending trust and adjust accordingly with more or less trust from there.

29. *"I'll keep my distance"* *"I care about you"*

    » President Theodore Roosevelt said, "People don't care how much you know until they know how much you care." Good leaders are sincerely interested in others.

30. *"Special treatment"* *"I'll eat last"*

    » People resent leaders with preferential treatment. Good leaders park in the regular lot and get in the back of the line in the employee cafeteria.

31. *"I'll be cautious in my communications"* *"I'll be totally transparent"*

    » Very few things should be confidential. In the absence of information, people often assume the worst. Be open about virtually everything.

32. *"We need super-stretch goals"* *"Our goals will be reasonable"*

    » Audacious goals belong in your shared vision. Shorter-term goals must appear achievable to avoid demoralizing people or encouraging them to play the system.

33. *"Maximize shareholder value"* *"Create value for our stakeholders"*

    » Former GE CEO Jack Welch said "maximizing shareholder value is the dumbest idea in the world." Maximizing value for any one group sub-optimizes other groups. That's self-defeating. Good leaders create good value for all their stakeholders.

34. *"Stay in your box"* *"We form lots of temporary teams"*

    » Rigid, hierarchical organization structures are obsolete. Good leaders are constantly forming and reforming temporary teams to attack problems and opportunities.

35. *"We're all responsible"* *"Who will do what by when?"*

    » When everyone is responsible, then no one feels accountable. Good leaders are clear about who will do what by when.

36. *"Do this, not that"* *"Let's achieve this objective"*

    » Micromanaging people shuts down their morale and creativity. Good leaders paint a vivid picture of the clear results desired and allow wide latitude in how people decide to get there.

37. *"Our values are a joke"* *"Does this fit with our shared values?"*

    » Most organizational values are ignored. Good leaders synthesize the shared values of their people and inculcate them into the DNA of the organization.

38. *"Here's my vision"* *"Here's a draft of our shared vision"*

    » Leaders come and go, so the leader's vision doesn't engage people. They really want to commit to a vision that they share. Good leaders synthesize that vision after deep connections with people.

39. *"He's a strange duck"* *"I'll coach and protect you"*

    » Some mavericks are committed to the vision and values of their organization, but are just different. They are often the source of innovative breakthroughs. Good leaders protect and coach those mavericks.

40. *"Toxic but gets results"* *"We don't tolerate jerks"*

    » High-performers who operate contrary to the shared values of the organization need to change or be terminated.

41. *"Culture is airy-fairy"* *"We can create the culture we want"*

    » Good leaders put the culture of "how we do things here" actively on the agenda and empower people to form and protect the desired culture.

42. *"That's not my job"* *"I'll help with that"*

    » Good leaders don't tolerate people who won't help their colleagues. They love people who step-up and assist.

43. *"Don't screw up"* *"I've got your back"*

    » Good leaders give opportunities to people to lead projects and tell them that they'll coach them and stand behind them whatever happens.

44. *"Rah-rah"* *"Let me touch your heart"*

    » Motivating people through hip-hip-hooray speeches and incentive bribes have a short half-life. People motivate themselves if they're inspired. Good leaders inspire the hearts of people.

45. *"Here's our mission"* *"Why do we exist?"*

    » Most mission statements are useless and not memorable. Good leaders synthesize a short, memorable, and noble purpose for why the organization exists that everyone commits to. Disney: "To make people happy."

46. *"Bullet-proof plans"* *"Quick pivots"*

    » The world is changing too fast to live with fixed plans. Good leaders pivot quickly with rapid mid-course corrections.

47. *"Send them to a training class"* *"I'll help you develop"*

    » Training classes are fine, but the best way to develop people is to give them challenging assignments and coach them.

48. *"There can only be one leader"* *"Leadership ebbs and flows"*

    » One leader with lots of submissive followers is a recipe for disaster. Good leaders see leadership as organic and dynamic, where many people flex between leading and following and working supportively together.

49. *"I can't do anything about this"* *"I'm standing up against this"*

    » Idiotic rules and unfairness surround us. Good leaders stand in front of the tanks of injustice.

50. *"Stick to your job and shut up"* *"Everyone here has two jobs"*

» Good leaders empower everyone with two jobs: their regular job and to be a steward of the desired culture with an irrevocable license to lead by the shared values. Culture is the legacy of leadership.

Hopefully, you've found some practical applications in these 50 leadership tips, or if your current workplace is hopeless, you've found why you should seek a better working environment. Bondage to unsatisfactory jobs with submission to bad leaders will drain your life. It's not an easy journey to learn about and find good leadership, but the trip is worthwhile. I wish you success on your quest.

And by the way, I never bothered to read the book or see the movie. I'm really not into BDSM.

Bob Vanourek is the former CEO of five companies and the co-author of the award-winning book Triple Crown Leadership: Building Excellent, Ethical, and Enduring Companies. His next book, Leadership Wisdom: Lessons from Poetry, Prose, and Curious Verse will be published by Motivational Press in 2016.

EXEMPLARY SERVICE IS ABOUT CROSSING THE LINE, AGAIN AND AGAIN.

Doug Sandler

My goal was not to be a big shot. My goal has always been to be a little shot that keeps on shooting. Over the years, I have found one of the biggest problems business owners is their lack of consistency; they stop shooting. Every once in a while they attain greatness (become a big shot), crossing the line from mediocre to great, but most of the time average, good enough and mediocre as their standard operating procedure and their results prove it. Greatness is not just achieved from being successful at performing tremendous acts of enormous proportion. Most of the time, greatness can be achieved through mundane, routine, everyday acts, done consistently with style. I am referring to things like returning phone calls and emails consistently, over delivering on every promise made, and consistently being on time for meetings and appointments. In other words, if you consistently show up, do your best and want the most out of the company you own or work for, you can achieve a superior grade from your customers.

In order to hit the big goals in life, consistency is key. Without it, you will struggle to gain the trust of those around you and probably fall short of achieving your goals. Consistent action with the little things builds trust, loyalty and relationships. Start with the little things, the easy things within your control and eventually you will find your consistency with the big things will start coming into focus as well.

I have built several businesses over the years and have found that consistency has been the key to every success that I have had. To be superior, you have to know what to be consistent with as you climb the ladder to success. Here are the five rungs of the ladder that I have had to climb again and again. Focus on these five time-tested areas as you build, revise, and strengthen your business model and go through your daily activities. Do not lose sight of them. Print them out and look at them daily.

"If 80% of life is just showing up, the other 20% will help you attain greatness. Strive for greatness."

While these five pillars may not be directly measurable on a balance sheet or profit and loss statement, stay consistent with them and success is just a matter of time.

HONESTY

It should go without saying but honesty is non-negotiable. Honesty needs to pass the mirror test as well. Can you look at yourself in the mirror and feel good about what you just promised, delivered or intended? Not only do you need to be honest with others, but you will need to be honest with yourself as well.

When you are honest with your customers, they will respect you more. Take off your sales hat long enough to understand your customers' wants and needs. Once you take a deep dive into their desires, work hard to develop a solution for them. Honesty plays an integral part because if you truly feel like are not a fit, be honest with your customer and tell them that key piece of information. Chances are very good you will be rewarded with future business, referrals, and a very appreciative customer. Keep in mind that not everyone is a potential customer, and that is quite alright. Also, don't confuse a spike of income with a happy customer, if the product or service you sold them is not consistent with their needs.

"If people like you, they will listen to you. If people trust you, they will do business with you." ~Zig Ziglar

With every customer you have and each prospect in your pipeline, your goal is to become their go-to expert and consultant. As such, here are some areas consultants focus so they can provide honest information to their customers and prospects:

1. Consultants provide unbiased information in the form of a competitive analysis.
2. Consultants work within the parameters of a prospect's budget to keep costs in line with vision.
3. Consultants understand finding a solution is not the only way to work with a customer.
4. Consultants take a deeper dive and discover the reasons behind the problem.
5. Consultants are not afraid of the truth. As a matter of fact they work hard to uncover it.

INTEGRITY

Honesty 301 is integrity. Since integrity integrates morals, principles, truthfulness and sincerity, it involves so much more than just honesty. While being consistently honest is very important, having integrity involves your entire being including the way you think, act and behave.

If honesty is a surface condition, integrity can be felt to the core.

Organizations that are run by leaders with integrity are constantly looking for ways to improve and get better in the eyes of their customers. Leaders that lead with integrity care. When an organization's culture has integrity at its roots, it is destined to be liked and admired. When integrity is consistently applied to business practices within the company's brand, it's message will be clear, precise and honest - a winning triple threat.

Organizations with integrity show it to more than just customers. Integrity is a commitment made by an organization to its staff, vendors, partners and anyone else coming in contact with their brand.

At the heart of providing consistent integrity, organizations continually work hard to make improvements to their policies, procedures, products, services and anything else affecting the experience they provide. There must be a consistent message that represents the integrity of company's products and services.

"Integrity is doing the right thing, even when no one is watching." ~C.S. Lewis

Organizations with integrity are consistently fair, honest and trustworthy. They have integrity because it is the right thing to do, even when it is not the easiest and most profitable thing to do. Integrity does not follow the balance sheet, but rather acts independently, rising above the value of currency, a closed deal or a signed contract.

TRANSPARENCY

There is an inherent quality about transparency that is very calming for me. In today's fast paced, often cutthroat world, there always seems to be an, "I win if you lose." undertone. Transparency can help reduce feelings of becoming the victim of an organization's agenda. There should be no winners, no losers, just players in the game. We are all on the same team, working toward a common goal.

Businesses that are transparent are more easily understood than organizations that put roadblocks, obstacles, and filters in the way of doing business with their customers. Similar to integrity, organizations that are consistently transparent become predictable to their market because of their openness.

"A lack of transparency results in distrust and a deep sense of insecurity." ~Dalai Lama

While their message remains clear, they are not afraid of the response that transparency can create if the organization's views are not lockstep with their market. Social media channels are an easy way to help organizations remain transparent today. Transparency leads to shared opinions, messages, ideologies and views. The important part for an organization's message is to remain consistent.

The idea of transparency transcends the messages that an organization shares with its stakeholders. It goes far deeper than that, a transparent organization incorporates policies, procedures, operations, management decisions and financial information as well.

What is so great about transparency is that it ends the market's feelings of doubt, judgement, and second guessing. No longer do customers need to worry if they read the "fine print." All the fine print is exposed and discussed and there should be no feelings of insecurity when using a brand's products or services.

LEADERSHIP

"The quality of a leader is reflected in the standards they set for themselves." ~Ray Kroc

Leaders are consistently good coaches.

Growing up, I can remember the coaches that helped me play my best. These coaches were consistent and predictable. They played me (and my teammates) when we had a good attitude, followed the rules and worked our hardest. When we had an "off day" or our attitude was less than stellar, we remained on the bench. As an adult, the coaches that inspire me follow the same pattern of predictable and consistent actions. They not only tell me the way, they show me the way, and are excellent advisors as well.

Leaders are consistently encouragers.

There is no better feeling than having someone standing on the sidelines and encouraging you to do your best. Cheerleaders lift your spirits when you are down, help you regain traction when you are slipping and turn a potentially negative situation into a positive experience. A great leader consistently understands there is more to life than winning and helps get you back on the path even when things aren't perfect.

Leaders consistently catch people doing something right.

Too often people are criticized. A great leader understands the importance of constructive criticism, but more importantly, will catch people in the act of doing something right. Think about how great it makes you feel when you are given a pat on the back for a job well done. Recognition does not need to necessarily come along with a big reward.

Just the words, "Nicely done!" will be appreciated by the receiver. Leaders that consistently find the good in a situation will be admired by those they are leading.

Leaders consistently empower others.

It's impossible to do it all yourself. At some point you will need others to help you. Great leaders empower others to get the job done. Delegation is a challenge for those that want to retain control, however, leaders that consistently empower others to make decisions, take action, and be in control are the most effective. With the ability to empower others comes the responsibility of understanding failure is a part of the road to success. Empowering others does not negate a leader's ability to take ownership and responsibility for failure. A great leader accepts responsibility for everyone on their team, does not blame others for failure and passes praise to others on the team as well.

Leaders consistently have vision.

Think about great leaders in business and technology. Technology leaders like Steve Jobs and Bill Gates, and business leaders like Sam Walton. Each of these men had great vision. They were able to see the future and determine the right moves for their organizations. Jobs and Gates created products and services by living in the future. Their vision was so clear that they were able to convince others that anything part of their vision was possible. If they had doubts or problems, they created the solutions. Sam Walton, founder of Walmart, had vision of providing quality products at a low price for people all over the world. He did not want to invent anything, but he did have a vision to build a more efficient way to move and distribute products. The people that follow Jobs, Gates and Walton did so because these leaders consistently had vision and developed a way to convert their vision into action while leading others.

Leaders consistently show gratitude

There is nothing better than getting a heartfelt, genuine, "Thank you!" for a job well done. When I was new in the business world, I had a boss that would go out of his way to say thanks. He would express his appreciation in a variety of ways. He would send cards in the mail, leave short notes on my desk, take me to lunch and show appreciation again and again. Over time, it was easy to see why every other department within the organization wanted to work with him. His consistent show of gratitude had a huge impact on those around him. Great leaders are consistent with their appreciation and gratitude.

POSITIVITY

One fact has remained true throughout my entire career dating back to my first job in 1977. While I may not have been completely thrilled with every task I was given, I kept my attitude and approach to each task positive. Part of our challenge in the workplace today is finding others that have a positive outlook. Keep in mind you are only responsible for your behavior and no one else's. If you find yourself working with someone who is less than positive (or negative), work hard to keep your head up and remain positive. Do not allow yourself to get caught in a downward spiral of negativity. I've said many times that negativity can sometimes be disguised as a television program, a LazyBoy recliner or a water cooler conversation. Remain positive, feed your brain with happy information and love the life you are given, you only have one chance to make it work.

"You can't have a positive life and a negative mind." ~Joyce Meyers

1. Focus on what you are good at doing, not just what your faults are.
2. If you look for a silver lining, you are going to find one.
3. Look for positive influences in your life including the people you associate with.
4. Be solution focused. Don't get caught in a rut of playing the blame game.
5. Know that you have a choice. Choose positive.
6. Share your positivity with others. Positive loves the company of other positive.
7. Appreciate the little things that are in your life.
8. Do your best not to compare yourself to others.
9. Stay in the present. Positive lives in the present moment if you look for it.
10. Keep your mind fresh, rested and ready to move. Negativity dwells on what was.
11. Always be a student. When you learn new things you will stay positive.
12. Be grateful for what you have. Focus less on what you don't have.
13. Don't let life happen, make life happen.
14. Communicate openly, freely and honestly. Be confident in your communication.
15. Smile with your entire being, not just your mouth.
16. Learn to reward yourself and not so critical when things go wrong.
17. Be patient with yourself and with those around you.
18. Don't settle for anything other than the best you possible.
19. Keep self-talk positive and provide yourself with consistent positive affirmations.
20. Be curious about your encounters and never be afraid to ask why.

There are many ways you can choose to be positive. The important thing is to be consistently positive, over a long period of time. Do your best to feed positive words to yourself. Although we are our own worst critics, you should be your best supporter as well.

Consistency will set you apart from others and put you on the proper path to success. As you approach business and the relationships that you have, be consistent with your actions and the five pillars. Work hard at remaining consistent like your career and your relationships depend upon it. As you remain consistent, others will begin to notice the changes in you. You have an opportunity to make an impact in this life. By remaining consistent with honesty, integrity, transparency, leadership and positivity you will create lasting results no matter where you go and what you do.

Doug Sandler has over 30 years of business experience as an entrepreneur, business owner, and leader. His book, Nice Guys Finish First is a #1 ranked Amazon Best Seller. He specializes in making connections, building relationships and strengthening connections. Doug is a nationally recognized speaker and writer for Huffington Post. Doug has been titled by a leading social media marketing company in the top 100 of Social Media Thought Influencers to follow.

Chicken Stir Fry

Serves 4

Ingredients

2-3 tablespoons canola oil or peanut oil
2 8-ounce boneless, skinless chicken breasts, sliced into 1/2-inch pieces
1 large yellow onion, peeled and cut into large dice
8-ounces sliced crimini mushrooms
1 red bell pepper, seeded and cut julienne
1 yellow bell pepper, seeded and cut julienne
2 cups broccoli florets
1 cup snow pea pods, strings removed
1 8-ounce can baby corn, rinsed and drained
kosher salt and freshly ground black pepper
2 tablespoons soy sauce
1 teaspoon sambal olek
2 cloves garlic, peeled and minced
1 tablespoon dark brown sugar
1 tablespoon Asian fish sauce
1 1/2 tablespoons lemongrass purée from a tube
2 teaspoons toasted sesame oil

Heat the oil in a wok or deep sauté pan over medium high heat until shimmering. Season the chicken liberally with salt and pepper on both sides and add to pan. Stir fry until almost cooked through. Remove and reserve. Add the onion to the pan and cook until soft but not colored. Add the mushrooms, season with salt and pepper, and stir fry until browned, about 3 minutes. Add in the bell peppers and broccoli and stir fry until crisp tender, about 2 minutes. Add the baby corn and snow pea pods to heat through.

In a small bowl mix together the soy sauce, sambal olek, garlic, brown sugar, fish sauce, lemongrass and sesame oil to make the sauce. Add the chicken back to the wok or skillet. Pour the sauce into the pan and stir to coat all of the ingredients. Cook for about 2-3 minutes to finish the chicken and heat the sauce. Serve immediately.

LEADERSHIP BEGINS WITH LISTENING

Greg Hartmann

One of the biggest "buzzwords" today in organizational change or organizational transformation is team building. Here's the simple fact: for the most part, team building doesn't work. Period. By the way, I didn't say that; major universities have shown much of what is referred to as "team building" is ineffective and does not produce lasting change in an organization. Consider this, team is an emergent phenomenon that happens as stable partnerships are built within an organization. In this chapter, we are going to look at some of the fundamental leadership models that build stable partnerships. The concepts I present are intended to challenge the existing beliefs and ideas that you feel have been the source of your effectiveness up to this point. I am asking you be open to some new and challenging paradigms. You are like a glass that is already full of water so no new water can be added to the glass. I am asking you to bring an empty glass to the conversation. Being able to receive new information is harder than we think it is. It requires suspending what we already know so we can hear something new. Remember, the artist always starts with a blank canvas. It is my intention to leave you with some food for thought and an opportunity to improve your effectiveness in leading teams and building organizations.

Let's first look at what's in the way of an authentic, collaborative "we" culture in most businesses or organizations. Usually the person at the top of the organization, the CEO, the President, the Director, etc. has obtained that position by being an effective, high producing individual. Many of the traits that enabled them (you) to obtain this position have also become a barrier. These traits, unless transcended, begin to limit their effectiveness in having their organization grow and prosper.

Nearly all leaders exhibit a top of the food chain, "better than" attitude. Sometimes this way of being and behavior is expressed very boldly and consciously. Mostly, however, it is nuanced and expressed in subtle ways that end up turning people off and undermining authentic collaboration and teamwork. These characteristics are often expressed as demands, ultimatums or "my way or the highway" communications with little or no thought given to their impact on others. By simply identifying this, we can elevate our communication to a more level approach. People often perform better when spoken with rather than spoken at.

Differences between leadership and management are not well understood. I've spent the better part of three decades engaged in the best practices of leadership and management. Only in the last decade have I begun to understand the differences between these two domains. As we move forward in this chapter, begin to separate the demanding, dictatorial and authoritarian communications of management from the engaging, supportive and collaborative communications of leadership. I want you to relate your communication from these two separate realms. If you are paying close attention to your communication you will begin to differentiate when your communication is management and when it is leadership.

What has had you be effective in running your business or organization is the management skill(s) you have acquired. While management is necessary as a foundation, it is insufficient to foster true collaborative leadership. For instance, the area of music. In order to fully express yourself as artist in the area of music, you must learn all of the notes, scales, modes, time signatures, etc. Once you have this foundation, your expression as an artist can begin to emerge. The learning and expanding of the fundamentals of business is what creates a great manager. To go beyond management and become a great leader, one must become an artist in communication.

LEADERSHIP BEGINS WITH LISTENING

It's become cliché that leaders are good listeners. What makes a difference is what you are listening for and where you are listening from. Most people don't take the time to consciously listen to their own point of view first. When we listen to our own point of view or, our own internal dialogue, then we can hear where we are listening from and what we are listening for. Good listeners are able to suspend their personal biases to listen clearly to the speaker's point of view. You as the listener are always listening from somewhere and for something. Being able to discern our predispositions or motivations allows us to really listen clearly and with less bias. By suspending our own point of view we can clearly hear what another is trying to communicate.

Once you have suspended your point of view, you can begin to listen for something you can align with and for opportunities to move something forward. It is possible to listen generously enough where we are able to include all that is being said by someone, and listen to capture the value or gold in what is being communicated. Great listeners are able to converse not knowing how that interaction should look or turn out. Rather, they enjoy the uncertainty that arises in the dialog and develop a skill in creating a field where people experience that they are a valued partner in the communication. This is the essence of true collaboration.

As you listen for the value in what is being communicated, you can hear what is being said and not said. You can hear yes, no and maybe. You can honor wherever people are at in the discourse. Understanding and having empathy and compassion for where people are in relationship to what is being demanded of them by the challenges in their work and life fosters deep, meaningful relationships that are the building blocks of team environments. Listening is a critical part of the art of leadership that you will be forever expanding and unfolding.

HOW WE LISTEN TO OTHERS

As conscious, functioning human beings we are judging, evaluating and assessing all the time. Mostly, we are mapping things on to what we already know. We agree or disagree, we like or dislike, we accept or reject, all consistent with what we already know and already believe. We find people who agree with our beliefs or views and call them our friends. You do however, have the ability to interrupt this automatic way of listening and consciously listen from somewhere and for something. Let's look at an example with regard to friends, colleagues, subordinates, staff, etc. You have a moment-by-moment choice to listen in way that diminishes another or in away that elevates or supports another.

For example, I am your boss and you report to me. I assign a task to you and you fail miserably. In the next moment I have a choice about how I am going to listen to you. Am I going to listen in a way that diminishes you, which would be listening through the filter of "you're a screw up", and "you can't do anything right". Or, am I going to listen in a way that elevates or supports you, which would be listening through the filter of "you may need more support", or "maybe my instruction wasn't clear enough". These are two entirely different places to listen from and will drastically effect how it goes in the next moment with this person. Incidentally, whichever place I choose to listen from, I will filter everything from that place and gather all the evidence I need to be right about either view. Listening from the first place does nothing to forward a nurturing, collaborative, "we" environment. Much of the high turnover in today's businesses and organizations could be eliminated if people simply took on the practice of discerning how they are listening.

The default place we listen from is the place that judges and diminishes others. We then find people that agree with our view or worse yet we gossip with others to get them to agree with our tainted view. In a collaborative environment where people are out to authentically create "team" and "we", this kind of listening is quickly differentiated. Again, this judging, diminishing filter is automatic and is often our first thought. (Your parents and our culture have trained you that way!) One important facet of the art of leadership is catching this and shifting how you listen to a supportive, "we" based context. Developing this area will require continued practice and will pay great dividends.

Leadership starts with you first. Though you may have people around you who diminish people and gossip about them, the key to shifting this is YOU modeling the behavior of listening to people in a supportive manner. As you build competency and consistency in listening this way, people will naturally begin adopting this way of listening. As this expands, the shift you will see in your culture or environment will be significant.

GAMES WHERE EVERYONE WINS

There is a whole field of study at the university level called game theory. While I am not able to give you all of the ins and outs of game theory in a few paragraphs, understanding some of the basic principles of game theory will go a long way in building a collaborative, "we" culture.

Game theory talks primarily about two types of games. Zero-Sum Games and Non-Zero- Sum Games. Zero-Sum Games are the types of games we are all very familiar with. These are games where there is a winner and a loser. These are the types of games we all grew up playing. Baseball, Football, soccer, etc. What all these games have in common is there is always a winner and always a loser. They are called "Zero-Sum-Games" because how much one team wins by is exactly how much the other team loses by. So if my team wins by 5, your team then lost by 5, so 5–5=0, hence the term Zero-Sum-Games. Zero-Sum-Games are also called strictly competitive games because there is always a clearly defined winner and loser at the end of the game. You could simply say Zero-Sum-Games are win/lose games or I win/ you lose games. Our society is permeated with professional sports and politics that are all about picking a side or team and having them win at all costs. Often, without any regard for the impact on others or those around them. So much of our culture, society and business structure is in this win/lose Zero-Sum paradigm; it is hard to think outside of it.

The other type of game is a Non-Zero-Sum Game, also referred to as a Win-Win Game. This is a game where we all win together or we all lose together. In looking from the Non-Zero-Sum Game perspective, we must really do some thinking to get outside the Zero-Sum Game box we're trapped in. We must begin to ask questions like: "How can I structure this so everyone wins?" or "How can I conduct this business transaction so both my company and my client win?" This perspective really requires a whole new place to think and act from.

We see this often within organizations where even though everyone is "on the same team"; departments are pitted against each other in a win/lose scenario. Years ago when I was less experienced and just starting my business, I worked in an engineering firm where this was the norm. We were a large engineering firm in the factory automation business. The "sales team" sold the project and the "engineering team" implemented it. Since there was limited collaboration between sales and engineering in the sales process, there was always "bad blood" between the two departments. The engineering team would say: "Why can't these idiots just sell what they know we can build?" The sales team would say: "Why can't these engineers give up being so rigid and be a little creative?" This went on and on, project after project. What neither side failed to realize is this Zero-Sum mentality resulted in reduced margins, lower profits and in some cases even lawsuits over projects not delivering on what was sold. This had a huge impact on ALL parties, not to mention the bottom line of the company.

The question is: "What would it have taken to restructure those two departments into a Win-Win, Non-Zero-Sum environment? Looking back from my current perspective, I can see a number of questions to speculate on that would engage the thinking necessary to create a Non-Zero-Sum, Win-Win environment.

Questions like:

» How could we work more closely in the sales process so both sides are collaborating on the solution?

» What would engineering have to give up or let go of to work effectively with the "creative" sales team?

» What would the sales team have to give up or let go of to understand and work within the capability of the engineering team?

» How could compensation be structured on both sides to encourage this type of Win-Win behavior?

» How could the interface between these two teams be designed to foster the collaboration?

Those are just a few questions that begin the kind of critical thinking required to foster this type of environment, but it is enough to give you an idea of looking from a Non-Zero-Sum perspective? If you are not responsible for where you are listening from and what you are listening for it is hard to create Win-Win games. Prior to this understanding of Zero-Sum and Non-Zero-Sum games, I did not even realize what was going on. I would go to lunch with the engineering team and it would be us against them with the sales team. We would gossip about "those sales people" and what a bunch of #$@&*% they were. The problem is on the next project, in the next sales cycle that was where we were all listening to them from. You could say, the sales team didn't stand a chance in winning with us. We were listening from our undistinguished bias, which was shaping and determining every future interaction with the sales team.

IN CLOSING

Leadership is an art. Art is often messy. If I can leave you with anything at the end of this chapter it's: "Get in and mess it up with people!" I don't mean cause trouble with people or annoy them. What I mean is have the courage to begin interrupting the status quo. Be willing to give up your preconceived notions and listen in a way that elevates, supports and nurtures those around you. Begin to speculate on: "how can I turn the Win/Lose games I'm in into Win-Win games?" Begin to ask yourself: "How would this look if I came at it from a we perspective rather than an I or me perspective?" Rather than relating to those around you who are struggling as inept or incompetent you could ask: "How could I support, elevate or partner with this person?" or "What resources do they need that would allow them to grow and flourish?"

Your leadership begins with how you listen!

Greg Hartmann is an internationally known trainer, speaker, program facilitator and cultural architect. He has spent more than 20 years engaged in personal and organizational transformation. He is one of the founders of Cultural Architecture, Inc. Cultural Architecture specializes in using proprietary, cutting-edge tools and models that foster the emergence of team and collaborative "we" based cultures within businesses and organizations.

WHY I BECAME A PASSIONATE ADVOCATE FOR WOMEN-LED VENTURES – AND WHY YOU SHOULD, TOO

Joanna L. Krotz

Before the turn of the 21st century, during the so-called "second wave" of feminism, I actually drank the Kool-Aid. I thought women could, should and would change the world. Catch phrases at the time were all about how the personal is political. It made a lot of sense to me—both then and now—because I could look around and see palpable, unacceptable gender inequities in the home, in the workplace, in government, at all levels. More than that, I could see that women's ways of thinking, talking, working and relating were often dismissed.

I figured that by working in media, I could develop messages and stories that would help bring about change for women and men that would redefine perceptions. I've been a top editor and manager at a string of national magazines, including at Time Inc, Meredith and Hearst, and I've been a commentator and editor with many online publishers, including MSN. I've spent years tracking and analyzing gender-based elements in the workplace, in culture, and in leadership and entrepreneurship. Over those years, I've interviewed hundreds of small business owners, male and female, and heard their stories and struggles. I've run my own small business for more than a decade, a New York-based custom content provider, which keeps me honest about ownership hurdles and triumphs.

My personal has indeed been political. It's been a tricky odyssey, a challenging journey of navigating between the Scylla of battling for recognition and the Charybdis of slow progress and setbacks. For sure, women's roles have changed—dramatically—over the past few decades, most everywhere you look. But honestly? I thought we'd be much further along by now in securing women's parity and prosperity.

Two decades ago, at the United Nation's Beijing women's conference in 1995, world leaders pledged to work toward having 30% women members in their national legislatures and parliaments. Today, a scant 44 legislatures among those 190 countries have met that goal. The US is not one of them. The 114th Congress, elected in 2014, boasted a record number of women. Sadly, that added up to only 104 among the 535 members of Congress, or 19% women in the House and 20% women in the Senate.

Don't forget that women today account for half the US population. Who represents us? Consider Congressional hearings on reproductive rights that consist of all-male committees and exclusively male expert witnesses called to testify about what women need or should have. Also the male-led majority in the House and lobbyist groups during the 2010 healthcare reform debate insist on "gender rating," or requiring that women pay higher fees than men for similar medical services because "women go to the doctor more." Restrictions on women's healthcare are fast becoming law, mandated by male-dominated state legislatures across the country. In August 2015, presidential candidate Jeb Bush—presumably running to be president of all the people, not just men—announced, "I'm not sure we need half a billion dollars for women's health issues." Public indignation and a social media firestorm forced Bush to retract that statement, but first utterances out of people's mouths are usually what they really believe.

Where are the legislators and policymakers who understand women's lives, needs and rights? Too few voices in the Congress are demanding solutions for the proliferating cases of rape on nationwide college campuses and throughout the military. And those few voices are certainly not male. Think how the thinly veiled beliefs about women's advancement, like Jeb Bush's front-line throwaway, reverberate in workplaces and C-suite corner offices nationwide. How far have we really come?

I believe we've now shifted from first generation discrimination into what many researchers call "second generation bias." What is that? The Center for Gender in Organizations at Simmons School of Management in Boston defines it this way: "Distinct from first generation discrimination involving intentional acts of bias, second generation gender practices seem unbiased in isolation, but they typically reflect masculine values and the life situations of men who have dominated in the public domain of work."

In other words, whereas workplace and other discrimination against women used to be blatant and condoned, nowadays it's subtle and, speculates Simmons, even occasionally unintentional.

What does this mean in practical terms? First, despite women's inroads into dozens of professions, men still make the rules and decide the teams. Second, challenges for women have moved beyond getting hired. We've pretty well accomplished that. Hurdles to clear now involve being valued and promoted. It's all about advancement.

By the career metrics men use—who gets the fancy executive suite, big cheese title, multimillion-dollar salary and power seat at the table—women are hardly fast tracking. As of 2015, only 23 CEOs in the S&P 500 are women, or just less than 5%. Likewise, only 25 women are Fortune 500 CEOs. Worldwide, a puny 8% of women CEOs steer companies with revenues of at least $500 million or more.

Let's be clear. The current American workplace is an entirely different playing field than the mid-20th century. Better educated and skilled, shaped by decades of advances and activism, women today have their pick of unparalleled options. Starting with the 1940s wartime reformation, once women integrate any working ranks—in construction, sports, politics, finances, unions, symphony orchestras, the presidential cabinet and on and on—the genie never goes back into the bottle.

But when you do the math, it's crystal clear that men continue to run things in government and business and academia. Despite the half-century since women entered the workforce, they are scarcely advancing into positions of real leadership or power—not even close given women's current levels of education, skills and experience.

A comprehensive high-profile study released in September 2015 by McKinsey & Company and LeanIn.Org, entitled "Women in the Workplace," surveyed 118 companies and nearly 30,000 employees. Its key findings: "Women are still underrepresented at every level in the corporate pipeline...." and, "...based on the slow rate of progress over the last three years, it will take twenty-five years to reach gender parity at the senior-VP level and more than one hundred years in the C-suite." The report analysts point out that common assumptions about women leaving companies because of difficulties balancing work-life and family challenges aren't the motivating reasons. Rather, according to "Women in the Workplace," the large-scale exits are directly owing to the effects of systemic and ongoing gender bias: "Women are almost four times more likely than men to think they have fewer opportunities to advance because of their gender—and they are twice as likely to think their gender will make it harder for them to advance in the future." Perhaps even more discouraging, "74% of companies report that their CEOs are highly committed to gender diversity. However, less than half of employees believe that gender diversity is a top priority for their CEO, and only a third view it as a top priority for their direct manager."

Is it any wonder so many professional women are opting out of male-run companies to assume the reins of their time, lives, families and futures? In fact, if you scan the horizon, you'll see change is looming, mostly because women are leaving corporate compounds to strike out on their own. We now have an entirely new playing field that tilts toward women's economic power and skills. For about a decade now, business media with serious male gravitas have been broadcasting the upsurge in women's economic influence. In a themed issue back in 2006 called "A guide to *womenomics*," *The Economist* announced "Arguably, women are now the most powerful engine of global growth." From *Fast Company* in 2011: "Women dominate the global marketplace." And in 2012, writing in *Time*, no less than President Bill Clinton distilled the essence: "Women rule." The rise of the global She Economy is shaping the future that's hurtling toward us. In turn, that's fueling unprecedented expansion of women's leadership.

What has shifted? The transformation began with women flexing their consumer muscle and lucrative purchasing power as CEO of the family amid a rising global middle class. However, the ripple effects of that economic impact are being increasingly bolstered and driven by women entrepreneurs.

Around the world, women are launching and growing their own businesses in never-before-seen numbers. In Western nations, it's typically because women are walking away from male-driven companies, weary of being undervalued or overlooked, and/or seeking greater control and satisfaction in juggling work, childcare, and broader interests. Among younger, well-educated women, it's often about gravitating to social entrepreneurships to find purpose as well as profits. In developing nations, it's usually because women have few other options to sustain themselves and their families. Study after study shows that when women in developing regions start enterprises, the results and income immediately benefit the community, the family and, especially, girls, who then can become educated.

Starting a business is hard and frequently all-consuming. Yet it's been attracting women at all levels, in every location and in greater numbers than at any time in history. Far from being Plan B for women who can't make it or a part-time stopgap for stalled careers, women most often start enterprises nowadays because in a wide range of circumstances it's so plainly the better option.

If women can't find the flexibility they need in a corporate setting, they figure they can do it if they set their own hours and agenda. When you're the boss, with or without employees, you have the satisfaction, the privilege and sometimes the indulgence of making your own compromises. No one chooses for you. That freedom can be liberating for women.

Ongoing challenges do not belie the dramatic inroads women have made across the business landscape. Likewise, urging women to start their own enterprises has nothing to do with whether selected women can perform as leaders of global conglomerates or commanders of corner offices. Of course they can. But, same as most men, the majority of women have neither the chops nor the drive to ascend to Fortune 1000 CEOs (though women have less of a shot at it).

It's precisely *because* of all the choices women fought for and secured, not despite them, that so many women now are questioning how best to expend their well-honed talents, passions and abilities. Why keep struggling for pay and parity within rigid corporate precincts when the lines keep wavering, the goalposts keep moving and the battle is never won?

It might just come down to time and money. How much of each is important to you? How much of each are you willing to sacrifice? How well can you adjust to the corporate sandbox? How much frustration and lack of recognition can you swallow?

We each only have one life, typically one family and, usually, only a couple of decades or so to build a career. In many respects, women have a broader continuum for work and life choices than men do, with many more potential roles and transitions.

So what's worth doing?

With difficult paths for women in the corporate arena, and having "leaned in" so long and so hard that thousands of women professionals are bent double. Women are increasingly deciding to run their own shows.

On every continent, women are now buying and selling new and different categories of products and services. They're creating new marketplaces, new classes of customers and significantly greater GDP for their regions and the world. And as we've all learned, money talks. Economic power has a way of leading to political clout.

Change happens by degree. Solutions surface locally. Opinions get shaped one person at a time. Focused on the day-to-day challenges and hurdles, women entrepreneurs mostly aren't aware or thinking about the reach and influence of their *collective* power and what they might achieve by banding together. But that perception, too, is shifting as women's business groups set up international networks through social media and technology that allows cheap new ways to connect in far-flung locations.

In the early 20th century, British and American suffragettes rewrote the rules of society forever by demanding that women have a voice and a vote in issues that affect their lives. It got messy and took awhile. Men weren't comfortable seeing women at the ballot box. Now, a century later, women are demanding greater power in business and across society. This is also taking awhile. Again, men are uneasy seeing women take charge. But more and more women are no longer waiting around for male approval or recognition. Instead, they're picking up the reins, and launching their own enterprises. Increasingly, women are gaining control of markets, influencing economic growth and investing in lives of purpose and satisfaction.

As the number of female-owned firms grows, it's become clear that women bring unique strengths to running a business that are especially relevant in the current climate of scant resources and ubiquitous technology. However, it's also clear that women have some characteristic gender weaknesses that often handicap their growth.

Women launch and grow businesses that are categorically different than companies run by men. Around the world, one business at a time, women's entrepreneurship is changing women's future. Lately, I've been eyeing that Kool-Aid one more time.

Joanna L. Krotz is the author of Being Equal Doesn't Mean Being the Same: Why Behaving Like a Girl Can Change Your Life and Grow Your Business, a call to action to women to become entrepreneurs to find parity and purpose, and The Intelligent Guide to Giving. She hosts The Woman's Playbook podcasts and frequently writes and speaks on women's advancement.

Pappardelle with Spinach, Mushrooms, Feta and Walnuts

Serves 4

Ingredients

2 tablespoons extra virgin olive oil

1 large sweet onion such as Vidalia or Maui, peeled, cut in half and sliced thin

4 large cloves garlic, minced

8-ounces sliced crimini mushrooms

4-ounces sliced shiitake mushrooms

8-ounces fresh baby spinach leaves

1 (14.5-ounce) can diced tomatoes with juice

1/2 cup crumbled feta cheese

1/3 cup toasted walnut pieces

kosher salt and freshly ground black pepper

1-pound pappardelle pasta, cooked al dente according to package instructions

1/2 cup reserved water from cooking pasta

Instructions

Heat the oil in a large skillet over medium heat until shimmering. Add the onion and cook until caramelized, about 10 minutes. Add the garlic and cook until fragrant, about 1 minute. Add the mushrooms to the pan and sauté until browned, about 3 minutes. Add the spinach, salt and pepper, and cook until wilted. Add the diced tomatoes with juice and cook until heated through. Add the cooked pasta to the pan along with the feta and walnuts and toss to coat the pasta. Add up to 1/2 cup reserved pasta cooking water to create a creamy sauce. Taste and adjust seasoning with salt and pepper. Serve immediately.

THE FOUR CONVERSATIONS YOU MUST GET RIGHT AS A LEADER

Wally Schmader

Almost all successful leaders understand that effective leadership really comes down to influence. Influencing outcomes, influencing direction, influencing decisions, influencing atmosphere and influencing people. The degree that a leader can successfully influence people and teams becomes their "lid" in their role. The only reliable tool we have to influence others is communication. Any leader or manager who is serious about improving his own performance should always start with improving his communication skills and techniques.

Influential leaders are great communicators. They know what to say and when to say it, and they understand that effective communication is a study. It does not come naturally, and it needs to be worked on the same way a leader might work on her technical skills. We have all worked with would-be leaders who never seemed to get it right. They would say the wrong thing at the wrong time. Or worse, they would say nothing when something definitely needed to be said.

Your communication skills are your #1 leadership asset. This is especially true in high-performance environments or in organizations going through a lot of change. Leadership communication skills is a very broad topic. Let's focus on effective one-on-one techniques. We are going to review the four conversations we must get right as leaders.

CONVERSATION #1 - THE CRUCIAL CONVERSATION

This is a must-have conversation for specific situations. No leader looks forward to a Crucial Conversation because of the stress associated with it. How do you know it is time for a Crucial Conversation?

- » Someone is underperforming and affecting the overall results
- » Someone is creating issues for the team (any kind of issue)
- » You are invested in them and they are not succeeding
- » It is not going improve without your intervention

Every situation is different, of course, but there are proven ways to have a Crucial Conversation. Most leaders will either avoid this dialog or go into it without any preparation. Top leaders know how to structure this talk for success with a conversation script.

Your Crucial Conversation Script:

1. Explain reason for meeting (performance issue)
2. This (issue) concerns me because...
3. Confirm their understanding of issue
4. Make a clear coaching recommendation
5. Confirm recommendation & have person repeat it back for understanding
6. Set up a review time and put it on both of your calendars
7. Clarify your confidence in the person

CONVERSATION #2 – THE ROCKSTAR REMINDER

This one is so simple, yet very few leaders ever do it. Here is the summary:

- You have someone on your team with amazing potential
- They are still learning and improving
- They may be hitting some bumps in their career
- You expect them to do GREAT things
- You need to tell them!

This is the Rockstar Reminder. It is as important as it is simple.

CONVERSATION #3 – THE NOW OR NEVER CONVERSATION

Every skilled leader has had this kind of dialog, and none of them look forward to it. The leader needs to understand that the key to this conversation is timing. There is always stress and emotion involved, usually for both parties. If a leader has a "Now or Never" conversation too early it will feel like manipulation. If the dialog happens too late, there won't be enough time for the person to make the necessary changes. That is why the timing has to be absolutely perfect.

The Now or never conversation should always follow a failed Crucial Conversation (#1). The person knows that their performance/behavior/issue cannot continue and has had some time to make changes. This person is now at risk.

The best way to prepare for a Now or Never conversation is with talking points. Lots of different things can happen in this dialog, so scripting your comments and questions is not the best way to prepare. Here are some effective talking points that will take the conversation where it needs to go:

"We seem to be stuck and we're running out of options"

"You are making a decision about your future with your performance, do you understand that?"

"Your potential in this role is as great as it ever was"

"I would hire you again if you walked in for an interview"

"This is the moment where things must change"

This dialog is the last chance a leader has to influence behavior. The Now or Never conversation is one that most leaders are unwilling to have. You can separate yourself from other leaders and managers with your candor and honesty.

CONVERSATION #4 - THE STAY INTERVIEW

As its name implies, the Stay Interview is the conversation you have with a proven and valued team member who you very much want to stay. This important tactic is routinely overlooked, even in high-performing organizations. Do you want to surprise and impress your team with truly progressive leadership? Learn how to conduct the Stay Interview.

How Do You Know it is Time for a Stay Interview?

The recommended strategy is to add stay interviews to your calendar, a quarterly schedule works best. Every quarter you will consider who on your team is really performing? Who might be being overlooked? Who is in a role that may have less recognition attached to it compared to other roles? Who seems to have a lot of upside? You are not really reacting to a certain accomplishment... you are paying close attention to sustained performance.

An important thing to remember is that you don't use the phrase "stay interview" with the candidate. That is an internal descriptor to help you remember what you are doing and why. As far as they are concerned you are scheduling time for a conversation with them about their position and performance.

Another important detail is that you do not want to schedule a series of stay interviews. These are occasional and important one-off conversations. Doing them too often will erase the positive effects.

HOW TO CONDUCT A STAY INTERVIEW

The meeting should be set casually, and not as a part of a formal performance review. You should ask the candidate if they can set aside some time for you on a certain day. Make sure your tone is upbeat and positive, and don't set the time more than a day or two into the future. You don't want this valuable person worrying for a week about a pending conversation with the Boss.

When the day comes, keep things very casual. The only formal part of the meeting will be your preparation. Start things off by thanking the person for taking the time to meet. Next, tell them you have been consistently impressed by their performance. Be specific here and note aspects of the candidate's work that are excellent. For the people you are doing Stay Interviews with, this should be easy.

Tell them you want to ask them some questions about themselves and their job, and that you would appreciate candid responses. Make it clear that they are in a safe environment with a leader that really values them.

GREAT QUESTIONS FOR YOUR STAY INTERVIEWS:

Here is a series of great questions for Stay Interviews. You will see a few that are very applicable to your situation and maybe a couple that are not. Add a few of your own questions to the list- maybe something specific to the mission or culture of your organization. Start with general questions and then move to more specific topics.

» How are things going for you?

- Are you enjoying work?
- What is the best part of your job?
- What is the part you enjoy least?
- If you could change something about your current responsibilities, what would it be?
- Do you ever have tasks that feel like a waste of time?
- Where do you see yourself in five years?
- Is there a task or process that is done outside of your responsibility that you think we could improve on?
- Is there something that you think we may be focusing on too much?
- Do you see any growth opportunities that you think we may be missing?
- How do you feel about our working relationship?
- Do you have any coaching tips for me?
- Do you know how valuable you are to this organization?

These questions, along with the additional questions you add to the list, will guarantee a positive dialog with your candidate. You will have opportunities to ask for more detail and possibly hear some great ideas... maybe even do a little brainstorming. The last question will give you an opportunity to tell the candidate how much you appreciate them and their great work.

Your Stay Interviews should take around 20-40 minutes. Any shorter and it wasn't a substantive conversation. Any longer and you probably started talking about other people or went off topic. 20-40 minutes is your sweet spot.

It would be hard to list all of the positive benefits of Stay Interviews. Many of the best outcomes will be invisible, but still powerful. You can strongly influence retention, culture, job satisfaction, expectations, working relationships, and much more. By adding the Stay Interview to your repertoire of leadership skills you will be placed in a small group of progressive leaders who know how to pay the right kind of attention to the right people.

Now you know the four conversations you must get right as a leader. Using these templates, along with your own thoughtful preparation, you will see your positive influence over people and outcomes grow exponentially. Communication skills are your #1 asset as a leader. I strongly recommend that you keep working on improving your skill set as a progressive and confident communicator.

> *Wally Schmader has over 25 years of successful hands-on experience developing and leading high-performance teams. He has worked successfully with senior executives, middle managers and front-line leaders and managers.*
>
> *He is a highly regarded leadership coach and described many of his strategies and insights in his first book "Full Contact Leadership: Dynamic New Ideas & Techniques for Today's Leaders". Wally is the Co-Founder of the Exceptional Leaders Lab, a community of progressive business and organizational leaders. Wally has been interviewed by Fortune Radio, the popular Join Up Dots podcast, and been a featured speaker at many conferences, forums and seminars.*

Pretzel Crusted Chicken
Serves 4

Ingredients

1 cup pretzel crumbs (Pulse salted pretzel rods in food processor to create crumbs)

1 tablespoon kosher salt

1 tablespoon freshly ground black pepper

1 tablespoon granulated garlic powder

1 tablespoon granulated onion powder

4 boneless skinless chicken breasts, 4-6-ounces each

1/2 cup spicy brown mustard

Non stick cooking spray

Instructions

Preheat oven to 450° F. Line a rimmed baking sheet with heavy duty foil and place a wire cooling rack inside. In a large shallow dish mix together the pretzel crumbs, salt, pepper, garlic powder and onion powder. Place 1 chicken breast in a large plastic zipper bag and pound with mallet until about 1/3-inch thick. Repeat with each of the remaining breasts. Coat each breast with the mustard and then place in the crumb mixture and coat completely, pressing to adhere. Spray the wire rack with non stick cooking spray and place the chicken breasts on top. Spray the top of the breasts and place in the preheated oven. Bake for 20-25 minutes until the chicken is complete cooked and the coating is crisp and brown. Let rest 5 minutes and serve.

SUCCESS

A "BALANCED DIET" APPROACH TO LIFE, WORK AND FAMILY

Scott Behson

Whether we're carrying the load at home or juggling the demands of career, family and other commitments, it can often feel like we're stuck running on a giant hamster wheel. It is hard to jump off the wheel, sit in the pile of cedar chips, shove some nuts into our cheeks, and take time to look at the bigger picture.

We'd be better off slowing down and attending not just to work and family, but also to all of the aspects that make up a full life. Life is not a marathon, nor is it a series of sprints. It's more like a decathlon with many different events leading to an over-arching goal – and each component requires a slightly different skillset. Work and family may come first, but we need to pace ourselves and spend some time thinking about how we can be more effective in all aspects of our lives.

A lot of people don't like the term, "Work-Family Balance." Some prefer "Work-Life Balance." I don't. After all, work is an important part of life and the two are not opposites or enemies. In fact, in many ways our experiences outside of work help us in our careers, and the skills and perspectives we gain at work can be applied elsewhere in our lives.

Others take issue with the term balance, and instead prefer terms like integration, fit, blend or success. But I like the word balance, so long as we have the right visual in mind. When some see "work-family balance," they think of balance as in a scale, seesaw, tightrope or balance beam in which there is a single, hard-to-find, precarious equilibrium point between two opposing forces.

Thinking about balance that way leads us (and, unfortunately, managers and employers as well) to think about work and family solely as trade-offs. I think this is the wrong way to think about it.

We need to stop seeing work and family as "either-or." Time for both work and family are very important components of a full, meaningful life, and there's more to life, too. If we don't reflexively see them as opposing forces, we may come to understand that both can enhance the other in helping to build a balanced life.

Therefore, when I think about a balanced life, I find it helpful to visualize a "balanced diet" rather than a tightrope. Just as a balanced diet requires more than two food groups, a balanced approach to life means time and attention devoted to the full range of life activities, not just work and family. A full, balanced life means attention to work, family, self, exercise, religion, community, extended family, friends, social needs, relationships and relaxation. All of these priorities are important parts of a complete, and rewarding life.

Sometimes we need to prioritize one aspect of life over others and temporarily slip out of balance. There are inevitable ebbs and flows in both home and work. Some work weeks require intense hours and/or travel. Some weeks, home requires our full attention.

The use of a tightrope metaphor frames temporary imbalance as a failure; anything less than 50/50 means a perilous fall. If, instead, we think about a balanced diet, eating too many carbs one day can be balanced out by extra salad the next. And it also helps us recognize that we need many food groups to be healthy – there are many important things in life that are neither work nor family.

Many authors and writers emphasize the need to protect family time from interference at work. Of course, as there are only 24 hours in a day and 168 in a week, work and family compete with each other for our two most valuable resources, time and energy. Time is non-renewable, and energy only renews itself slowly over time. It is only natural to focus on the conflict between work and family.

However, it isn't always that simple. In many ways, work and family enhance each other. In fact, they are two of the main components of a full, meaningful life – success in both is vitally important. In fact, time and energy spent at work can make us more effective at home, and time and energy spent on parenting can make us more effective at work. For example, after becoming a father, I learned to be more organized, efficient, empathetic, and to better differentiate what is/is not truly important. There is research evidence that I am not alone in experiencing work-family synergy. According to a study by the Boston College Center for Work and Family:

» 64% working parents agreed that their family gave them knowledge/skills that made them better employees
» 61% agreed that family life made them use their time more efficiently, helping them be better employees
» 82% agreed that family life made them feel happier, helping them be better employees

A more recent follow-up study by the folks at Boston College also shows those who, because of workplace flexibility, have more time with their kids are:

» Happier at work
» Less likely to voluntarily leave their company
» More engaged at work
» Report that their work performance is improved by having enough time with family

So, it works both ways. Conflict and synergy. A balanced diet metaphor helps us think in terms of synergy. It reminds us we don't have to choose between work, family, and the rest of our lives. We can choose enough of each to be successful and that, as a result, we'll be more effective in all the aspects of our lives.

There's no sense in choosing just steak or just potatoes, let's take enough of each to make a great, balanced meal. A balanced diet extends far beyond steak and potatoes, or bacon and eggs, or spaghetti and meatballs, or PB&J (or any other yummy two-food combination). It's more like Thanksgiving dinner. Turkey and stuffing , cranberry sauce, sweet potatoes , corn, green beans and some weird Jello-fruit thing. There would be wine, beer, mashed potatoes, and my wife's awesome lemon-poppy seed cake and far too many other desserts to list.

To many, this sounds nice in theory. But is there actually enough time to devote to our full range of priorities? I know we're all busy, and some face extraordinary circumstances. But, I submit that, for most of us, if we honestly examine our time usage, we can uncover and find the time necessary.

There are 168 hours in a week; this gives us a jumping off point for examining our time use and making positive changes.

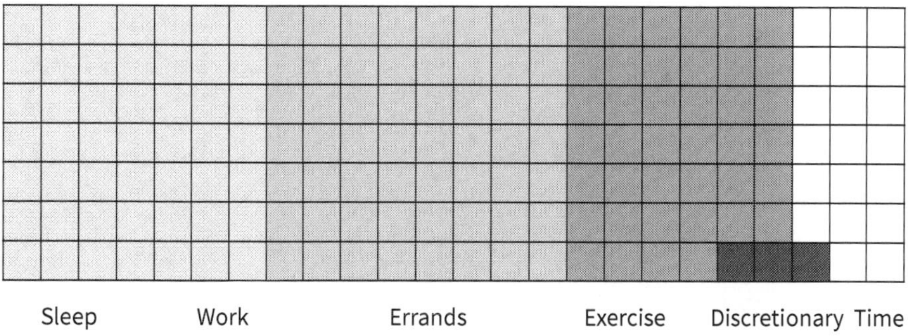

First, let's take away 49 just for sleep. Don't try to cheat on this. If you are getting less than seven hours a night, you are probably not resting enough, and your decreased energy will take its toll on the rest of the hours of the week.

So you've really got 119 hours. Let's assume you're ambitious and subtract 56 for work. This means working eight hours a day, seven days a week – or, if your weekends are off-limits, 11+ hours a day on weekdays only. I know some of you put in more time than this. However, outside of very few professions (and peak times at others) no one really needs to – so if you do, you are probably working inefficiently or being pressured to uphold unrealistic expectations.

Subtracting all 56 hours, that leaves you with 63. Now let's take out two more chunks of non-fun activity – 7 hours per week of commuting, and 33 hours per week of errands and housework, ranging from cleaning and shopping to changing diapers and cooking. A decent slice of this time represents time with family, but more the "have to do" stuff rather than the "want to do" stuff. At this point, you still have 23 hours remaining.

Maybe you've been saying you don't have time for exercise, but it seems you do. Exercise makes you more effective the rest of your work week and at home. Let's devote 3 hours to that. This leaves you with 20 hours of free time- just about three hours a day- to do whatever else makes you happy and healthy. Use this time to pour into your relationships with your children, spouse, church, friends, community or extended family- with some time left for personal renewal.

I find it helps to set long-term goals and then schedule in specific times to meet these goals- if not every week, at least regularly. If time with your friends is important to you, but (like most of us) you have allowed more pressing demands to crowd out social time, is there a way to schedule some time in during 20 hours a week? If we feel like we're drifting away from our spouse, is there a way to use two of the 20 discretionary hours each week to hire a sitter and go on a date? If we feel rushed during family time, is there a way to designate one evening a week without any distractions, shut off our screens, and build a new family tradition? I bet that, with a little bit of effort, we can do this.

So, let's end this chapter by converting our priorities into specific goals, and thinking of ways we can schedule our priorities into our discretionary time.

Parenting/Family	My example
6 Month Goals	- Spend an extra hour/week with my son - Increase his confidence going into baseball season
Ways to Schedule in Time	- 1 hour every Saturday morning playing catch or taking to batting cage

Parenting/Family	
6 Month Goals	
Ways to Schedule in Time	

Spouse/Relationship	
6 Month Goals	
Ways to Schedule in Time	

Extended Family	
6 Month Goals	
Ways to Schedule in Time	

Friends/Social	
6 Month Goals	
Ways to Schedule in Time	

Physical/Exercise	
6 Month Goals	
Ways to Schedule in Time	

Relaxing/Recharging	
6 Month Goals	
Ways to Schedule in Time	

Hobbies/Interests	
6 Month Goals	
Ways to Schedule in Time	

Religious/Spiritual	
6 Month Goals	
Ways to Schedule in Time	

Community Service	
6 Month Goals	
Ways to Schedule in Time	

Career	
6 Month Goals	
Ways to Schedule in Time	

Financial	
6 Month Goals	
Ways to Schedule in Time	

If we want to live a successful life, we need to be sure we address all of our most important priorities. A balanced diet approach can help us get there.

> *Scott Behson, PhD, is a professor of management at Fairleigh Dickinson University, a national expert in work and family issues, and was a featured speaker at the recent White House Summit on Working Families. He's the author of the Amazon #1 best seller,* ***The Working Dad's Survival Guide: How to Succeed at Work and at Home*** *(Motivational Press, 2015), the first book of its kind to provide advice and encouragement for working fathers, helping them to achieve success in their careers while also being the involved, loving dads they always wanted to be. Scott founded and runs the popular blog, "Fathers, Work, and Family," dedicated to helping working fathers and encouraging more supportive workplaces. He writes regularly for the Harvard Business Review Online, Huffington Post and the Good Men Project, and has also been published in TIME and The Wall Street Journal. He frequently appears in media, including MSNBC, NPR and Fox News. Scott also has worked with Fortune 500 companies as a consultant, and has served as a keynote speaker at major events.*

PERSEVERANCE

Deborah Riley Magnus

A few years back I went through a training session where the instructor asked everyone to describe themselves in just one word. It didn't take me very long to come up with mine. It was perseverance.

I was born in Boston in 1969 and grew up in the projects of South Bronx, New York City. The thing I remember most about living in New York was the fires burning almost every night. The last fire I experienced was my family climbing out of a burning apartment onto a huge fire ladder. We rushed out trying to avoid the plaster from the ceiling dripping down like melted icing on a cake. One bit of plaster burnt right through my brother's jacket giving him third-degree burns on his shoulder. After that my family was homeless with nowhere to go. For a while, we stayed mostly in cars and sometimes slept at strangers' homes.

My father was black and my mother was white and back then that was not accepted. I will always remember a night my father was badly beaten by the police, just because he was with my mother. It was strange because he was usually the one doing the beating, both to my mother and all of the kids. My family was about as dysfunctional as possible, with alcohol and drug addiction affecting our daily lives. When I was 10 my father got so drunk that he beat me with his huge belt buckle and split my head open. My parents had no choice but to take me to the hospital. I was taken into state custody for my protection. But it wasn't very long before I was sent back to live with my parents.

We made money with shrink wrap art, and we had paper prints that we would attach to pieces of wood and cover with a liquid that hardened like glass. We would sell those wooden pictures on street corners coming back and forth from the box truck we lived in as we traveled back and forth between Boston and New York. Years later, one of my first jobs was delivering newspapers and I was unnerved to realize the delivery van we drove around was a pretty good replica of the van we drove around and lived in for years. But we did what we had to do to survive, to persevere.

The first real apartment I can remember was in Worcester, Massachusetts, and it was a house of terror. Some nights I could hear my mother screaming, dishes and glasses breaking, thuds from her being hit, and more screams. There were nights I would stay up all night scared, and many other nights I would have to go to the bathroom but I would hold it all night because I was terrified to leave my room. After that I learned to climb out of my bedroom window. I would shimmy down the railing, go to the bathroom outside, and run to the end of my street where I would call 911 from the payphone and tell the dispatcher that my dad was beating my mom. I would run back to the house as fast as I could to make sure I got there before the police, so my father didn't know it was me who called. This went on for a quite a while, until the night finally came where the police got to the house before I got back. My father knew and I was terrified. It wasn't long before he got drunk again and I took a serious beating. But you know what? Even after that, I still climbed out of my window and called the police on him regardless of what he would do to me. I didn't know it then, but I was learning a hard lesson in perseverance. In a sick way this helped me become the strong and fearless person I am today.

When I was around 13, my mother escaped from my father with us kids, and we lived in shelters for a few years before settling into one of the poorer areas in Worcester. I never saw my father after that. The first school I went to long enough to make friends was Elm Park Community School. Unfortunately, most of the friends I made were from the same type of environment as me. Today many of them are alcoholics, drug addicts, gang members, in and out of jail, living in poverty, or all of the above.

A lot has changed for me since then, but Elm Park Community School is still a big part of my life today. Instead of getting into trouble with the kids, I visited a speaker every year to talk about perseverance. I have a keynote called Broken Chains that's about breaking through unhealthy generational cycles. I teach kids that just because they grew up a certain way doesn't mean that way has to be their destiny.

I was a very angry, insecure, and aggressive kid who got into a lot of trouble because of my lack of coping skills. When things didn't go my way the only thing I knew was to become aggressive and I got into many fights. Fighting was about the only thing my father taught me growing up. He taught me kickboxing and how to defend myself, but he also personally taught me how to take a serious beating. If I cried when he beat me, I got beaten harder. This came in handy when I boxed in my twenties – when I got hit so hard that I saw the stars it didn't bother me. I kept going. Fighting is where I found my confidence. Although I don't advocate street fighting, kickboxing helped me continue to exercise perseverance. As you can image, with my anger and aggression, things got much worse in my teens when I was introduced to drugs and alcohol.

I wasn't interested in schoolwork and was sent to an alternative high school, which I dropped out of. At 17 I got a job working in a call center setting up appointments for sales reps who sold $1500 Kirby vacuum cleaners. Then at 19, I ended up in another call center calling homeowners and getting them to take credit card applications over the phone. I was actually really good at those call center jobs. Thinking back, I believe it was because I was stubborn; someone saying no to me just made me try harder. Perseverance kicked in. I actually enjoyed the jobs too, both because I was good at them and because they were flexible enough for my dysfunctional lifestyle. But I knew I needed to go back and get my GED, which I did, in addition to completing a Ford Motor two-year college automotive program. After graduation, I got a job at a new car dealership, but because of my attitude it didn't last long. I ended up taking a half dozen jobs that all ended the same way – with me quitting or being fired. I didn't respect managers and in return they didn't respect me either.

Not long after this, my mother started a local trade magazine and she hired me to sell advertising. My career options were slim pickings anyway. I was pretty much unemployable because showing up to work on time was something that didn't interest me. However, no one could argue that I wasn't good on the phone. That's how I ended up working for my mother's company for 14 years. I developed excellent sales skills through cold calling numbers right out of the phone book and knocking on doors. I was a selling machine at work, but my personal life was a mess.

As I got older, I got angrier and drank more so I didn't have to deal with my inner problems. This led me to a lot of trouble and run-ins with the law. I simply did not care what happened to me because I carried so much pain inside. I figured I deserved to either be in jail or dead.

While working for my mother's company two very significant things happened to me. The first was the birth of my amazing daughter Jaquilyn. Because of the state I was in at the time, unfortunately, I didn't spend a lot of time with her for the first few years of her life. (But looking back, the silver lining is that she wasn't subjected to my lifestyle at the time. She never saw me at my worst, and I'm thankful for that). The second significant thing was getting myself into trouble with the law one time too many. I was sentenced to a six-month state-run alcohol and drug rehabilitation program and three and half years of probation once I got out. I didn't realize it at the time, but the judge who sentenced me gave me the greatest gift of my life. I believe now that the program was the turning point for me to become a better person.

In that rehabilitation center I was introduced to an older lady who convinced me that if I wanted to change my life I had to humble myself. I had to ask God for help. I wasn't raised in a religious family and I didn't think praying would work, but I was desperate and had nothing to lose. I remember the first time I got on my knees in the rehab. I made sure no one was around. I literally put my knee on the floor and then jumped back up. I didn't do what most people consider prayer–talking to God–but taking that simple action was the start to my new life. That continuous, daily action helped me change my attitude, and when I got home I changed my environment. I got involved with people who didn't drink or do drugs and was introduced to local AA, which is still a massive part of my life. As I write this, I am six days away from my 13-year anniversary of sobriety and I still go to three meetings every week. Sobriety hasn't been an easy journey, but the one thing I did and still do today is get on my knees. No matter what happened in my life, I persevered with my quest to remain sober. I truly believe that is why I am who I am, and where I am today.

Not long after getting sober, my then 10-year-old daughter Jaquilyn said, "Mom's friend makes lots of money in real estate. You should get into real estate." I didn't think much of it, but the next morning when I woke up, I couldn't get it out of my head. "Why not?" I thought. After 14 years, I didn't love working for the family business anymore and wanted to try something new. So I went online and signed up for a real estate course.

When I got licensed, I signed with Keller Williams because Steve, the person who recruited me, offered me the option to tele-market for his team. I could earn money just for calling and setting appointments. I started right away and Steve taught me how to call for-sale-by-owner (FSBO) leads. We checked all of the magazines, websites, and newspapers, and I tried my hardest to set appointments. It didn't come easily but because of my history of cold calling, I was able to get seven listings within my first month in the business. That may sound easy but I must have spoken with over a thousand people to find those seven. I remember days when people said, "Don't call me!" or "Take me off your list!" or "If I wanted an agent I would have called you!" These were of course all followed by clicks of the phone hanging up, but I did not give up. I persevered!

After about six months on Steve's team I decided that I didn't need to be on a team anymore, so I went solo. I focused 90 percent of my efforts in FSBOs, which was pretty much all I knew back then. I had a good first year closing about 40 transactions. I remember back then I absolutely loved real estate, so much so that I couldn't sleep. I stayed up all night working on websites, learning scripts, and doing whatever else would help me get better at my job and sell more. After about two years I started my team with a buyer's agent. I had built a fairly successful team and around 2006 we started closing about 90 homes a year. In real estate, the national average for agents is about six homes, so you can see how my perseverance paid off.

I kept pushing to become better at selling real estate and it worked. I became a top agent in Worcester and in 2009 the city government asked me to present on a new program that they were rolling out for first-time home-buyers, called Buy Worcester Now. My job was to serve as spokesperson for the real estate community and train other realtors on the program. I prepared for the conference as much as I could and felt pretty good about my presentation. When I showed up to present at the new high school, I was surprised to be speaking in front of a seemingly massive crowd of 400 realtors. I got very nervous, and to be frank, my presentation was a disaster. I remember leaving there embarrassed, covered with sweat and telling my girlfriend (now wife), "I will never do that again." And I meant it!

After my disaster performance I couldn't believe it when the city called me again to present at the Local Board of Real Estate. And I also couldn't believe I agreed to it. Well, I practiced more, calmed my nerves, and I did a thousand times better. That was when I knew that speaking and training was what I wanted to do. I found my calling. I never looked back from there. I took Dale Carnegie training, I took every "train the trainer" training, I went to every class I could, I studied speakers, formed a relationship with Jairek Robbins, (the son of personal development guru Tony Robbins) and got to know another half dozen other professional speakers, who I do events with today. Over the past couple of years I became a Keller Williams University Certified Instructor and I have had the opportunity to teach in dozens of market centers and different regions. In 2010 I presented at a KW event in front of more than 10,000 people and I'm proud to say I was completely comfortable on stage.

The most gratifying moments for me are when people from all over the country tell me things like, "I got my first listing because I took your class," or "I used one of your scripts and I got an appointment," or "I started exercising again because I heard you speak," or "Now I get up earlier for work because of your session." But even more than helping professionals hone their skills and advance their careers, I love being able to hear a pin drop in an auditorium of 200 sixth-graders because they can relate to my story. Speaking, presenting and helping people is my passion! When I read Simon Sinek's book *Start with WHY*, I knew right away that I had the same vision in life: "Inspiring others to do things that inspire them." This shows up everywhere in my life today.

I know I defied all odds to be where I am today and I want to encourage others to do the same. I have an amazing second daughter, Samara, who will be three years old in a few months, and a beautiful wife, Vee. My older daughter, who apparently served as a wise career coach for me at only 10 years old, has grown up to become an amazing and successful woman, and ironically, a sales trainer just like her dad.

Today I own a coaching and speaking business and I'm just finishing writing my first book. In 2014, my team received an award for being the number one productive team at our Real Estate board. But the most beautiful and important thing is that neither of my daughters had to experience a childhood like the one I experienced. This, in itself, is my greatest accomplishment by far. Thinking back to the instructor who asked us to describe ourselves in one word, I'm confident I got it right when I said perseverance.

RABBIT HOLE PROBLEM SOLVING

A day doesn't go by without some sort of problem or challenge. It's what keeps us on our toes. This particular thought process links all the way back to our fight or flight days when a saber-tooth tiger represented a serious problem to be solved, quickly.

Sometimes a little chaos is needed to hone those thinking-on-our-feet skills. Great minds are broad minds; they see things linearly, circularly, in bursts of sparkles, and with utmost clarity. However this is only after shifting gear and getting off the main road. One might call this style of problem solving side-street thinking or a nomadic method of dealing with issues. I call it Rabbit Hole Problem Solving and it can be effectively used for any quandary or setback life presents.

There are seven techniques for Rabbit Hole Problem Solving, and it begins simply.

1) Look at the Problem Differently – Problems come in all sizes and shapes. They might be small day-to-day inconveniences, or major business issues requiring quick resolution. Our initial reaction to the problem sets the tone for either finding a perfect solution or dwelling on the peripheral elements at hand.

Most people immediately focus on the problem and how it affects them. It's easy to sidetrack our thinking to encompass the person responsible. The problem may present such a large challenge that it twists our imaginings toward nonproductive places, no matter how improbable. When this happens, the smartest thing to do is take a deep breath and see it from the other person's perspective. Was the problem caused by a misjudgment? A misunderstanding? Miscommunication? On your part perhaps? We're all human and mistakes happen. Most times a shift in our point of view can make all the difference.

The first and most important step is to forgive the person responsible for the mistake, especially if that person is you. This is the first cleansing breath before meeting the Mad Hatter at the bottom of the rabbit hole. There's no time for baggage, so let it go. This technique requires a little compassion, a little understanding, and a lot of patience. Granted, the problem has landed in your lap, but it is ineffective to focus on blame over solution. This particular technique helps clean out emotions that has no place in your problem solving efforts.

If your toddler spilled the milk, it's a perfect teaching opportunity while you mop up the mess. However, if your assistant manager leaked company information through social media, other actions may need to be taken. Seeing the assistant manager's point of view may or may not change the outcome, but it will empower you to know you have heard all sides and responded without a knee jerk emotion.

If you are the kind of person who bristles and sees red when trouble looms its head, you may find great help in stepping out of your own head and looking at the problem from a different point of view. Practice this approach everyday and everywhere; while driving, shopping; working, planning and interacting with friends. It's one thing to imagine we know how another person thinks; it's far more advantageous to truly care enough to understand. This technique can smooth every part of your daily problem solving responsibilities.

2) Toss Out Old Solutions – We all have tried and true solutions to most of our recurring problems. Too much traffic? You know of an alternate route. Too many interruptions? You can always close your office door. Missed deadlines by your support staff? Occasional rewards can make easy work of that problem. Your wife wants the bedroom painted? It doesn't seem important to you, but rather than argue you begin to choose a color you both like and purchase a few paint brushes. This list can go on and on because there are at least a hundred little problems every day that we've created acceptable solutions for. But have we?

Are you finding that your support staff has stopped meeting deadlines when not offered a reward? That your idea of blue paint and your wife's idea of blue paint are completely different? Obviously rewards and paint chips aren't working. Now what?

Get creative and break old problem solving patterns. This technique begins with the daily little issues but can build wonderful flexibility for those big surprise problems that come up when you least expect them. It's a little like keeping your knees soft so that you can shift easily from one tennis volley to the next. It will uncover an unexpected ability to shift gears, to solve problems beyond your normal process.

Start small when adding this to your problem solving repertoire. Think about that daily drive to work. Plan on three or four possible alternate routes. Consider leaving for work earlier or later. Think about changing your schedule. Visualize how these possibilities can seamlessly fit into your life and implement as many of them as possible.

By doing this with small daily challenges, you will discover that your mind works faster and sharper when a saber tooth tiger arrives on the horizon. It's now conditioned for flexibility and logic in the blink of an eye.

3) Try Imagining the Opposite – We like to think that we are logical and rational at all times but we also know the truth. Emotions and fear jump directly into the mix the moment we recognize a problem and the need to solve it. Like the technique above, this particular method requires practice on the small issues. Big problems often come like a tsunami, giving us little time to play creatively with resolution building. In order to get your muscles limber and use this technique well, you'll be doing a few sprints with the White Rabbit through the red rosebuds.

Are you the kind of person who recognizes a problem and immediately determines to call for help? Or are you the person who struggles to fix the issue far too long before actually seeing results? Chances are you're both. If you know cars, your first go-to solution might not be calling the auto club. If you know little more than reading the gas gauge, staring at the monster under the hood will not solve your problem, no matter how long you tinker.

As adults we like to think that we learn something new every day, but how many times do we learn them by choice? Booking yourself for a basic auto mechanic's class is a wonderful way to use this particular problem solving technique. Of course there may be times when playing with the engine isn't practical, but in order to create peace of mind and a clear path to solving other more serious problems, it's a good skill to have. Knowing how an engine works is an excellent entry into a broader understanding of how business and relationships work

You may not currently have a situation requiring that you speak another language, but learning one does something wonderful for you. It builds a strong confidence base that there's not much you can't learn and do efficiently.

Listening to classical music may open your mind to structure and harmony you hadn't thought about when facing an issue. Shifting gears and trying something completely the opposite from your normal activities will open your eyes to other ways of thinking and communicating.

Look around at your life, including your personal relationships, your career, your hobbies, your leisure time, and even your dreams for the future. Look at how you've already set up a solution for most of the things that come up. Now, imagine trying the opposite. The rewards will sharpen and polish your skills for more and more complex problem solving ahead.

4) Wear the Correct Thinking Hat – Remember the imaginary thinking hats we wore in nursery school? That was the beginning of problem solving for us all. We've carried that concept into our adult lives, only we have all limited ourselves to specific hats for specific situations. The Mad Hatter wears one hat, it's all that crazy dude needs. You don't live at the bottom of the Rabbit Hole; you live in the real world so your thinking hat has to be a lot more bendable and multidimensional.

Actually, there are six thinking hats that I know of.

Emotion Hat. This hat is red hot and has a hair trigger, ready to go off whenever we assume it to be appropriate. Understandably, finding your spouse with another lover might be an appropriate time to explode with emotion, but are all other times also appropriate? Understandably you need to wear this hat briefly to experience the emotions and let them pass.

Negative Hat. This hat is usually right on the heels of the emotions hat. It struggles with holding on to the negativity of the problem too long. Like the emotion hat, this one also deserves its time to brood and huff. Just don't let it go on for too long before moving on to the rest of your thinking hat wardrobe.

Facts Hat. After we filter through the emotion and negative anger, there is the *Facts and Nothing but the Facts* hat. It fits very well, no matter how hot our heads were earlier. It's the logic hat that helps us learn everything we can about a problem before plowing in to find the best solution.

Positive Hat. Okay, this one is a little silly but extremely important. This hat helps us look as closely as possible at the problem in order to locate the positive things about the issue. Can something be improved because of it? Will an employee be more careful because of it? Will you be more specific with instructions because of it? It's the positive hat, so be sunny and bright and find the good in this problem.

Creative Hat. This one has glitter and bouncy balls and colorful rainbow explosions all over it. This hat helps us look at every single possible creative solution to the problem, including solutions that will prevent it from happening again. This hat allows us to think circularly, swerving around to see the idea from several angles. I often imagine Johnny Depp when thinking of the Creative Hat.

Practical Hat. This is the last hat we put on when effectively and efficiently solving problems. This hat takes everything into consideration—all the emotion, negativity, facts, positives, and creative concepts that have run through your mind—and creates a powerful resolution to the problem.

Every one of these thinking hats are at work all time inside your mind. When an issue arises, often we take it as a personal affront to our already overloaded day. The thinking hat problem solving technique simply suggests that when it's time to solve a problem, use ALL of your thinking hats, use them in the order above, and let them show you the way to practical and powerful solutions.

5) Willingly Drop Down the Rabbit Hole – Down here at the bottom of the Rabbit Hole things look different. They expand with creative options and colorful pathways to a multitude of solutions. This technique is way out of the box. It is a kind of role play situation and works best when playing with another person.

Pretend it's a game. Ask the other player to present a problem, and you offer a solution. At that point the other player must complicate the problem further and further until all your problem solving skills are used to the fullest to find a perfect solution. Be lighthearted with this. Create scenarios that are impossible and inventive so that the solutions stretch your abilities to the limit.

By dropping down the Problem Solving Rabbit Hole, you've brought all your brain's sparks and insights to the foreground. This way, when a real problem presents itself, you simply think differently, quickly, and more efficiently.

6) See the Bigger Picture – Most of us aren't the president or vice president of the company or organization we work for. We trudge through our day, hoping for an annual raise, and never raising our heads above the cubical walls that enclose our work world.

Open your eyes and ask yourself a few important questions. Are you challenged enough in your job? Do you want more from your career? If so, then this is the first and most important problem for you to solve and it requires only one thing—seeing the bigger picture.

For your career, seeing the bigger picture means understanding the whole company and industry you work within. Recognize it as an organism or machine where you play a role. Look carefully at the working parts to help you identify the role you'd rather be playing. Examine the pistons and cogs of this machine and your wonderful problem solving capabilities will show you a path to moving up the ladder.

When looking at any problem, it's vital to really take flight and view the situation from above. If something on the edge of the problem isn't identified and considered in the solution, it will return with a vengeance at a later date. Every day take a few moments to close your eyes. Use your mind's eye to take an airborne tour of everything around you. You'll be surprised how often a few moments like this can spot a problem in the making. Seeing the bigger picture is a proactive as well as an overview problem solving technique.

7) Prepare to Hunker Down and Do the Work – A problem with a solution requires something rather visceral and tactical. It requires action on your part. Yes, it may be a solution that a specific department will handle. It could be a solution your kids need to physically do. It might be a solution you've chosen a professional to implement. Either way, you must be present. I'm not suggesting micromanagement. I am suggesting that you be a part of the process.

One thing we all know is that no solution is perfect. They all require a little tweaking. Being a part of the process keeps your nose in the activity and your mind working quickly to direct any modifications as needed. It's never wise to pass off a solution, no matter how large or small. Tweaks and adjustments should never be left to others. See it through and make sure it succeeds then be sure to thank everyone who worked on the solution with you.

Hunker down and do the work when it's best for your own hands to create the solution. The solution may be that your child needs a tutor, but consider taking a few hours a few times a week to be that tutor. If your staff needs to work better together, consider being part of the activities that will teach them how to do that. If your friends like the beach but you like down hill skiing, find a solution where you get a tan, and they get a few skiing lessons.

Too often we throw a solution at a problem and brush off our hands. We do it in the name of efficiency. We do it because we're above the dirty work or maybe we do it because we don't trust ourselves to learn how to be part of the process. Problems beware. Roll up your sleeves and jump right in. It's good for the soul and even better for a successful solution.

Deborah Riley Magnus is an author and an Author Success Coach. She writes both fiction and nonfiction. Her nonfiction focuses on helping authors use their creative skills to market for sales success.

Cajun Style Sautéed Zucchini, Tomatoes and Olives

Serves 4

Ingredients

2 large shallots, peeled and sliced thin

4 small zucchini, trimmed, halved lengthwise and sliced into 1/2 moons

1/4 cup New Orleans style chopped olive salad, drained (use 2 tablespoons of the olive from the jar to cook the shallots and zucchini)

1 cup cherry tomatoes, cut in half

kosher salt and freshly ground black pepper to taste

Instructions

Heat the oil from the olive salad in a medium skillet over medium high heat until shimmering. Add the shallots and cook until soft but not colored, about 3 minutes. Add the zucchini and season with salt and pepper. Sauté until lightly browned, about 3 minutes. Add the olive salad and the cherry tomatoes and cook until just heated through. Serve immediately or allow to cool to room temperature.

STOP TRYING TO BREAK BAD HABITS! CHANGE THEM FOR SOMETHING BETTER

John Patrick Hickey

When it comes to dealing with bad habits in our life, most success-minded people have a good idea on how to handle them. After all, when you have a passion to achieve and realize your dreams, you cannot allow something like a bad habit to get in your way. It's true that habits like smoking, drinking too much, over eating and drugs are big issues and have many deep roots to deal with. But the fact that they are so big causes us to face them with determination and if necessary, seek help along the way.

A reality that few people tend to think about is how we deal with the little, less threating habits that easily stay hidden from the rest of the world. Habits like the inability to get things started, negative thinking, moodiness, laziness and the like. These are never thought of as real "bad" habits and we do little about them. The problem is, these so called "little habits" can bring down your success faster than many of the larger battles ever will. As Benjamin Franklin once pointed out, "Little leaks sink big ships."

There is a verse in the Song of Solomon that says, "It is the little foxes that spoil the vine." It's not always the big issues that undercut and weaken us. Small cracks in our character and behavior can bring us down just as easy. It may take a bit longer, but the destruction they bring is just as real.

So, how are we to deal with this problem? My first suggestion is for you not to quit these habits. You heard me, don't fight them; don't stop them and do not pay attention to them. The only way to overcome the "little foxes" in our lives is to replace them. The more we fight and try to "break" them the more attention we give to them. They become our primary focus and therefore they gain power they do not deserve or require.

The less attention you give to them allows you to give attention to the things you should do. It is impossible for two different habits to control a portion of our lives at the same time. It's the one who get the attention that has the power. Remember this well: what you do, be it good or destructive; is always up to you. You are in control and you make the decisions.

I want to share with you some decisions you must make in order to achieve success over these little foxes. Each one is vital in overcoming bad habits by replacing them with good, healthy habits. The stronger each of these decisions are the more power they will generate so you can be the success-minded person you know you are.

#1. DECIDE WHO YOU WANT TO BE

Many success-minded people who are familiar with setting goals may think, "I have known what I wanted for a long time. " Let me make this clear, I am not saying for you to decide what you want to do, but who you want to be. There is a big difference between the two, one between success and failure.

Allow me to give you an example. Let's say that your goal is to become a writer. You have always loved writing and it has been your dream for some time now. You may not have done much to achieve this goal, but it's what you want to do. So you follow the steps for goal setting and write it down in detail so you can review it and set up your next action.

All that is great, but it is only part of the journey to achievement. However, this is where many people leave it. They decide what they want to do but they can't seem to get beyond that. That is because they do not know how to be the person they need to be to achieve the goal.

Ask yourself this question: "If I achieve my goal as a writer, who will I be?" Don't make the mistake of saying you will be the same person you are today. That is not true. If you were the same person you are now then you would get the same results. If we want to achieve different results, we need to be a different person.

This may sound confusing at first. Think of it this way, you are not talking about changing your character or your personality. What you are changing is your thinking and behavior. When we look at those "little foxes" in our life you will find that it is all thinking and behavior. The good news is, our thinking and behavior can be changed. You can improve your character and develop your personality, but you will still be you. Your thinking and behavior on the other hand can be drastically changed if you choose to do so.

Try this little exercise. Sit down at your computer or with a pad and pen and write out a description of the person you need to be to achieve the success you seek. Would you need to be more focused? Someone who takes action right away or one who needs to plan things out first? Or do you need to be outgoing and friendly? What about thoughtful and disciplined?

Try to find someone who has achieved the success you are looking for and seek what they do. How do they behave? What is their thinking process? Look at their daily habits. Remember this, as Tony Robbins always says, "Success leaves clues!" There are things that successful people do that can be learned and when followed, can bring the same results.

Never think that you will achieve success by doing it your way and by finding a new path to follow. Successful people have discovered that the principles of success have always been and always will be the same. It is the people who learn these principles and act on them that reap the benefits of their thinking and behavior. I love the words of great author and success expert, Jim Rohn who said, "Success is neither magical nor mysterious. Success is the natural consequence of consistently applying the basic fundamentals."

As you decide who you want to be, write it down in as much detail as you can. Close your eyes and think about being that person. What do you feel like? How do you see the task ahead of you? How will you act towards other people and how will you face the challenges ahead? What will be different in your thinking and behavior when you are living as the successful person you choose to be? What will you look like, how will you dress and how will you hold yourself, talk and laugh? I know this seems like too much detail, but it all moves you toward actually being the person you want to be. Once you have finished this assignment you are ready to make the next big decision.

#2. DECIDE WHAT YOU NEED TO DO RIGHT NOW

A truth that you must come to understand and make an active part of your thinking is that nothing happens without action! Nothing! It doesn't matter how much you want something, how detailed you planed it out or how much knowledge you may have on the subject, without action nothing is going to happen and your success will be as far from you as one who has no dream at all.

Pablo Picasso once said, "Action is the foundational key to all success." Look at the lives of successful people throughout history and you will see that they all have one thing in common, and that is the ability to take action. Action is the power behind every dream, it is the force behind every success and the drive that changes a simple goal into a hard reality.

Success-minded people have learned that with each new goal comes a new set of steps. These steps are the path to follow from setting a worthwhile goal to achieving it. Action steps helps us stay on track and not run down every rabbit hole we find along the way. They are never taken by chance, but are planned and followed with diligence.

Once you know where you want to go and who you need to be, the time has come to put action behind that vision. Knowledge, no matter how wonderful, is only information without action to back it up. It is taking action that brings about change. Just knowing where you want to go will never get you there. It is only when we put that knowledge into action that we can see great things happen. As American businessman, Joel A. Barker so clearly put it, "Vision without action is merely a dream. Action without vision just passes the time. Vision with action can change the world."

Start by asking yourself a simple question: "To be who I wish to be, what do I need to do right now?" To find the answer to this question you may need to start at the end and work backwards. Start by thinking about who you wish to be. What will your success look like? What will that look, feel and sound like? Now, start to work backwards to where you are today.

Break this down into steps. To be the person you wish to become, what do you have to achieve? How will you think once you have achieved your goals? How will you walk and talk and connect with other people? When you have discovered the answers to these questions, start putting them into action. "But what if I'm not at that point yet?" You may ask, "How can I act successful when I am not? Isn't that faking it?" The answer is simple, yes it is. So what? If you want to be successful tomorrow you need to think and act successful today.

I understand that many have a hard time with this one. No one likes the idea of fake it till you make it. That is not what I am advocating. If all you do is pretend to be a successful person, you will never be a successful person. What I am encouraging you to see is that you are the person today that you need to be tomorrow. If you wait to believe in your success you will never do what is necessary to usher that dream into reality.

If you wish to be successful you must first believe that you can be. Hoping that you will be successful will not cut it. Believing in the success you seek is the first step to actually achieving that success. Many people never become successful or achieve the dreams they desire simply because they do not believe they can. Here is a fact that all success-minded people must embrace and believe. You can achieve the success you desire if you are willing to do what it takes to achieve it. If you are unwilling to do what is needed to succeed you will not succeed. It is that simple.

I am not telling you to pretend that you have succeeded at your goals. I am telling you that you must believe you can succeed and then do what is necessary to accomplish that. It is a matter of faith not one of pretending. As St. Augustine said, "Faith is to believe what you do not see; the reward of this faith is to see what you believe."

What do you need to do today to begin to see that success? Is there someone you need to talk to, a book you need to read or a class you need to take? Find what your first step needs to be and take that it. Do not take it tomorrow or the next day. Do not wait till things are just right or when you feel comfortable. Take action today! Right now!

Here is a principle that will be key to all achievement. When you set a goal, whether it's short term or a lifelong goal, take decisive action within 24 hours. Waiting longer than 24 hours will decrease your chances of getting anything done. It does not matter how small or large the step is, just do something to start the process. Once you have taken that simple step, take the next, and the next after that. You will discover that you can move forward and achieve your goals faster just by taking action right away.

You have heard that there is no time like the present. The truth is there is NO time like the present. Now is all you have. Yesterday is gone and there are no do overs. Tomorrow will not get here till today is done. If you are going to take action do it now. Now is all you have, but when action is taken, now is all you need.

#3. DECIDE TO BE THE PERSON YOU NEED TO BE

Now that you have decided who you would be once you achieved your success, the time has come to start being that person. This has caused many to now move beyond their current state. There are two fears that hold people back from becoming all they can be. The fear of being seen as an imposter and the fear that success will cause negative reactions in your life.

Let's first look at the fear of being an imposter. We have all heard the saying, "Fake it till you make it". For most of us, that is a repulsive idea. It makes us feel that we are pretending and being dishonest with ourselves and others. Success-minded people put a lot of weight in things like integrity, truth and transparency. The idea of faking who you are is something we just do not want to do.

I am in full agreement with this. But what about being who we are? I believe that we were all born, as Zig Ziglar puts it, "...with the seeds of greatness inside us." Your goals and dreams are more than wishful thinking. Our dream is in fact who we were created to be. It is amazing how many people do not believe their destiny will be anything they would desire. They think for some reason that what they were created to do will be unpleasant and a sacrifice.

The reality is if you were created to be something, that once achieved, would fulfill you. You would be living in your perfect fit. It's not unpleasant but the very thing we all strive for. You were not created to fill a space, you were created to make a difference. You were created for greatness.

If you know that you were created for the dreams you are pursuing, than you know that you are already the person who will achieve those dreams. You do not have to become who you already are. You only have to achieve the fullness of that reality. So why not start living in that reality now?

Another myth we believe is that achieving success will make us something we do not want to be. I have heard many times how people do not wish to achieve their dreams or be successful because they think they will become selfish and a jerk. The fact is, if you are selfish and a jerk as an unsuccessful person, you will be selfish and a jerk as a successful one. Likewise, if you are kind and caring to others as an unsuccessful person, you will be even more so as a successful person.

To become the person you wish to be you only have to see yourself as that person already. The only thing you are waiting for is the achievement of the dream, not the creation of the person. Who you are is one who knows the right things to do in order to succeed and does them.

Once you live the reality of success in your life you will have no place for the little foxes to live. You do not have to fight them you only need to live as you know a successful person lives. It is not the habits you stop that make the difference, it is the habits you start that will drive you to the success you seek.

John Patrick Hickey is a Certified Personal Development Coach as well as being certified in **DISC** *Assessments and evaluations. John Patrick specializes in communication, goal setting and the discovery of a person's key purpose in life. John Patrick is the author of three books, Daily Thoughts: 90 Daily Readings for Success-Minded People, All You Have Is Now: How Your Approach to the World Determines Your Destiny and his newest books with Motivational Press, On The Journey To Achievement, and a new Kindle book, Oops! Did I Post That? Online Etiquette in the New Digital Age. He is also a speaker, instructor and well-read blogger. To read more from John Patrick Hickey or to get his books, training and book him to speak to your church, business or group, visit our website at http://www.growthcenter.net or www.johnpatrickhickey.com.*

IMAGINE... MAKING A DIFFERENCE

Joel Caldwell

Bonnie had gotten to the point in her life where she couldn't hide it anymore. She had felt an emptiness for so long it affected her appearance. Her face showed every year of her life and then some, and everyone guessed she was older than her actual age. She was a manager in a large corporation who felt that she had spent most of her life going through the motions and it only seemed to be getting worse. She was coming to see me because she wanted to live differently. She wanted to make a difference.

I can identify with Bonnie and you probably can as well. We all get to places in life where we question what we're doing and whether we're making an impact on the world. We want to know that what we are doing is important. But how can you identify what is important and overcome the obstacles to achieving your goals?

As you look through the chapters in this book, you'll find great advice on health, business, and relationships all with the idea of creating a new you. But once you've developed the new you, how will you use those improvements to make a difference in the world? This chapter illustrates the essentials for making an impact.

Know Your Passion

Teresa walked across my high school parking lot toward me the same as always- in a foul mood. Whenever I saw her, she seemed to have a sullen look on her face. As usual, she wanted to talk. More specifically, she wanted help. Teresa had recently discovered that her boyfriend had been cheating on her and she was looking for a place to vent. That place always involved me. Teresa was like many of my friends. Whenever they experienced problems in their lives, they gravitated toward me. I never asked them to talk and, at 16, I certainly had no words of wisdom. Maybe I was just a good listener or somehow made people feel comfortable. Whatever the reason, I was the sounding board and I was good at it. Helping people navigate their problems became a passion of mine. That passion has turned into a career and eventually become a strong part of my identity.

I see many people in my practice who are looking for success, however they define it. They want to know if they are on the right road and the changes they need to make. I tell people that wherever your passion and abilities intersect, it is there you will find success. That is where you will make an impact on the world. Your abilities are God-given. Your passion can be developed without limits. The first step in making your impact is identifying and cultivating your passion.

It is striking to me how many people respond to my question, "What are you passionate about?", with a blank stare. It's too easy to go through life focusing only on your daily to-do list and completing your to-do list doesn't usually make the impact you want. For that, you must pursue your passion.

If you have difficulty identifying your passion, think about the things you enjoy the most; the aspects of your day you look forward to; the events in the world that illicit the strongest emotions, the last time you felt a real sense of accomplishment. These can all be clues to recognizing and unlocking your passion.

You will know your passion when you find it. You will become excited to pursue it, and it will give you a sense of purpose to your life.

PASSION IN ACTION

So what happens once you've identified your passion? Now what? Knowing your passion alone doesn't make a difference in the lives of others. The greatest challenge for most people] is translating their passion into action.

Peter Frates discovered his passion in his early 20's. He was a college baseball player who was diagnosed with amyotrophic lateral sclerosis (ALS) in 2012. As he began to lose control of his bodily movements, he was determined to do something to combat ALS in the world. He began aggressively fundraising and advocating for research. During the same year he was diagnosed with ALS, Peter won awards for his advocacy work in raising awareness of the disease. In 2014, Peter and his friends developed the Ice Bucket Challenge in order to raise money for ALS research. It became the greatest fundraising campaign in the history of ALS initiatives. Peter's passion for finding a cure for ALS became obvious to him because of his own struggle. What makes Peter's story so great is not his passion, but his ability and determination to put his passion in to action.

How do you convert passion to action? What need exists that best utilizes that passion? Peter knew that he could not single-handedly develop a cure for ALS. However, he saw a huge need for increased funding for research leading to a cure. That became the vehicle for using his passion to make a difference.

If, like Peter, your passion involves a cause, how can you effect change? If your passion involves a talent, how can you best utilize that talent to make a difference in the lives of others? There are countless needs in the world. Each one is awaiting someone with the necessary passion to make a difference.

OVERCOMING YOUR FEAR:

You've identified your passion as well as a path to make an impact. So what's holding you back? What keeps you from making the necessary changes? If you are like most people, you are likely giving in to your own fear.

My family and I recently made a trip to Walt Disney World. We had made several times before, but this visit ended up being a little different. When most think of Disney World, they think of nice family rides, parades, and costumed characters. These are all reasons I enjoy going there. However, there was always one ride I actively avoided: The Hollywood Tower of Terror. I do not like heights. More specifically, I do not like being dropped from high places. My children always ignored this fact and encouraged me to ride anyway. I had managed to turn them away consistently until this most recent trip. I had grown tired of watching seven year olds exiting the ride while smiling and laughing. "How bad could this be?"I thought. I decided to ride in spite of my fear, and I found myself leaving the ride smiling and laughing like those seven year olds. I had faced my fear and that fear was replaced with joy.

We all have fears that become obstacles to achieving our goals. For you, it could be a fear of failure or a fear of rejection. Maybe you have a fear of giving up your familiar life in favor of a more impactful life. What would that life look like and what exactly might you have to give up? What if your choices don't work out? Could you get your old life back?

These are the types of questions that keep you from doing anything different with your life. You have a vision of where you want to be and you may even have clarity on how to get there. However, your fear of the unknown can keep you from realizing the impact you long to have.

In order to overcome your fear, understand the potential of your impact. When you can see where you want to be, your fear is failing to get there. You will have overcome your fear when the fear of not making an impact becomes greater than the fear of personal failure.

As I was exposed many times to my children wanting me to ride the Tower of Terror, the nature of my fear changed. My fear of the ride diminished as my focus became more about how I saw myself. Was I going to let my fear of this ride keep me from an enjoyable experience with my children? More importantly, as I refused to ride, what was I teaching them about having courage and facing their fears? The answer to that question became scarier than the ride itself.

As you experience fear that holds you back from positive change, consider what you may be missing, and how giving into that fear is incompatible with the impact you envision.

SMALL IMPACTS ADD UP TO BIG CHANGES:

If you are like me, having a vision for making a big impact is easy. That requires only the ability to dream big. It can be fun to think about performing for a larger audience, providing food for the hungry, or growing a successful business from scratch. We hear stories about people who do this all of the time. But how do they get to the point of making such large impacts? What is involved in pursuing those dreams? The truth is that no one gets out of bed one morning and starts making a worldwide impact. You don't just happen to become President of the United States or an Oscar-winning actor. Those achievements are built over time with many intentional steps. The impact you are looking to make is built the same way.

My dream has incorporated becoming an author and speaker. I want to share my own life experiences and insights to help others in overcoming difficulties and achieving their goals. I am still not where I want to be but I have come a long way.

I will always remember a publisher sharing with me about the importance of building a platform. In particular, he conveyed how an online presence can make a major career difference. I have never been the most internet-savvy person. Early on, I had no website or social media accounts. I always viewed those as something other people did and the thought of creating anything online was intimidating. Nevertheless, I researched how to set up a website and how to create an effective social media strategy. I did this not because I wanted to be active on social media, but because I knew it was essential to having the impact I desired. I mean, no one enjoys starting on Facebook or Twitter with zero followers. I felt like the tree falling in the forest that no one is around to hear. Does it make a sound? Truth be told, I am in the early stages of building that platform, but I work through those frustrations by always keeping an eye on my goal.

As you look to make your impact, know not only where you want to go but have a plan to get there. Don't get discouraged by the number of steps in your plan. Instead, look at each step as an opportunity to make a smaller impact. Those smaller impacts will grow over time to become the goal you originally envisioned.

The first presentation I made was to a group of 14 men at a breakfast in the basement of a church. I was not paid for this and speaking in a venue like that was never my goal. However, I still look for opportunities like that. The intimate setting helped create a great dialogue which had an impact not only on those in attendance but me as well.

What may feel like a small impact to you could actually make a big impact for others. And the greatest impact you make may not be found in actually achieving your goal, but in the process of pursuing it.

NOW IS THE TIME:

When we think of making changes in our lives, we tend to consider change as something that's going to occur in the future. When you think of starting an exercise program, volunteering your time, or developing a budget, the best day to begin always seems to be tomorrow. That's because making significant changes is never easy and can often be stressful. Rarely is change something we look forward to, even when we believe it will result in personal growth or be beneficial to our community.

I challenge you to think of change in a different way. That's because the change you are attempting to make is so meaningful. What you are trying to accomplish is more than a diet or exercise program. You are using your passion to make an impact on the world. This is your opportunity to make a difference.

I know how important it is to follow your passion and I believe that your greatest calling is to make an impact with your unique blend of gifts and abilities. I encourage you to not think that tomorrow is the best day to start pursuing your goals. Start now! If you think about it, there is something you can be doing in this moment that gets you closer to making the impact you envision. And isn't that the point?

The whole reason you are reading this book is because you have identified areas of your life which can be improved. Embrace whatever change comes with that. Discover your passion. Make a difference.

Dr. Joel Caldwell is the author of "Living Larger - Discovering the True Riches of Life". Dr. Caldwell has worked as a psychologist since 1999 treating children, adolescents, and adults. He is currently in private practice in central Florida. Joel can be reached through his website at drjoelcaldwell.com or via email at **drjoelcaldwell@gmail.com**

Chicken Cutlets with Shishito Peppers, Mushrooms and Olive Salad On a Bed of Spinach

Serves 4

Ingredients

2 tablespoons extra virgin olive oil + 1 tablespoon
4 chicken cutlets, 4-6-ounces each
1 large red onion, peeled, halved and sliced thin
4 large cloves garlic, minced
6-ounces shishito peppers, stems cut off, sliced in half, seeded
8-ounces sliced crimini mushrooms
1/2 cup New Orleans style chopped olive salad, drained
1-pound fresh baby spinach leaves, thick stems removed
kosher salt and freshly ground black pepper

Instructions

Heat the 2 tablespoons of olive oil in a large skillet over medium high heat until shimmering. Season chicken cutlets on both sides with salt and pepper. Add to the hot oil and cook on each side until golden brown, about 3-4 minutes per side. Chicken will release easily when ready for flip. Remove to a plate and tent with foil to keep warm. Add the onions to the pan and cook until soft, about 3-5 minutes. Add the garlic and cook, stirring, until fragrant, about 1 minute. Add the mushrooms and season with salt and pepper. Sauté until browned, about 3 minutes. Add the olive salad and stir to heat through.

Meanwhile, heat 1 tablespoon of olive oil in a medium skillet over medium heat until shimmering. Add the spinach and season with salt and pepper. Cook until completely wilted. To serve divide the spinach among 4 plates. Top each with a chicken breast and then with the vegetables. Serve immediately.

IMAGINE, 30 DAYS TO A NEW YOU! AUTHENTICITY, THE 5 KEYS TO UNLOCKING THE POWER OF PURPOSE

Elisabetta L. Faenza

YOU CAN'T JUST ADD WATER...

When I was invited to write a chapter for "IMAGINE, 30 Days to a New YOU," I asked myself: What is the one, non-negotiable step in creating a new self? What can I share with the reader, keen to get themselves on track for a more fulfilling and rewarding life and career that will actually make a difference?

First I needed to think about the concept of 'A New YOU,' what does that imply? The word – reinvention – immediately popped into my mind, and I realized that the process of creating something new out of something already in existence is the process of reinvention. Then it struck me that to have value, impact and flow in the world, reinvention actually might be about stripping away a patina. Like refurbishing a piece of furniture that may have gathered some nicks and dents, layers of paint and perhaps even some dodgy repairs. Reinvention in this sense is about stripping back the additions, and the false layers to reveal the original, and then see what purpose it is fit for.

THE POWER OF REINVENTION

In this fast-paced world, reinvention is a necessary part of entrepreneurial and business evolution. Without reinvention individuals and organizations run the risk of being left behind, losing relevance and market share. Those who are able to adapt to rapidly changing environments survive, while those who don't, perish.

Many of us were directed into our careers by well-meaning family members, educators, and career's advisors. If like me you are an X-Gen or Baby Boomer (Moderns), then you were probably never asked to reflect on what you wanted out of life. Over time you may have found what you were good at, or could be paid well for. You adapted your skill set and personality to suit the dominant paradigm of your field, and got more and more competent. All the while feeling that something just wasn't right, but never stopping to address the issue. For many of us, the careers we were trained for no longer exist. If the pundits are right, then Millennials (Post-Moderns - the generation born between 1981 and 1999) will experience four to six career changes in their lifetime. So we are not alone, and our angst is all too obvious to Millennials...

"Millennials perceive their parent's generation as a generation riddled with mistakes. The pursuit of the perfect house, matching BMWs and in-ground pools at times outweighed the importance of family. Looking to the future, Millennials want to balance their work and family lives. They want to be home for dinner, and companies are beginning to implement programs where this kind of lifestyle is possible."[1]

"...Millennials are concerned with other things. Money is important and they do enjoy making it, however, they long to be part of something bigger than themselves. The workplace doesn't define them to the degree that it did for too many Boomers. Millennials want to lead a balanced life. They want to be happy at home and happy on the job – money is somewhat secondary."[2]

1 Moore, Karl and Snell, Margaret, *Working More Effectively with Millennials, excerpt appeared in Forbes Leadership; Aug 14, 2014*

2 Ibid

Regardless of your generation, if you are reading this book, then chances are you might be at a crossroads. This is because either what you've done for the last ten or twenty years is no longer working, or it no longer rewards you as it once did. So you picked up this book, flipped through the chapters and decided the wisdom within it might help you get yourself back on track.

What I want to offer in this chapter is that instead of just doing what you've always done by painting another layer over the top of the former you, take a moment to strip back the layers and re-discover the real you. Take a leaf out of the Millennial's book and meet your authentic self. Take this opportunity to re-discover what excites you; what rings your bell, and more importantly, what you can contribute with a happy heart and mind. Then from that base you can reinvent yourself for a purpose that will carry you through the next stage in your life. This, however, requires self-awareness.

WHAT MILLENNIALS HAVE TO TEACH US

Millennials are empowered by self-actualisation. While Baby Boomers longed for security through love and belonging, and X-Gens sought importance and self-expression through individuality; Millennials are driven by a deep need for self-actualisation via a bigger purpose, connected to their authentic self. Lucky for them they got to do this before too many layers of paint were added. It's no coincidence that for the most part, in the West, Millennials were born the most affluent generation in human history. The lower rungs in Maslow's Hierarchy of Needs[3] ladder have been taken care of by their parents, freeing them to climb the ladder quickly and expertly. They have the benefit of being able to recognise their authentic self, while X-Gens like me, or Baby

3 Maslow, Abraham, H., 'A Theory of Human Motivation,' All About Pyschology, 2011.

Boomers have to get out the paint stripper. It makes sense then that we might learn a couple of things from the Millennial generation about what authenticity in the workplace might look like, and it might just make our businesses easier for Post Moderns to connect with.

Karl Moore, professor at Desautels Faculty and Forbes Columnist, has extrapolated four basic principles about authenticity from the work of leadership experts - Kevin Kruse, Jon Mertz and Maureen Laufenberg:

1) "Authentic leaders need to be **self-aware** and **genuine**. Before they will be able to encourage and support self-authenticity among Postmoderns, Moderns must be aware of their own strength, limitations and emotions. A starting place for excellent leaders is self-knowledge and awareness. Moderns need to demonstrate their weaknesses and be more open in communicating their feelings. They need to acknowledge their imperfections and mistakes. Give up trying to present a perfect façade, it is untrue and, thankfully, a bad thing with this generation.

2) Authentic leaders need to be **mission driven** and **focused on results**. They must focus on the goals and missions of the organization before their own self-interests. They do not allow the lure of power, money or ego to limit their ability to get the job done. They connect with people and motivate them to pursue common objectives. They embrace the idea of community; one focused on doing something worthwhile in the world, in a way that reflects excellence. Throw out those books on power and how to get it and keep it.

3) Authentic leaders lead with their **hearts**, not with their **minds**. They are concerned with the well-being of the group. They follow a guiding set of empowering principles which lead them to consider all actions taken should result in increased well-being for all involved. They emphasize trust and respect to create an empathetic, supportive environment. Karl has been shadowing senior women leaders. His research (along with many others) seems to suggest that many, but not all, senior women leaders over 45 are good at being empathetic. If you

are not, take the time to lean back and watch some senior women show this trait in action – a great chance to learn.

4) Authentic leaders focus on the **long term**. They evaluate the possible future impacts of their day-to-day activities. They strive for sustainable and enduring results, rather than those which are immediate and short-lived."[4]

This emphasises the urgent need for reinvention within business, within leadership and within all areas of coaching and training. If we persist in the old paradigm driven by profit and power, we risk being left behind, and losing relevance. When you imagine the new you, visualize yourself aligned with your deeper values and beliefs, making a difference and most of all never having to pretend to be anything you are not.

Dan Pontefract believes that Millennials can help existing organizations and the generations that run them to understand the meaning of purpose. He provides some startling statistics about Millennials' worldview:

1. 75% of Millennials believe: "Businesses are focused on their own agendas rather than helping to improve society." Put differently, if Millennials are about to make up half of an organization's population, at least 38% of the employees will be vehemently against the company's existing mission, beliefs and operating practices. As the report indicates, Millennials are sending a signal to redefine the definition of business, "Suggesting that the pursuit of a different and better way of operating in the 21st century begins by redefining leadership."[5]
2. Millennials are just as interested in how a business develops its people and society as they are in its products and profits.
3. Public relations firm Edelman, for example, revealed some

4 Opcit, Moore.

5 Pontefract, Dan, 'FLAT ARMY: Creating a Connected and Engaged Organization,' Wiley, 2013.

interesting results in its 2015 Edelman Trust Barometer research. Edelman annually surveys over 33,000 people across 27 countries asking questions about their trust in the institutions of government, media, business and non-governmental organizations. The survey addresses employees from all generations. What struck me, however, was when the firm asked Millennials about the perceived drivers of change. 54% of Millennial respondents believed that greed was a key driver of change within their workplace, while less than 30% believed it was to improve people's lives, or make the world a better place."[6]

"But what they are doing infinitely better than GenX and the Baby Boomers (Moderns) is pushing society to actually put purpose on par with profit. I define the *Purpose Mindset* as individuals who are "passionate, innovative and committed to a meaningful and engaging workplace that serves all stakeholders." This seems to be the epitome of a Millennial's DNA in the organizations where they work."[7]

It seems to me, that rather than trying to train Millennials to fit into the existing paradigm, we could learn a lot from them, creating more meaningful lives for ourselves and healthier organizations that positively impact the world.

Being authentic by revealing your true self is challenging, especially if you haven't done it before. Some of the world's most prominent individuals and brands struggle with being authentic, and are instead addicted to the adulation and popularity of their false, public persona and paying a fortune to maintain that façade. Scandals inevitably arise and are driven by the conflict between the public and authentic self. In the social media driven, 24-hour media cycle, it's too hard to be someone you are not for any extended period of time. It is far easier and

6 Ibid

7 Ibid

requires a lot less effort to be authentic and lead from your core, but it does take practice. Don't be discouraged when you find this difficult to implement.

I've worked with individual entrepreneurs, writers, speakers, business owners and major corporations to help them uncover their purpose. During that time I've identified 5 Key Characteristics of Authenticity that will allow you to Unlock YOUR Purpose:

1. Mindfulness – be aware of your behaviour, what engages you and gradually rid yourself of the behaviours that do not represent your authentic self, your core purpose or your deeply held values. This is the paint-stripping step in the process, and is crucial
2. Honesty – be willing to admit when you make a mistake, own up to errors or weaknesses. This will free you to put more energy into the things you do well and easily
3. Focus – don't allow distractions or the priorities of others to hijack your time, energy or activity, unless they are in alignment with the priorities of your authentic self
4. Flow – notice where your energy moves with ease, and where it is blocked. Chances are that every time there is a block it is because you were trying to be someone you are not, or engage in a behaviour that does not represent the real you. Go where the flow is
5. Feedback – commit to a continuous process of growth and refinement. As you reinvent yourself, notice how you feel and what you achieve. Pay attention to the feedback life is sending you and make small adjustments to keep you on track. Your relationships, health, quality of sleep and how good you feel in your skin each day, as well as your financial wellbeing, will be great indicators

Just by being aware of these characteristics, you'll naturally steer towards exercising authenticity, which your Millennial customers, stakeholders and staff will love.

Ultimately though, being authentic will allow you to Unlock the Power of YOUR Purpose, and live the life you've always imagined was possible.

Elisabetta is an expert in human performance, specialising in the application of the latest research in epigenetics - how our genes and environment interact - to optimise organisational and societal outcomes. With 30 years of experience working with individuals, corporates, transnationals, non-profits and government agencies, Elisabetta maximizes individual, team and organisational performance.

Elisabetta's journey was prompted by a childhood diagnosis of a rare genetic condition, which led her on a quest to understand how our bodies and the environment interact to switch genes on and off. As a clinical hypnotherapist and performance mentor, Elisabetta has assisted thousands of individuals to change unwanted behaviours, recover from trauma, and achieve personal and career goals

With a Masters in International Relations, Elisabetta also has a keen understanding of the global trends that effect business and individuals alike. Elisabetta is the author of Nemesis (True North, 2015), The Energy Code (Motivational Press, 2014), The DNA of Bullying (No Trees, 2014), The Energy Bucket (No Trees, 2010), The Infidel (True North, 2015), Veritas (True North, 2015) and was librettist for the musical 'D'Arc, the Legend of Saint Joan.'

To discover more about how Elisabetta L Faenza can help you discover your authentic purpose, go to: http://elisabettalfaenza.com

THE UNSPOKEN WORDS OF SUCCESS

Michael Jenet

Words are not just a means to communicate, they help us describe our reality. We don't just think in images. We don't simply see with our eyes, our brains process what we see into words so that what we 'see' are words like tree or leaf or rain in our head. These are the unspoken words of our mind's inner dialogue.

Words, therefore, give us the ability to define the world around us. They help us understand what we see and hear and smell and touch. These words are not spoken aloud, but are the silent thoughts of our mind. It is these unspoken words of our mind that we must master if we seek to improve our lives. Those who succeed, by whatever standard you define success, are those who understand the power of these silent words and learn how to harness that power to their advantage. Here then, are the *Unspoken Words of Success.*

We begin with three influential words. Unlike the rest of this list, however, these are words that you absolutely must forget! That's right, these are words you have been taught all your life and now, you must un-learn them. Strike them from your working vocabulary, forget you ever heard them or learned their definitions, for these first three words can do more harm to your life than any other words in the English language.

The first of the Unspoken Words of Success is WORRY. When we worry about what might happen, or could happen, or in some way project an outcome before it actually happens we are physically damaging our chances of success. When you find yourself worrying about something your physiology comes under attack. Your muscles tense, you're breathing either shallow or rapidly, your face contorts with lines and your jaw tightens. Your posture slumps and your mind pictures multitudes of negative images for you to focus on. You are literally attacking yourself physically over something that hasn't yet happened.

For many, this act of worrying feels like a defense mechanism against being let down should things not turn out the way they hope for. However, they are damaging themselves physically and mentally time and time again, far greater than the one time they might endure if their worry came to pass. You should spend at least as much time focusing on the outcome you want rather than what you worry it might be. Focus your energy, your physiology, and your mind on what you want, not on what might (or might not) happen.

The second word you must absolutely forget, is DOUBT. Yet another word that attacks our physiology before we have even begun our quest. When you doubt yourself, or the outcome, you immediately hinder your ability to succeed without even taking one step towards the outcome.

A baseball player who doubts he can hit the ball will not swing as straight or react as quickly as one who is sure he will succeed. The actor who yearns for a part in the play will not appear confident, nor perform as flawlessly, as the one who is sure of their role. Your body listens to those unspoken words and when you doubt something your body responds physiologically. Doubt is simply a thief who takes away your success before you lift a finger to grasp it.

If you do not doubt, but instead go forth with all the confidence of a child who has not yet tasted the bitter fruit of defeat and give it your all, and you do not succeed, what is the result? You will have done all you can, put forth your best effort, and you will walk away knowing that this was simply not your day; at least you can hold your head high knowing you did your best. Doubt your outcome at the beginning, however, and you will only walk away knowing you didn't really try.

The third one we should forget fastest of all, is FEAR. Most of us, for most of our lives, will never need that 'fight or flight' response built into our nervous system that early humans used to stay alive. Fear of something that can actually harm us is good, but most of us tend to fear that which we cannot control; that which is unknown to us, or something we do not wish to happen.

In each of these cases we are once again talking about the future, about something which has not yet happened. Fear, unlike our two previous words, prevents us from moving towards our goals at all. We become paralyzed, unable even to take that all important first step.

The trick, in removing fear from our vocabulary, is to defeat it as often as we can. That seemingly insurmountable task is actually rather easily accomplished. You may have heard the notion that to defeat fear you must do the thing you fear. That alone can seem daunting until you learn that the trick to doing what you fear is not to do it all at once. Rather do it slowly, little by little. Afraid of speaking up in groups? Start by asking one question. Just one, and build from there. Afraid of talking to people you don't know? Begin by simply saying 'hello'. Nothing more. Simply say hello to one person. Tomorrow, say hello to two. Keep going until saying hello becomes easy and then build on that. By taking on your fears a little at a time and ultimately ensuring their defeat you will find that the word itself no longer holds residence in your mind.

Having committed to un-learning the first three words in our list, let us now turn to the foundation of our Unspoken Words of Success vocabulary, the first being ATTITUDE.

William James, often called the Father of Psychology, once wrote "It is our attitude at the beginning of a difficult task which, more than anything else, will affect its successful outcome." Attitude, then, is what we must hold in our mind in place of doubt and worry. Many people base their attitude on what happens to them and miss the key to their success, namely that they have a choice in what attitude they present to the world.

Life really does reflect back what we give it, and our attitude towards everything we do is the most important factor in determining our success or failure at any given endeavor. We get out of life what we expect from it, and our attitude determines that expectation. Having an attitude filled with expectation, joy, happiness, enthusiasm, love, kindness and many other emotions of positivity will create greater success in every area of your life.

Beginning with attitude as the base, we now move on to GRATTITUDE. Have you ever seen a child opening a large pile of presents? They rip open the first package and before they have even registered what the first one is they're already reaching for the next one. By the time all of them are open, most get tossed aside for the favorite one, and even that loses its luster after a short while. Why? Because they are not grateful for anything and therefore are grateful for nothing.

We cannot fully take the next step on our journey until we have completely and fully moved into our current step, we must learn to be grateful for what we have now. Begin your day with an 'attitude of gratitude'. Learn to be grateful for all that you have and all that you are. Everything, good or bad, that you have experienced and achieved so far has made you who you are today. You could not be you without your past. Do not mourn what you have not done or seen or achieved, you are you without them. Celebrate today by spending a moment being grateful for everything. Only by this act of gratefulness for all you have in your life can you be truly ready for more to come your way.

APPRECIATION, the next word on our list, is often confused with gratitude. The difference is that you can be grateful for the sun in the sky without appreciating it. You can appreciate a nice meal that you're eating and yet not be grateful for it. Learn to appreciate all that comes your way. Appreciate the struggles for they give you strength to conquer hurdles ahead. Appreciate your family, your friends, and your loved ones for they are the ones who truly care about you. Appreciate what you have and where you are in life for you have earned every bit of it.

Nowhere is appreciation more important than in ourselves. Too often we sell ourselves short with those unspoken words in our mind. When you stop and think about it, as a human being, you are truly amazing. No one has your DNA, or your way of seeing the world. No one has your unique view of life, your sense of humor, your wonderment, and your wit. No one is exactly like you. Appreciate you for who you are. You shouldn't devalue something simply because you haven't used it correctly. That would be like buying an expensive watch, never setting the correct time, and blaming the watch. Just because you haven't used it correctly doesn't mean it is any less valuable.

The same is true about you. No matter where you find yourself at this point in your journey, or where you want to go, you are still amazing. Appreciate all your greatness and hold a positive attitude moving forward and you will be amazed at how valuable you really are.

Next on our list of Unspoken Words of Success is DREAMS. Dreams are the antidote to fear and what we must use to replace that word now that we have forgotten it. As children our dreams are vivid, grandiose, outrageous, and completely achievable. We blindly and passionately believe in our dreams, until someone tells us to stop. Little by little, we lose faith in ourselves. Our dreams become silly, far-fetched, and unrealistic until we wake up one day and no longer remember what they were.

Your passions are the coming attractions of your Dreams. They are the preview of your noble purpose. Each of us has something that only we can do a certain way. Your uniqueness endows you with skills, perceptions, viewpoints, and passions that combine in a way that no one else can. It is this melting pot of who you are which gives you your passion and noble purpose. Every day you push that away you deny your gifts to the world.

Fulfilling your dreams, pursuing your noble purpose, accomplishing your passions in life are what will truly make you successful. Spend time with your dreams, cultivate them, fuel them with your passion and success will seem but a fleeting byproduct of the amazing journey of your life.

Albert Einstein was once asked what he thought the meaning or purpose of life was. He answered that we are here to serve our fellow human beings. SERVICE is the next word on our list. Those who have achieved success in life know that the true secret is to do more for others than they do for you. This is true in every area of life.

Providing more in service, giving more, caring more for your loved ones, and conducting business better than anyone can do in return is the key to being successful. Our goal should not be to climb a ladder of success but rather to help others achieve new heights. It is not about getting more from others but giving more to them that matters. Only by being kind to everyone, can we ever hope to see kindness in return. Make serving and giving more to others your mission and watch success come to you in ways you never imagined possible.

You are what you think.

This axiom has been handed down through the ages from the Bible, in Proverbs: 'For as he thinketh in his heart, so is he', to the aforementioned William James who wrote a whole book on the subject, *As a man thinketh*. It's true, you are basically the sum of your thoughts. Rather than discus where those thoughts come from, however, let's focus on our next word; BELIEF.

Every successful person has ups and downs on their journey to success. There comes a time, however, when the climb reaches that all important tipping point. A time when your success will come down to you and you alone. It is in that moment that your success will be won or lost, based on your Belief in yourself. When everyone seems to doubt you, when all seems to be going against you, when there is nothing left, you must reach deep inside of yourself, and hold on to your belief.

There is a famous poem called "Thinking" by poet Walter D. Wintle. The last few lines of his poem sum it up best:

Life's battles don't always go / To the stronger or faster man, / But soon or late the man who wins / Is the man who thinks he can!

PERSISTENCE is perhaps the most often ignored of our list of Unspoken Words of Success. If there are three words that are more important than any of the words on our list in terms of your success, they would be the following; don't give up.

» JK Rowling was turned down by 12 major publishers for her Harry Potter story.

» Stephen King's first novel was turned down 30 times.

» Babe Ruth famously hit 714 home runs in his career. He also struck out 1,330 times.

» Bill Gate's first business was a complete failure.

How committed are you to your own success? Are you willing to stay with it until you achieve your goals? How many 'rejections' are you willing to face? Will you fail twice as much as you succeed, like Babe Ruth, and still push on? You must, above all else, never give up on your dreams and goals. Only by this practice of unrelenting persistence will you truly have the life you dream of.

Now we come to our final word of the Unspoken Words of Success. I originally thought that this word was 'authentic', but that word has become far too overused today and has lost much of its true meaning. The last word on our list is BRAVE. You see, being honestly, truthfully, authentically YOU takes guts. It's not easy un-learning Worry, Doubt, and Fear. To begin each day with the correct Attitude, focus on

Gratitude, and Appreciating what you have is difficult to do. Working on remembering and cultivating your Dreams, being of Service to others in everything you do, and Believing in yourself despite what everyone says; this is what BRAVE is all about.

Make these unspoken words your battle cry for success every day. Discover Your Brave!

Michael Jenet is the author of the International Book Award Finalist book "ASK: The Questions to Empower Your Life" and the recently published book "A Better Life". He is a self-proclaimed recovering CEO-turned author and speaker. From boardroom presentations, to TEDx, to audiences large and small, Michael Jenet transforms people's lives through storytelling and motivational presentations.

THE "TATTERED" YOU VERSUS THE "MATTERED" YOU: RISING ABOVE THE UNDERTOW OF YOUR NEW LEADERSHIP LIFE IN FIVE SIMPLE STEPS

Rick Jetter

Being a leader can be a tough *life*. It's not all glory, either. Sometimes, that is just a myth. Sometimes, leaders feel like they are swimming in a never-ending ocean, that the undertow will pull them underwater once and for all and no one will care. CEO's, entrepreneurs, and business men and women from all walks of life. School Superintendents, software designers, runway models, police chiefs, moms, and even movie stars striving to be good role models each day. We are all leaders of some sort. We lead teams of people, our children, or small businesses that we hope will become something *bigger* someday. We feel irreplaceable, but we're not—according to those who can fill our seats with another *body*. With another *somebody*. And your legacy will be forgotten very quickly. Or will it?

You've been *tattered*, shut down. Your ideas have been thrown overboard by those you lead, those you try to impress. You've tried shared decision-making, but no one buys in. Your competition becomes your own employees that you hired. Your biggest fans might really your biggest enemies in *disguise*. And you don't even really realize that they are doing the "Julius Caesar" behind your back. Plotting. Waiting for your downfall.

You've had one too many drinks after work, perhaps. Your day becomes blurred because you can't make heads or tails if it is breakfast time or "pass-out" time by the television. You wake up the next morning not remembering what the final score was to the Monday night football game that you don't remember turning on, either. You search for a newly pressed shirt, negotiate with yourself if you are going to shave or wash your hair or skip a day, and then have to get out there to do "it" all over again. Do it all for others. Make them love you. Make them want to march behind you. After all, you've worked so hard to get to the top, but now you feel *faded*. You just want that feeling to go away. Just support your family. That's all you wanted, but you didn't want the stress that goes along with the job that is no longer a desired career. You feel trapped with few options. You want to feel great like you once did when you were on top of your game. Invincible. Indestructible. Charismatic. Persuasive. Powerful.

We've all been there. We've had our ups and downs in life. Nothing in life is perfect. It shouldn't be perfect and we know that deep down inside, but it is difficult to see the path that became so burdensome and treacherous for us along the way. A natural part of life just like the seasons we experience outside our windows. Summer heat turns to Fall, with Winter freezing our souls, but Spring providing rebirth and rejuvenation. It's a cycle, a rut you fall into. It will go away, but only if you let it go away. You can and will tread the water that is trying to pull you down as you make your way into a lifeboat and then hopefully a speedboat once again. All you have to do is follow five simple things to bring you back, bring you up, and bring you forth to greatness.

1. GET DRESSED & BE THANKFUL

This is your first task. Some refer to this first step as "show up." Well, you *have* to show up. Get out of the mental gutter that you are in by grooming yourself to be the best that you can be. Consider Dan Waters from Battle Creek, Michigan who works in a warehouse for a sports manufacturer. He has a middle management position and his office is along-side one of the packing lines on the main floor. He has a cement office, a few pieces of drywall around him (to set him apart from the forklifts), but he always wears a tie to work, shaves himself each day, and carries a gorgeous leather briefcase to work, a gift from his wife.

Dan wakes up each morning, gives thanks for being alive, and then goes out to make "it" happen. His co-workers talk about how uplifting Dan is around the office. He makes people laugh, smiles himself, and leaves mystery gifts in the lunchroom with a different name labeled on it once a month for an employee who does good work, struggling with challenging life events, or who is improving each day and giving 100% effort on the job.

Dan "gets dressed" and exudes the positivism that leaders should model for others. Whether you are a stay-at-home mom or a CEO of a multi-million dollar company, your spirit and smile comes directly from either a shirt that is "tattered" or one that matters. Effective leaders show up, are humble and thankful, and become role-models for others by taking care of their own *basics* in life. Once the basics are satisfied, you can move on to greater innovations of your creative mind. There is a way to feel *physically* good, which directly impacts you *mentally*.

2. GET EXCITED

The second step for you is to click the "refresh" button and re-acquaint yourself with what makes you special, extraordinary, and talented. Sometimes life is not all that exciting, but we are in control of how we move our lives forward. Do we stay in the status quo or make new things happen? Do we settle for contentment or take risks that will enable us to jump onto a new "S" curve?

For instance, take Betsy Peterson from Gulfport, Mississippi who owns and operates her own unique T-shirt business for over ten years. Business was good at first, but then it plateaued. Betsy's usual orders came through each day, but her flame started to burn out in terms of her lack of drive for seeking new customers. Betsy was successful, locally, but that was the extent of her business model.

She always had a love for computers. She even went to a Community College and received an Associate's Degree in computer technology and programming. One day, one of Betsy's customers came in to pick up an order. The customer told Betsy a quick story of how he was mailing Betsy's T-shirts to his daughter in Illinois while she was away at college.

Getting ready to leave, the man looked at Betsy and said, "So why haven't you gotten a web-site up and running where people can simply buy your awesome, unique T-shirts online? Everyone has a website." Betsy was satisfied with her current reality—being a local supplier of T-shirts to a clientele that appreciated her and came back for consistent orders. But once this became boring for Betsy, a new spark ignited her passion to become excited about her business and her own talents all over again.

Not a novel idea, but still something that was lacking in Betsy's business was the basic task of building a web-site with a shopping cart feature. The result? Betsy now ships her T-shirts across the globe from hundreds of on-line orders and her store, still located in Mississippi, receives thank you notes from clients in countries, such as Singapore and Sweden. Effective leaders get excited about something new and when that is no longer "new," they find something else new.

3. GET CONNECTED

Spice up your life by getting some advice from others or creating new relationships. It sounds basic and easy because it is. It was easy for Bob Peterson, from Buffalo, NY who worked in various telemarketing firms for most of his life. Bob is a family man who made a decent living by working on a telephone to book appointments for door-to-door sales representatives in the security-systems business. Bob's number one philosophy which made him the top performer in his company was, "You have to say hello in order to get a hello back." The more calls Bob made, the increased probability that Bob would land more sales.

When you put yourself out there, you are going to meet new people, experience new frontiers, and perhaps find a new niche that will steer you into new directions. As you put yourself out there, don't hold back by not asking others for their help or advice. A simple, "Hey, I was wondering if you could help me . . ." can open your eyes to pathways that you never saw in the first place. Effective leaders ask for help, they don't shy away, and they get connected to others in order to do great things. Social media is a great way to connect, but so is talking to those you normally wouldn't because you withdraw from anything that threatens your comfort level. Push yourself to get *connected.* Effective leaders have thousands and thousands of connections. You never know who can help you out someday when you need it.

4. GET GROUNDED

Robin Baker from Perryton, Texas struggled with alcohol for five years after her husband passed away. She finally made a decision to get some help after her children gave her an ultimatum that she would never be able to see her grandchildren again unless she got clean. Robin had a few relapses, but was finally successful in becoming sober because she grounded herself and realized what mattered most to her: her family. They were her strength for helping Robin move from a state of dark depression to a state of happy expression.

To this day, Robin loves seeing her grandchildren grow up, play sports, and enjoy the magic of Santa Claus at Christmas time. Effective leaders know where they come from, what their vices are, what is most important to them, and what they need to do to make themselves whole. Getting grounded moves people from conceited to humble and from "living to work" to "working to live." Remembering where you came from, what you learned, the mistakes you made, and the hearts you've filled. This will exude confidence and appreciation in the leadership moves that you make next.

5. EVALUATE YOURSELF & COMMIT TO IT!

Are you living in a small world—your own little world—or are you doing something to help the planet? Are you giving back to the community? Are you putting yourself first or last? Remembering the greater good takes your daily successes and shares them with others so that you can do something for society. Your tasks might include writing a book, getting to the gym, or making a difficult decision to quit cigarettes so you can enjoy your children for many more years.

Whatever you do, you have to honestly evaluate yourself and make changes that are empirical, not *invisible*. You have to feel something different in your life in order to take yourself more seriously. This is going to be your hardest task because self-evaluation is never comfortable. However, if you invite discomfort, you will never be surprised by it. All you have to do is give it a try and if you are hesitant in doing this, evaluate yourself in private. Go to your bedroom and lock the door. Write a list of what you want to do in order to re-shape or renovate your life. Remember, effective leaders know when to slow down and detour themselves to a pit-stop for a "changing of the tires."

Now, go from "tattered" to "mattered" again. This is your one chance . . . your one life. Cherish it. Seize it. And know that you *matter*. Realize that when you are gone, you will have "mattered," while leaving a terrific legacy behind you for others to cherish and appreciate.

Effective leaders work through these five simple steps for personal and professional growth and success. There is no reason that any undertow should pull you down into a sea of drowning and heartache. Put on a life vest and swim to the shore of a new "you." After all, you are important.

Rick Jetter, Ph.D., is a multi-genre author, expert consultant, and motivational speaker. To learn more about plugging into Dr. Jetter and having him speak at one of your upcoming events or train your group, visit http://www.rickjetter.com or e-mail him at drjetter1@gmail.com.

Salmon Burgers with Lemon Dill Sauce

Serves 4

Ingredients

2 (7-ounce) cans salmon, drained
2 eggs, slightly beaten
1/2 cup Panko (Japanese breadcrumbs)
2 shallots, peeled and minced
1 poblano chile, stem cut off, seeded and finely chopped
1 lemon, zest only
kosher salt and freshly ground black pepper
Canola oil for frying
4 soft burger buns with sesame seeds
Butter lettuce and tomato slices for serving
1/2 cup good quality mayonnaise, preferably Hellmann's
2 lemons, juice of both, zest of one
2 tablespoons chopped fresh dill
kosher salt and freshly ground black pepper to taste

Instructions

In a large bowl mix together the salmon, eggs, Panko, shallots, poblano, lemon zest, salt and pepper. Form into 4 burgers and chill for 30 minutes. Meanwhile preheat the oven to 400° F. Heat about 1/4-inch of canola oil in a large oven proof skillet over medium high heat until shimmering. Add the cold burgers to the pan and cook until browned on each side, about 3-5 minutes per side. Place the pan in the hot oven to finish cooking through for about 5 minutes. Toast the insides of the buns.

In a small bowl whisk together the mayonnaise, lemon juice and zest, dill salt and pepper. Spread the sauce on the bottom of each bun. Top with a salmon burger, tomato slice, lettuce and more sauce. Serve immediately.

STEPS TO SUPERSTAR COMMUNICATION

Karen Southall Watts

Superstar: a person widely recognized and sought after for his or her talents. Many of us know one, and if not we've certainly heard about them or seen them through media—Superstar Communicators. They easily handle the routine tasks of communication like getting a message across quickly and effectively absorbing information. Superstar Communicators are described as great conversationalists, good listeners and masters of the written word. As speakers they inspire and often give listeners a feeling that a speech is "just for me." Their face-to-face speaking style has just the right amount of energy to be engaging, but not frantic, and they listen to others in a way that makes people feel valued and understood. When they write, Superstar Communicators are clear, concise and often quotable. What's the secret to this magical ability to connect with others? Is it something we common folk can master? Absolutely.

While they give the appearance of being natural and relaxed, it's important to realize that Superstar Communicators take communication very seriously, and so should you. In the same way that champion athletes review game videos and actors get director's notes, accomplished communicators earnestly reflect on feedback as a part of their constant improvement plan. Feedback on communication can be as simple as being asked to repeat something in a conversation or as complex as a file full of editor's comments. The real difference between Superstar Communicators and everyone else is what they do with feedback.

We all have individual styles when it comes to communication. However, sometimes personal preferences can morph into weaknesses or blind spots over time. Feedback from your audience, whether it's in a one-on-one conversation or in the comments section of a blog, can alert you to areas where you need to improve. Are you using unnecessary or confusing jargon? Do you make hasty assumptions about your audience? Is your style very stilted or outdated? Superstar Communicators carefully digest and apply useful feedback while holding on to their unique flair.

One of the most important steps you can take toward becoming a better quality communicator is to stop multitasking. Multitasking and wallowing in business has become an odd badge of honor in some circles. However, the truth is that just appearing busy doesn't mean you are getting anything done, and juggling a variety of tasks at once only insures that nothing gets the attention needed for excellence.

Multitasking can be a good coping skill, especially during moments when business or life gets out of control. However, as a first line strategy for accomplishing goals multitasking is a poor choice. Divided attention lowers performance for all of the jobs you're attempting to balance at once. In communication divided attention translates not only into lackluster results but also as a lack of respect. People can easily tell in telephone or face-to-face conversations when your attention is not truly focused on them.

I recall being on the telephone with a close associate several years ago when I felt this first hand. We were discussing a joint project when I realized I was being multitasked.

Me: "What are you doing?"

Associate: "What are you talking about?"

Me: "I can tell you're doing something else...what is it?"

Associate: "Uh...how can you tell? Never mind. I'm just trying to finish up these emails to customers."

Me: "Well, call me back when you're finished and we can refocus on this."

Despite the fact that I could not see my associate or hear any distracting sounds like keyboard clicks or even background noises, I knew that our communication was suffering from divided attention. The episode has become a long-running joke between us now, and helps us to maintain a better communication dynamic.

Written communication as well can suffer greatly from divided attention. Whether a short text or a full length blog post, most readers can usually spot half-hearted efforts. Lapsing focus is responsible for countless typos and misunderstandings. In a culture that now boasts the **tl;dr** abbreviation for "too long; didn't read" it is essential that your written messages be of the highest quality possible.

What this says to your audience is, "I have something more interesting or important happening now than my communication with you." Superstar Communicators never allow their audience to feel second best. Full attention not only shows respect toward others, but it will also improve the quality of your communications and allow you to accomplish more of your goals.

One evening, as part of my own desire to improve my communication skills, I attended a panel discussion on multicultural business communication. The moderator asked some general questions and then turned to each of the experts on the panel for a reply. One gentleman in particular told slightly funny and clearly rehearsed stories every time he was called upon. Unfortunately, his polished responses had nothing to do with the questions presented or the overall topic. He was more concerned about looking good than actually communicating with the rest of us. In the end, his choice of grandstanding and performing instead of connecting with the audience in real dialogue made him look unprofessional and desperate for attention—two qualities I doubt he wanted to be associated with his brand.

There are a lot of reasons someone might memorize a few things before a key communication situation: nervousness or shyness, the desire to remember important details, or eagerness to share a special story. Yet, it is important to realize that another way to show respect and take a step toward becoming a Superstar Communicator is to forego the canned speech and participate in the conversation that is actually happening.

The next step is to blend the old and the new. Language, technology and cultural norms are always changing. Using newer methods to connect with your audience does not mean abandoning the foundation of communication. The key is to embrace technology carefully and in a managed way while holding on to the basics of clear messages and audience knowledge. Make sure your posts, tweets, videos and other public communications are accurate reflections of your personal brand crafted for your particular audience.

The ever-growing sea of electronic devices and social media platforms can be intimidating. Even those who grew up with technology can struggle to get their message across while avoiding social gaffs. Here are some tips to aid you in blending old and new communication features:

» Start every communication with an assessment of your audience and their readiness for your message. This can be as simple as asking, "Is this a good time to talk?" or watching for body language cues. When speaking to a group, ask for some background info ahead of time and when you arrive "read the room" for energy level and tension. Before you click "send" or "post" make sure your written messages match the audience and platform where you plan to place them.

» Manners still matter. One of the ways Superstar Communicators make others feel heard and valued is by employing good old-fashioned politeness. Even with the brevity of social media there is still time enough to thank others and acknowledge their comments gracefully. The same rules that apply to face-to-face interactions extend into the virtual world: don't ask brand new contacts for huge favors, keep your language clean and professional, and resist the urge to engage in nasty arguments.

» Global exposure means understanding diversity is no longer optional. Superstar Communicators realize the world is a diverse place and that in order to connect they need to continually expand their knowledge and understanding of others. Spend time learning about people outside your inner circle. When posting worldwide messages pay special attention to language that implies racial or cultural insensitivity.

Superstar Communicators never hesitate to directly address their personal shortcomings. One way to combine the steps of utilizing feedback and building your understanding of diversity is to ask colleagues from other cultures questions. This is designed to improve your communication with those who don't share your background. Improve your multicultural business communication by asking:

How can I show you respect when we first meet?

What would you prefer I call you when we speak professionally?

How important is it to you that we have a firm schedule and stick to planned topics?

Can you share some tips with me for communicating with professionals from your country?

Never try to bluff your way through, but work toward a genuine understanding of your audience. Most professionals are willing to give you honest and kind feedback when you demonstrate a true desire to improve your ability to communicate across cultures.

Once you've committed to taking these steps, it's important that you don't forget the basics. Dazzling conversationalists, talented copywriters, and inspiring public speakers build their panache on a foundation of solid techniques. Advice to use humor with caution, practice and proofread, and stick to the truth has been around for a long time, because it works. A key part to excellent communication is the often forgotten foundational skill of listening.

Listening is the frequently neglected side of the communication cycle. Many times we become so involved in crafting and delivering our own message that we forget to pay attention to the information coming in from others. Superstar Communicators are accomplished listeners. When applying "active listening" they are subtle and natural and avoid sounding like amateur therapists simply parroting back words. You can do this as well by listening deeply for the emotions and messages behind words, and by asking out right for clarification when needed. Asking someone to expand upon their ideas or to provide you with more details is a good way to convey genuine interest and respect for them. Listening extends beyond paying attention to the words and feelings in a conversation; it includes patiently absorbing silence. A good listener does not rush to fill every empty space in a conversation. They allow silence to happen, and in doing so, make room for others to complete their thoughts or consider new information.

Being comfortable with silence is one of the many ways to convey confidence. An aura of confidence, comfort in your own skin, is a key quality. Thankfully, those not born with charisma and an air of confidence can learn the behaviors necessary to broadcast self-assurance. The first step is to incorporate preparation, rehearsal, and a backup plan into your high stakes communications. Nothing enables you to relax and enjoy communication like the knowledge that you are well prepared. This is especially true with formal communications tasks like presentations, speeches or facilitating meetings. Experienced communicators research and rehearse and also have a *Plan B* for the unexpected like Teleprompters that fail, mics that pop, and other technology that refuses to cooperate.

Assurance, born in part from great preparation, shows in many ways. To move toward Superstar Communicator status you need to practice and master a few techniques. For face-to-face communication and especially occasions where you will be broadcast or recorded pay special attention to your tone of voice and body language. Listeners respond best to strong and sure speech spoken slowly enough to be understood and with natural inflections. Don't use a questioning tone, rising at the end of sentences, when you mean to make a statement. Keep your body language open and relaxed. Whether speaking or writing, purge your messages of qualifying language to reinforce your confident tone. Words like perhaps, just, only, or maybe suck the strength out of your statements. Use them with caution.

The final step is to make sure your communication always has "***ah quality***." No, I don't mean the relaxing feeling of slipping into a hot bath. Superstar Communicators fill their messages with ***ah***:

- A-accuracy
- H-honesty

One of the main reasons readers, listeners and viewers repeatedly return to Superstar Communicators is because they believe in the quality of the message. No amount of slick delivery can substitute a genuine message. Even if an audience can be fooled once, they seldom return to take in messages from communicators who have treated them with a lack of respect or violated their trust. You can certainly take your time developing into a Superstar Communicator. It might take a while to learn to focus and listen with intention or to write messages that cross cultural boundaries. However, you cannot wait to make the commitment to filling your communications with accurate information and honest motives.

Superstar Communicators are mere mortals like the rest of us. However, they have decided to augment their natural talents with a dedication similar to that of other virtuosos. By giving high quality communication a place of importance in their lives, and doing the necessary work, they make insightful and impactful communication look natural and easy. Follow these steps with perseverance and it's possible for anyone to transform from everyday conversationalist, speaker or writer, into a Superstar Communicator.

Karen Southall Watts is a "professional encourager" as well as trainer, coach and author focusing on entrepreneurship and management topics. Her book, Messenger: The Entrepreneur's Guide to Communication came out through Motivational Press in the summer of 2015. The fastest, and easiest to spell, way to find her is @askkaren on Twitter.

THE NECESSITIES OF SUCCESS

Mark & Tori Baird

Success is accompanied with discipline, focus, drive, patience, endurance, and a will to win. These are the personal characteristics of top achievers. We have a goal in mind that becomes our lives' central purpose. We work tirelessly in achieving our dreams, regardless of what obstacles we face along the way. We are relentless in the pursuit of our future. But we must not ignore the present: our health, our family, community service, and fellowship with friends. Being successful at these things will result in personal contentment and enrich the lives of others along the way.

In order to be successful, be recognized as a leader, build a profitable company, or happily in love, one thing above all else is needed: Good health. To pursue any of these without making robust vitality your primary priority is folly. Too many extraordinary people throughout history have fallen far short of their potential due to chronic illness and a premature death.

Successful people are commonly workaholics. Fourteen to seventeen hour days, 7 days a week, year after year, wears down a person's heart and brain. A coronary attack, a stroke, or both is commonly the result- as Jesus said, "What does it profit a person to gain the world, and then to lose their soul?"

It is vital that every motivated individual knows that success is not an end, but a moment in time. We struggle so hard and devote more than we knew was possible to get to the pinnacle. But when we finally get there, we soon realize that our work has just begun. Staying at the top usually takes more effort than the getting there.

The same effort and diligence that it takes to be a business or financial success is the same effort we must apply daily to the fortitude of our physical, mental, emotional and spiritual composition. Our bodies are our 'mother ship' without it, we aren't going anywhere. Those of us that practice a comprehensive plan for constant self-improvement live more fulfilling, happy and meaningful lives.

An unfortunate talisman of many exceptional, genius, creative and successful people that first taste success is a proclivity to celebrate and indulge in their accomplishments and prosperity to extremes. Particularly by abusing drugs and alcohol. How many great, entrepreneurs, musicians, artists and actors do we read about every year that accidently kill themselves? How many of the newly rich become quickly addicted to alcohol and a myriad of other chemicals? That or they over-indulge in eating rich foods and become ill. Financial success also can cause us to spend too much on non-essentials, which can lead quickly to going back into debt. This leads to depression and sometimes suicide.

In some ways, we adults remain children throughout our lives. In fact, the shared personality trait among those that achieve fame and wealth is an active, child-like imagination that has no boundaries. It is paramount to balance that exuberance with mature self-control and focus on the lasting instead of the temporary.

Successful people immerse themselves in a powerful tide. It is the global current of business that flows in and out of every country on earth. How much we earn is thoroughly connected to everyone else's economy too. It is cause and effect. Even though our endeavor or enterprise may be only a drop in this vast ocean, we are susceptible to its forces and storms. This is equally true of our physical health. Life contains seas of stress that we all must swim through sometimes. These endurance tests can weaken us. That is why the ancient Greeks left us with this: "A strong body makes a strong mind."

Humankind's brain was not built solely for work and the pursuit of material success. A host of horrible health consequences are usually the result of doing so. When we ignore our brain's and body's needs, it creates stress. Multiple scientific studies have proven that experiencing stress over a prolonged period of time is detrimental to physical, mental and emotional well-being. It is a negative force that can lead to many chronic health issues.

Poor health issues can rob any of us from grabbing a hold of the prize we so earnestly devote ourselves to possessing. We must restrain our innate desire to get to the top when it crosses into the time that we eat, sleep, exercise, and play. Keeping our body and brain at optimal health has to be our number one priority, every day.

Healthy people are attractive people. If your eyes are clear and white, if your complexion is rosy, if you exude vitality, and if you have a friendly and engaging personality, then you are a 'good looking' man or woman. You may be bald, grey, or even 'ugly'. However, if you exude health and treat others with respect then people will find you attractive.

Being attractive is big bonus when competing for the mountain top. Women already know that this is true when they are dealing with men. Someone who is strong and fit and has a vibrant countenance when meeting with decision makers, has a tremendous competitive advantage over a rival who do not. Whether we like it or not, this is the truth in the real world. Fit and healthy people are magnets. And they generally acquire more clients and achieve greater rewards.

Although having a strong body and mind is extremely vital to success, too many of us fail to make it a precedent in our daily lives. Making more money and all it demands takes the dominant place in our lives. We deserve to enjoy the fruits and riches of our long and hard labor, but many of us need to change some unhealthy habits in order to make that happen.

How do we get anything done? We plan for it. We put it into our schedule. Whenever I have an important call or meeting, I always put it in my Google calendar 24 hours, 12 hours and 1 hour from the appointment time. I have learned how distractions can make me forget even the most imperative engagement. So, I am conscientious and send myself reminders. Missing such conferences will shortly destroy my reputation and become a negative mark on my integrity. In like manner, we must make a schedule for the daily maintenance of our health, or it will have detrimental effects too.

What makes up a 'successful' person's life? The pursuit of a goal makes up the majority of our waking hours. In addition, we cannot exclude attending to our other essential needs in order to live a rich and fulfilling life. We must include good nourishment, exercise, time with friends and family, personal time, and rest.

Nourishment should be thought of holistically. It involves what you feed your body and your mind. It also means nurturing your soul. For instance, courage and love are more than feelings or thoughts. They are reflections of the person within us, our individual spirit and nature. This is our personal essence, separate and transcendent of the functions and feelings of either the brain or heart. A well fed and healthy soul has no less of an effect on our personalities, countenances and physical health.

Just like our bodies and minds, with effort, we can improve our souls too. It takes introspection and an honest appraisal of our convictions and beliefs as well as seeking answers to the questions of all humanity (God? Morality? After-life? Faith...). These are innate queries that arise out of our souls. Taking time to be alone without distractions to meditate, contemplate and pray is foundational to good health.

Our souls are reflected in our personalities and behavior. Here are some character traits that form a solid foundation for building success:

Courage is a critical quality to develop. It requires making wise and precise decisions while under fire. It may begin as fear that suddenly pushes adrenaline through your system that we all experience when faced with a potentially ominous challenge. It is the transforming of that fear into a calm and effective confidence that makes us courageous.

Another vital quality to acquire is gratitude. Always be grateful for what you have, no matter how much or little. Add humility to your thankfulness, respect others and learn from those that have gone before you.

Nourishing our bodies necessitates our practicing self-control. I do not say 'having' self-control.' That is not a naturally inherent possession of our personalities. It requires conscientious choice and willingness to go against powerful, personal desires. Once practiced successfully, it becomes a power one always possesses. Having once tamed your affections, you always have the knowledge that you can do so again. It is a matter of endurance that with daily application becomes a preference and then a way of life. This is the same lesson we apply when doing well in school, being an athlete, a parent, spouse, etc. It all begins with the will to change, and that requires Self-Control.

There are ten thousand 'healthy' diet plans, but there is only one that works: Eat food that is good for you and eat it in moderation. Acquiring and maintaining a healthy weight is not at all complicated. It is this simple.

Regular exercise should accompany a truly nourishing intake of calories. Exercise strengthens muscles, bones, arteries and organs. The health benefits of regular exercise are impossible to ignore. The benefits of exercise are ours for the taking, regardless of age, sex or physical ability. The advantages to our life include a more positive, youthful outlook and a robust sex life. Prevention magazine reports, "Physical activity keeps blood flowing and boosts oxygen consumption, both of which help your brain function better. Exercise also makes the brain work more efficiently, which reduces risk of heart attack, stroke, and diabetes."

Personally, I ride my bike at a moderate and consistent pace for 90 minutes and swim 1500 meters (40 minutes) 5 or 6 times a week, alternating one or the other day by day. I am 65. I did not start out by doing this. It has taken methodical improvement, since my heart attack a little more than a year ago.

Healthy, reciprocal relationships are an important ingredient to happiness. No amount of success is worth the effort if it does not reward us with an elevated, positive sense of well-being. And nothing will do that better than being loved. Studies conducted by the Centre for Ageing at Flinders University followed nearly 1,500 older people for 10 years. It found that those who had a large network of friends outlived those with the fewest friends by 22%. The Mayo Clinic cites these health benefits to building intimate relationships:

» Increases sense of belonging and purpose.
» Boosts happiness and reduces stress.
» Improves self-confidence and self-worth.
» Helps cope with traumas, such as divorce, serious illness, job loss or death of a loved one.
» Encourages changing or avoiding unhealthy lifestyle habits, such as excessive drinking or lack of exercise.

What difference could an extra hour of sleep make in your life? A study cited by WebMD measured the effects of creating disturbed sleep patterns on 10 young, healthy adults. After a mere four days, three of them had blood glucose levels that registered as pre-diabetic.

Naturally, a lack of proper sleep will have a negative effect on many areas of our lives. For instance, couples frequently complain that they are "too tired" to have sexual relations. Sleep deprivation also increase the severity of physical pain. Drowsiness will affect the quality of anyone's work. It is also a safety issue: How many fatalities on the road and seas are caused from a driver being too tired? Your mood, your weight, your mind and love life are all positively impacted when we get an adequate amount of rest. Discipline yourself to sleep 7-8 hours a night and to get a 10 minute nap in the middle of each day: Your life will greatly improve.

To achieve our fullest potential we need to be healthy. Our minds need to be sound, our emotions hopeful and happy, our bodies well cared for. We need close relationships with significant others, and personal reflection too.

A "successful person" is someone that fulfills their whole human potential. As we grow towards that goal our lives become of more valuable to ourselves and others. The true leaders of this world are those of us that aspire always to be the best that we can be in all areas of our outer and inner lives.

Take good care of yourselves, fellow voyagers!

Mark and Tori Baird are nationwide personalities who have appeared on multiple TV, radio and press outlets, including FOX National Business News, NBC Nightly News. And People Magazine featured them as "Heroes Among Us." Both US Presidents GW Bush and Obama have recognized their efforts and given them Presidential medals.Their blog ranks 27,000 out of all US websites. Their book, "An American Crisis: Veteran Unemployment" is a best seller. Their next book, "The Patriotic Business Plan: Strategies for Sensational Success" is being published this Spring by Motivational Press.

Asparagus Soup
Serves 4

Ingredients

2 tablespoons extra virgin olive oil

3 tablespoons unsalted butter

1 1/2 large sweet onions such as Vidalia or Maui, peel, cut in half and sliced thin

4 large cloves garlic, peeled and roughly chopped

2 large bunches asparagus, woody stem trimmed off, cut into pieces

1 quart low sodium chicken stock

kosher salt and freshly ground black pepper to taste

Instructions

Heat the butter and olive oil in a large saucepan over medium high heat until shimmering. Add the onions and sauté until soft, about 5 minutes. Add the garlic and cook until fragrant, about 1 minute. Add the asparagus and sauté for about 5 minutes. Add the chicken stock, salt and pepper and cook until the asparagus is tender when pierced with a knife. Using an immersion blender purée until smooth. If you don't have an immersion blender you can purée in a blender or food processor and return to the saucepan to reheat. Served immediately.

WHAT ARE YOU WAITING FOR?

Aneeta Pathak

We talk a lot about commitment in the workplace these days, but little discussion of what this actually really means. Commitment is a very important word in life; it is an essential part of our job as well as our personal life. To achieve even the simplest of goals we have to learn the meaning of commitment, whether it relates to personal or business goals. Without commitment, we cannot achieve anything. In other words, commitment is action; we have to show commitment over and over again in all your actions. Genuine commitment to our job separates us from the rest by the way we embrace the most difficult or challenging task.

Think about this; everything you ever achieved sprouted from a commitment you made, from your book, your job, your family, and your house. You kept whatever commitment you made even though you had to face foreseen and unforeseen hurdles. Once you have committed yourself to something, your mind becomes like a homing pigeon. You don't want to think about other choices; your mind is set on your goals.

The Cambridge English Dictionary defines commitment as *"a willingness to give your time and energy to something that you believe in, or a promise or firm decision to do something"*

Although it is usually taken for granted what the word 'commitment' means, in my words is. ***"The power of constantly reminding ourselves that we have to do what we have promised to ourselves and to others***

– commitments are non-negotiable".

Now it is your turn - just take a few seconds, and think deeply about this word and ask yourself this question:

Am I genuinely committed? As a parent towards my kids? As an author towards my readers? As an employee towards the organization I work for?

I believe that on a daily basis we try to confront our level of commitment at every stage of our life: at the office, at home, among our friends, and towards society. Our determination to commit ourselves must be consistent if we want to see ourselves successful in all areas of our life. Commitment is the common factor that will help us to unleash our passion, excel in what we do and focus on our goals.

When you have committed yourself to achieve the goals you have set, you must refuse to allow any obstacles to fritter away your focus.

Most of the time when you make a commitment, you promise yourself to design a way of doing things that you believe will result in the development of happiness and excitement.

When commitment is implemented, your principles become your regular habits of doing things. We know that a high-level of commitment is required to become a competent and efficient employer or employee. When you are committed to your work, you accept no excuses but only results. If you make a commitment to improve your performance at work, your commitment will yield its fruits as you're being congratulated by your boss for your extraordinary performance. If you make a commitment to increase your physical fitness, your will feel how committed you are when you will find yourself looking forward to go to the gym or choosing to eat a healthy meal. If you are truly committed, you will easily move through a change with no intention of looking in the rear-view mirror. I strongly believe that the best things in life come with a commitment. Do you agree?

Commitment is more than just a promise; it involves decision and dedication to do things, in a constant manner. Having consistency about an appropriate attitude, commitment and performance at work is crucial for both your personal and team success. If you want to show consistency all the time, you need to stick to your plans and goals. Most likely, you will get off track now and again. When you are lost, or challenged by shifting priorities; get right back to your plan and start moving forward. Even if you are challenged by shifting priorities, all you have to do is to revisit your goals and see if they still apply.

By bringing energy and initiative to your job everyday shows your commitment. If you care about your work and organization, this will show in the results that you produce. When you show commitment you will demonstrate leadership potential to your boss and can definitely lead to career opportunities.

I believe that we will always need someone to remind us of what's important, even though we think that we can remember everything-

From my perspective as an Executive Assistant, here are some key elements that have helped me in my line of work where commitment was established towards my employer and peers. Would you like to add them your commitment Zen?

» Contributing to effective relationships and understanding others
» Giving proper attention to details
» Being cooperative with your boss by helping on major projects
» Taking the initiative to complete tasks and respect deadlines
» Helping your boss to achieve his/her professional goals
» Taking pride in your work
» Focusing on the organization's corporate mission, vision and values
» Looking for new challenges to expand your horizons
» Overcoming obstacles by demonstrating a problem-solving attitude

When we make a commitment, we have to fulfill it, while recalling that total integrity is expected from us. If we fail to commit, we hurt the credibility of our peers and no wonder we will hurt ourselves too! Always remember that your duty is to honour and fulfill any commitments you make.

One of my favourite quotes from Tony Robbins – ***"Stay committed to your decisions, but stay flexible in your approach"***

Personally, I see this quote to be very insightful. Once we set our goals, we stay focused and never give up or change our minds. Obviously, you will come across obstacles that will block your way and you will find yourself in a standstill. Do not worry; you are smarter than you can imagine. Stop and think about other techniques that you can use to achieve your targeted goals. Always remember that there are distractions everywhere. If you are truly committed to your goals, you will never back down. If you focus on your commitment, it will help you to embed a winning mindset, overcome limiting beliefs and clear any blocked energy.

Trust is a major component of the foundation of successful interpersonal relationships.

Aneeta Pathak is a Senior Executive Assistant at Empire Life Insurance in Toronto and supports the Senior Vice President of Insurance and Investments. She is also an International Best Selling Author – "Shine-Secrets of Extraordinary Executive Assistants", her first book was published in April 2014. She has also co-authored another book with Justin Sachs and other industry leading experts – "A New Year to a New You", published in January 2015.

SELF HELP

DIG YOUR DIFF (DIFFERENTNESS)

Rick Clemons

Science tells us – in an international study conducted by Marcus C. Feldman of Stanford University, 2002 – that we Homo Sapiens (humans) are 99.9% alike in our DNA. That's certainly enough reason for worldwide group hug, wouldn't you say? After all, we love to be with people we know, like, and trust. Right? Or is that only in business transactions? Uh, no! We, creatures of human intellect, love, love, love to be part of something greater than ourselves. It's our groupiesque (yes it's a mashed up word, so get over it already) mentality that feeds our hunger to break bread with other soul brothers and sisters of like mind and spirit. Yep, it's all rainbows and unicorns until we discover our differentNESS (same as differences, just a sexier form with a few more curves) gets in the way of our Guinness World Record attempt for the largest group hug. It's also the moment *sameness* rears it's ugly little head, screeching like fingernails on a chalk board, "Don't abandon me. Please don't betray me!" And so it begins.

Regardless of who you are, the number of social likes in your Facebook profile, hearts flitting by on the screen as you Periscope, or the credentials or lack thereof that follow your name, someone somewhere doesn't *dig your differentNESS*. Conversely, there's a high probability those same people want to force you onto the comfy couch of *sameness* with them. "Aw, c'mon. Jump on the comfy couch of *sameness*," they cry! Be careful. It's a veiled request. While it may make sense in the moment to support the scientific findings of 99.9% alike, you might want to consider shifting your loyalties to the .01% that makes you uniquely you – a leader, an activist, a world changer, a stay-at-home dad, an entrepreneurial mom. That one percent isn't all about hair and eye color, and the build of your body. No, no, no. It is about you being a better you.

Too often, in a rote zombie state, we shlup onto the tufted, down-filled couches of *sameness* to keep our inner circles from feeling like we just gave them an abandonment wedgie. No one likes that feeling of misguided undies in their gluteus maximus crack (butt crack) – literally or figuratively. Our pals, mates, buddies, chums, friends, and family yearn for us to remain that person they've come to know. Remember, it's about that group hug moment. But, what about *differentNess?* What about those burning desires to be our own uniquely defined individual? How often have you stood by as your individuality went up in flames? More often than you'd rather admit. Right? If so, then douse that fire. Watch the hopes and dreams of others expectations for you go up in flames. It's time to lovingly say, "Sameness be damned!"

Now before you get panicky up in your head about going against the fabric of society, take a deep breath and ask yourself this one question, "What's missing from my life that I really want?" Go ahead. Ask away. This book's not going anywhere while you respond. It's also okay if you end up with a mini War and Peace response to that question. But beware of the thought speed bumps ahead like...

» That's too selfish. What would my husband think?

» I can't afford that. It'd be wasteful.

» He/she will never be interested in me. I'm not their type.

» That's just too weird. Everyone will think I've lost it.

» I'll do that when I have more free time or when the kids are grown. That's what a responsible person would do.

Truth is, each of those speed bumps (excuses), have two common threads...

1. A deep-seated need to be in *sameness* with others.

2. A fear of exposing your *differentNESS* to the world.

Each of these statements reeks of spoken and unspoken rules. Ones we've become accustomed in order to march to the universal beat of *sameness,* even if it makes us miserable. Don't rock the boat baby. Or is it time to *rock the boat* in your life and *dig your diff*? If you want to bring about long-lasting, pat yourself on the back change into your life, then the answer is a resounding "YES." LET'S ROCK THE BOAT BABY! It's time for you to DIG YOUR DIFF! But how?

STEP 1 – GET CURIOUS.

Curiosity killed the cat! Right? Poor kitty (I miss my two greatly), but that's not you. You're not going to die during your curiosity expedition. You're simply going to open up, play with wonder, and expand what might be possible. Possible only when you give yourself permission to ask and explore the following questions.

» How might my life be different?
» What could be possible?
» Where might I find more success and happiness in my life?
» Who might I bring into my life?
» When do I find my curiosity being squelched and why?

These questions will change the trajectory of this adventure you call life. The trick is, GRANTING PERMISSION! You MUST give yourself permission to board the CURIOSITY EXPRESS. Day in and day out, you practice – consciously and unconsciously – giving permission for others to run your life. Yet, when was the last time you gave yourself that same latitude? Without granting permission to be curious for your own sake, then you're just being curious because someone told you to be curious.

GIVE YOURSELF PERMISSION NOW TO BE CURIOUS ABOUT WHAT COULD BE!

STEP 2 – BE COURAGEOUS

If the Cowardly Lion of Wizard of Oz can do it, why can't you? Why can't you summon up the courage to be who you are? Because it makes you feel vulnerable. You're exposed. There's no hiding when you shed the façade and say, "This is me!" Raw, naked, humble truth is frightening but at least it's not a lie!

In her work, Brene Brown, talks extensively about vulnerability, courage, and truth – she's fully exposed in what she says. She's walking the walk, and talking the talk. Yes, she's *daring greatly,* and she's also taking a skinny dip in courageousness. Granted she's a gifted scholar, researcher, and Oprah Winfrey protégé – all of which makes her a prime target for the naysayers of the world. And, what does she do? She bravely steps into her courageous heels, dons her cloak of vulnerability pride, and strikes a power pose stance of *digging her differentNESS*. No apologies whatsoever for basking in the glory of her own *differentNESS*. All because...

> Vulnerability sounds like truth and feels like courage. Truth and courage aren't always comfortable, but they're never weakness.
>
> — Brene Brown

The challenging, yet simple formula for mustering up courage to do anything, and specifically for *digging your differentNESS, is*

Truth + Vulnerability = Courage

Open the doorway to practice. Yes it is a practice. Practicing this formula means undoing years of false beliefs and releasing the future *what could be's*. In other words, let go of the past, let the future become, and be in the moment. When you trust your truth in the moment, allow raw vulnerability to be exposed and the courage to be who you are and have always been will lead you courageously to your destined future. Practice, practice, practice. Just like yoga and piano, being courageous in your truth and vulnerability takes practice to make it a habit...not to make it perfect!

STEP 3 - EXUDE CONFIDENCE

You may have just cringed, reading the words *exude confidence*. If so, that's because the picture on the silver screen of your mind just played one of two scenes.

Scene #1 – I have no confidence to exude.

Scene #2 – People will think I'm cocky if I'm confident.

Scene #3 – I have a PH.D. in confidence, so no worries.

Well good for you and you can skip this step. NOT!

Regardless of which scene played out in the theater of your mind, the credits are rolling and the cast of characters who need to master the fine art of *confidence* includes everyone on the planet...even those with the PH.D.'s in Confidence. There isn't a soul on the planet that is fully confident, 24/7. If they say otherwise, then they are cocky, with a capital "C" not confident. The fact that everyone needs more confidence, begs two questions...

» Why do people need confidence?

» How does one create more confidence?

Why do we need confidence? Truth is, we don't need confidence. We tend to use the word *need* as frequently was we change our underwear. Please tell me you change your underwear frequently. If not, that would be a great way to IMAGINE being a new you in the next 30 day- changing your underwear frequently! Anyway, back to this *need confidence* syndrome. None of us needs confidence. If we don't have confidence we're not going to thirst to death or die of hunger. Ok you might, if you don't have the confidence to ask for food or water, but that's a whole other book – Basic Life Requirements for Dummies!

Instead of need, let's change the word to *want* or *desire*. Usually we *want* or *desire* to be more confident for various reasons:

» Confidence lights up our lives with love, or creates more success in our careers.

» Confidence helps us train for the New York Marathon or pass the State Bar Exam.

» Confidence keeps us focused to write our first manuscript or to keep trying when the odds say, "Sorry, no babies for you!"

Regardless of the situation, we desire confidence in order to experience a myriad of other emotions. Each of the previous statements, in and of themselves is focused on the outcome we derive from confidence. Yet, what we really want and desire is to experience the emotion from that outcome.

» Love in our lives leads to feelings of acceptance and desire.

» Success in our careers leads to feelings of accomplishment.

» Crossing the finish line at the New York Marathon leads to feelings of pride and triumph.

» Finally becoming pregnant leads to feelings of joy and happiness.

So why do we want and desire confidence? In order to feel something that we're lacking in our current state of being.

We now have a slightly better understanding of why we desire confidence. Now the question is how to create confidence. Simple, take two CONFIDENCE pills and call me in the morning. Just kidding. If it were that simple then there'd be no reason to be writing this chapter.

In order to build confidence we have to clear up a misconception. Confidence is not an aphrodisiac for the ego. It may feed the ego, but true confidence is not about feeding the ego it is about aligning with your core values and beliefs. Wait, what? Think about it. When you lack confidence, it's because you are faced with something that is out of alignment with your core values and beliefs. It may also mean that you're attempting something, or trying to be some way that is not fully aligned with how you see. If you're fumbling with this concept, take your time peeling the layers away from this different way of seeing. To smoothly peel back the understanding, ask yourself one question. "What value or belief is causing me to lack confidence?" Think back to a time, maybe just this past day or week, when you felt a lack of confidence or experienced low self-esteem. What value or belief, is getting in the way of your confidence? These questions are the litmus test of uncovering your confidence leaks.

Once you identify the value that is out of alignment, bring things back into alignment to experience higher levels of confidence. As for those beliefs, try to determine if the belief is coming from a grounded state of being or from an award-winning screen play you've conjured up in your mind. If it is a grounded belief, then go back to aligning with your values. If it is a conjured up belief, then it is time to address and change that belief. Get CURIOUS and COURAGEOUS about how changing that belief will make you more confident, improve your life, and up your happiness quotient.

STEP 4 – COMMITMENT - THE WASH, RINSE, AND REPEAT CYCLE

We've already established the practice of changing our underwear, so now we're going to establish the practice of doing the laundry of our life for higher levels of confidence.

The COMMITMENT phase is literally a mirror image of the metaphorical pile of laundry – the one literally in the hamper mimics the pile in our lives. Once the laundry piles up, it's time to do the laundry. For most people, this laundry cycle happens like clockwork. Yet, we can't seem to practice doing the dirty laundry of our lives. Washing, rinsing, and repeating the steps to bring more CONFIDENCE into our lives so that we can DIG OUR DIFFERENTNESS! Metaphorically speaking, the more we do the laundry, washing and rinsing out the stains that steal our confidence, the sooner we can wear the clean clothes of pride in the world.

HOW DO YOU DIG YOUR DIFF (DIFFERENTNESS)?

Step 1 – Get Curious. Explore and find ways to wash and rinse away the feelings of self-doubt and unworthiness.

Step 2 – Be Courageous. Stand tall and proud in the lion's den, knowing your differentNESS will set you free.

Step 3 - Exude Confidence. Align with your values and dump negative beliefs that hold you back

Step 4 – Commitment - The Wash, Rinse, and Repeat Cycle. Stay committed to the life long journey of *digging your diff.* It's a fabulous adventure that you're allowed to repeat, so you can grow, by being curious, courageous, and confident.

Now get going! It's time for you to go dig your diff!

Rick Clemons is a the author of Frankly My Dear I'm Gay, the founder of the .1 Project, a make you think speaker and podcaster, who creates ways for people to dig their diff in the world so that they can stop apologizing for who they are and start living as who they are meant to be!

30 DAYS TO A NEW YOU

Steve Lentini

When I was invited to contribute to this book, I started thinking about how to open the chapter and in reading James Allen came to this perfect passage. In his book The Path of Prosperity, James Allen writes, "All that we are is the result of what we have thought; it is founded on our thoughts; it is made up of our thoughts. Thus said Buddha, and it therefore follows that if a man is happy, it is because he dwells in happy thoughts; if miserable, because he dwells in despondent and debilitating thoughts."

In listening to clients describe their world it is always clear, with no exception, that their thinking **is** the difficulty....the thinking that they were blocked and their insistence to continue to complain about problems...***was the problem!*** What you can begin to do in 30 days to a new you is to "change how the world is experiencing you."

Look at everything that occurs and everyone in your world today as a reflection of you. Your thinking has created all of this so what kind of thinking has brought you all these people and situations? Would you describe each as positive or negative? Happy or Sad? Remember it's all you. People that bug you, situations, or jobs, etc. that are frustrating or "blocking your success" are in your life because you created them... to help you grow. People that bug you are showing you a part of you that you have not yet embraced. You created them in your thinking because you had to learn "just how obnoxious you are" for example, if you have obnoxious people in your life then it's really you not knowing that you also show up that way. As you begin to embrace that you are also obnoxious sometimes, your thinking switches to "oh, he doesn't bother me anymore and voila, as you changed your thinking- things changed. You changed. You are the only one that can change in all your relationships, your job, etc. As you keep changing how you describe situations and people, things will change. You are now beginning to "live from the inside out." Begin the next week to journal about all the "others" in your life, all your "situations", what do they tell you about your thinking? How do you speak about all of these?

You may need a coach to help you "hear yourself". How do you describe others in your world? How do you describe your career, job or do you think of yourself as a "failure" or do you feel blocked? People who are having challenges in succeeding or simply living happily describe their world much differently than those who are living happily and succeeding.

A good way to discover what I call a "default" pattern is to listen to how others describe their world. Are they a complainer? Do they sound powerless to change their world? Do their words match what you see about them? Would you describe them that exact way? When things don't go as you expected what do you "default" to? Do you begin complaining and feeling powerless? You might be tempted to say "Steve....my house burned down....how did I create this?" What I know is this...that circumstances can only affect you in so far as you allow them to. If you allow circumstances, outward things to make or break you, you are allowing them a power they do not deserve. You have the power to describe them as a gift- a blessing in disguise- as something designed to get you a new house, or something that you recognize now that you resisted. You can make it whatever you want.

Don't give the outward any power. You can be a "power-full" creator or a "power-less" victim, it's your choice. Which sounds more fun and a part of 30 days to a new you? Begin over the next 30 days to paint yourself a new you, a new picture of your life. Begin to visualize it and think of yourself as there already. Begin to use your words to describe that success.

Purify and dwell in loving thoughts of kindness, love, trusting and honest, good natured and charitable thoughts. James Allen said that "he who has realized the Divine within himself recognizes it in all beings, even in the beasts". "Birds of a Feather Flock together", based upon your thinking and speaking, you have attracted to yourself what you have sent forth, and surrounded yourself with people similar to you. Begin each day to simply believe this, that you are the creator of your world, believe it without a doubt in your heart and soul. Meditate upon this daily until you realize this power is true. You will begin to see the folly and fragility of of circumstances and you will discover the power of a happy and "self-managed" soul. A soul that has decided upon its power and its own happiness. The Universe is a reflection of you...your world and all that's in it is now a decision of yours and it is just waiting for you to change it.

As you send out love and kindness, you will find it and as you give generously, you will find the same coming back to you. Test it over the next 30 days as you imagine a new you; write me and tell me about what you experience. I know it to be true and I would never suggest to anyone to "follow my way". It's not my way, I have discovered this to be true by living a life of pain and anguish over outer circumstances. I have settled for less than the best for myself and then railed over "just how unfair it all was."

When I was ready, my teacher appeared and showed me how my thinking was unfair. She showed me that how I was describing my world became my world. It's the Law, it's totally impersonal. Once I followed the Law, my life changed because I had changed. I have a quote that describes the Law "If you don't like your experience of the World, change how the World is experiencing you." Now I get to keep what I have learned by teaching it. You are always getting what you are giving- Cause and Effect. Your thinking and speaking are the Cause and the Effect in your life. Who you are surrounded with and all the "circumstances" are a reflection of you. That is the gift of the Law, by taking stock of your life, the Law reflects your thinking as a gift to show you what you need to change or not. You do not need to go on a search, the minute you change, things will begin to change as well. In 30 days, 30 hours, 30 minutes, in fact the next 30 seconds, begin to think about your new life. Become excited about it now, feel in awe of the splendor of it coming. It will come, your new life...it has to. It's the Law.

Everything in the Universe is in Divine Order. Instead of beating yourself up about what you have created...think of it as all being necessary to get you to pick up this book and change. Everything has been created by you as a lesson in growth. If you resisted it all up until now, what you resists persists. It has persisted in showing up as a "knock upon your door" and the Universe will keep knocking until you get it. A Divine Gift to get you change your thinking, to get you to realize your power and the second you get it and the second you "wake up" you get the new life. As you change what you think about and speak about, you will recognize and use your power in a new way. It's as if I was asleep to my power when my life was not working and when I woke up, it was like jumping into a dream. I jumped into my dream and started driving to my new, desired destination. My life felt like a nightmare, repeating the same scenario nightly but with different characters. I had a story about what I would accuse them of and it seemed real. When I learned that I had created them all to get me to change, it all made sense. I now had the power to choose who was in my life and how it all played out by changing my thinking. It's a journey too, not a destination. I have to keep working at changing my thinking daily. So I have to remain at a level above my thinking. I have to become the Observer of my thinking.

Get the book "Are You Ready to Succeed" by Srikumar Rao. He teaches about developing this "Level of thinking above your Thinking." You cannot change your thinking until you stop believing it and begin to notice the patterns of thinking that do not serve you. As you faithfully develop this new level of thinking above your thinking, you will realize how your thinking has created your world.

For example, if you are a complainer, you bitch and moan about your lot in life, you blame your parents, your employer, your spouse, or the unjust powers in the Universe and none of these things are the cause. You have believed this thinking and given it further power by speaking about it in your complaints. Your ears have heard your words and programmed your future. Stop all the complaining, worrying and fretting; the blame lies within you. You are the cause, the cause is within you and where the cause is, therein lies the remedy. James Allen writes, "The very fact that you are a complainer, shows that you deserve your lot; shows that you lack that faith which is the ground of all effort and progress. There is no room for a complainer in a universe of law, and worry is soul-suicide." It's the continual complaining that draws more and more for you to complain and worry about.

"Life is best lived from the inside out." Make yourself worthy of more in the next 30 days, by being the best you can where you are. Stop complaining about your circumstances. By accepting where you are as your own creation, and being your best, things will change as you accept your own power. You cannot move forward until you master your own circumstances. Would you give a million dollars to a five year old? Are you that five year old standing behind your mom in the supermarket having a tantrum because you cannot have what you want now? Immediately? Once you accept where you are, new things will appear because you are being the best right version of yourself. If you desire a new home, make the one you're in look as pretty and nice as you can. If you desire a new job, become the one with the best attitude, always do your best. Bless your current conditions as the ones you're created over the next 30 days and beyond and you will be amazed at what shows up. No one and nothing holds the evil you think they possess for the evil is within you. Change your mind, reshape and mold a new you. Over time all of your "self-proclaimed" evils will turn into blessings.

Over the next 30 days, search unceasingly inward to find and root out all the thinking that has brought you to where you are. Break the chains that have bound you. Accept responsibility for what you have created and do not beat yourself up. Instead think of what I tell my clients, "Imagine not knowing." The irony is not lost on me that Imagine is what I suggest to my clients and that I have been invited to contribute to a book titled "Imagine, 30 Days to a New You."

Do not take my word for all of this. Do your own research. Make your life over the next 30 days the experiment. Whatever you decide will manifest or not. You decide. Are you a victim of circumstance and a slave to them, destined for a life of misery and failure? Or have you fallen asleep to your power and have picked up this book to wake up to your power? Will you accept this and change your thinking? I love the fact that it is all up to you. Find the one that sounds more enlivening, more power-filled. The one stirs you to believe you can have a new future in 30 days and beyond.

Find the gift in your journey up until this point. You found this book, is that a coincidence or is it your own frustration finally nudging you with thoughts like "There has to be more for me, I have a dream, why not manifest it?" Was it this kind of thinking that got you to pick this up?

I think ***YES, YES, a thousand times YES.***

Steve Lentini is a passionate, powerful, dynamic, inspirational speaker and teacher of Divine Principles and Universal Law. Lentini Sales Leadership and Universal Sales Training are Steve's creations. His passion for helping others succeed is legendary and due to his own frustrations and failures, led him to study for the past 35 years the power we all have to create our own future. His upcoming book published by Motivational Press is "Sales Success for the Rookie, How to Succeed at Sales Right from the Start." You can reach Steve at 917-805-1088 and at steve@stevelentini.com. His websites are as follow for more information; www.stevelentini.com and www.prosperityinstitute.com.

BE THE AUTHOR OF YOUR LIFE

Jan Johnston Osburn

Life changes when you make a commitment to yourself that you are going to live the life you love and be the person you want to become. In essence, be today who you want to become tomorrow. The changes churning within you come to fruition only when you recognize you have a choice in the way you want to live. If don't chose the option to change life, it's not going to change.

It's as simple as that.

WITH THE STROKE OF A PEN . . .

When you are born and bequeathed life, it is as if you were gifted an unopened, blank book. Imagine this book as having a golden embossed title with your name etched artfully upon it. As you open this book, every blank page symbolizes a new day in your overall life journey. Single pages are grouped together into chapters and those chapters form your novel. How you go about writing that book is up to you. You are the author of our life. You are the author of your book.

So as the sun awakens and makes its dawning entrance, with the stroke of a metaphorical pen, our life is also being written. Playwright Edward Bulwer-Lytton said, *"The pen is mightier than the sword"* and our destiny is designed by how we pen our story. What we write shapes our lives and the stories we write transforms us. But, one thing is for certain. If you don't like the way your story is unfolding, you *can* write a new chapter with a new outcome.

KEY ELEMENTS TO YOUR STORY

Imagine with me for a moment. Imagine you are picking up your life book, you open it, and you begin to read it. As you turn the pages, you can see where you lived through an array of emotions, actions, circumstances, and events. You had your ups and downs. You laughed, you cried, you won, you lost, you faltered... and you grew stronger. You can see where people entered your life and where people exited your life, sometimes through great sadness or sometimes as a necessity of survival.

But what if you flipped to the last page, what is it your book would say about you? What story would it tell? Would it be powerful and compelling or would it be filled with pages that had little impact to you? And, would it bore you?

When you read a book, you read about the experiences that have molded the characters, the trials, the misfortunes, and the turning points that have tested them. We shouldn't be frightened to tell our story in a way that lingers in the minds of those who read it. Our story should make people believe in us but even greater, it should make us believe in ourselves.

Wonderful stories are captivating and complement the meaning and purpose for what we are trying to accomplish. A noble story is critical for dreaming and yet most of us hesitate when given the opportunity to share our stories. Or when we do craft a story, we do so poorly. And, it doesn't matter what chapter you are in now because each day grants additional opportunities to inscribe something fresh.

Until the final sentence has been engraved, there is still time to change your story.

All great pieces of literature from *The Great Gatsby* to *Gone with the Wind* develop their influence from common basic characteristics and the story, just like your life, is constantly evolving.

HOW TO WRITE YOUR STORY

One of the most miraculous philosophies about our life, is that we too, can persistently update, amend, or augment our story as we grow. We can develop and transform by our desires and new encounters. It matters not what happened on page one or how you were born into this world or even the family in which you were born into. What matters is your desired outcome. And, writing your life story with what you desire is easier if you understand the key elements to your story and the power you yield. All great books have key elements and your life is a great book. Those elements include:

» The Protagonist

» The Antagonist

» The Struggle, Inner Conflict, and the Turning Point

» Character Development

» Notable Characters

» Redemption

As you go about writing your book, think about how those elements play into your story.

A Protagonist – The Protagonist is the central character in the story. If you haven't guessed, this is you. A Protagonist may also be called a hero. You can't have a story without a main character and you are the main player in your life, not a bystander on the sidelines. There is something unique about the protagonist that makes them interesting. Something that stands out and makes the reader curious to learn more. A Protagonist who knows what they want turns the story into something far more gripping than a character who sits around and waits for the story to happen *to* them.

For thought: Have you ever thought about what makes you memorable? Unique? How will you make things happen *for* you and not *to* you?

An Antagonist – In life, we all have forces or people that stand in opposition to us. In literature, this is the Antagonist. While it is common to refer to the antagonist as the "bad guy", in some cases they may exist in a form of inner conflict. The antagonist may also represent a major threat or obstacle to the main character just by their mere existence, without necessarily targeting them. The antagonist doesn't necessarily always mean "the bad guy" but can be someone who can stand in your way of accomplishing what you need.

For thought: Do you know what threatens your success? Are you writing a story so that you can overcome any such obstacle and one of triumph and victory? The job of the writer is to design a story in which the protagonist foils the attempt of the Antagonist. The Protagonist should always be prepared to contend with the antagonist.

The Struggle, Inner Conflict, and the Turning Point – This inner conflict is often a major theme of literary works and life is rarely without some form of conflict. Being the main character in your story means that you must come to possess awareness by knowing your internal conflicts. Conflict manifests itself in terms of desires, choices, and consequences and they are all basic elements to any plot. They also lead to turning points.

A turning point comes to life when the Protagonist realizes that the choices they have made in the past no longer work for the life they want today. What reels us in is the instant when the main character breaks with the past and sets off to grab something new. Their world has changed in some intriguing way that will force the protagonist to discover and reveal new insight for their future. If those elements of awareness are missing, our story falls flat and it won't move the Protagonist toward a resolution they are seeking.

For thought: If you have internal conflicts, are you working toward awareness and toward your turning point? Are you at the point where you've recognized that your past no longer works for your future?

But stories are not complete without Character Development, Notable Characters, and Personal Redemption themes. You can't write a best seller without these important attributes.

Character Development – As the story unfolds, the Protagonist undergoes change. Being the central focus heaps momentous responsibilities on the shoulders of a protagonist. There's probably no justification for change more compelling than some internal reason or some driving force. Character development deepens with reflection and turning life experiences into life lessons.

Notable Characters - A book is not nearly as entrancing if it had just a main personality and the antagonist. Great books are filled with other memorable characters. They make the most mundane day fresh and exhilarating. Unforgettable characters make the story come alive and they're one of the most important aspects to a good story. They're distinctive to every book and they make us feel different emotions. They help us see the world in new ways. They help us to re-think our own lives and motivations and affect us in a manner so that they live on in our memories for years.

Who do you surround yourself with in life that gives you a different perspective? Who inspires or motivates you? Who helps you step outside of your comfort zone so that you live more experiences? Evaluate the characters in your life to make sure these are the people you want in your book.

Redemption - Successful stories contain themes of redemption. Our story generally gets increasingly complicated as we bring in more characters, themes, and drama. Redemption is seen as when something in the story starts really bad, we make poor choices, or there is some sort of negative event or failure that leads to a temporary downturn. The redemption comes in the form of the transition into some positive outcome from those downturns.

BUT HOW DOES THIS APPLY TO LIFE-CHANGING INSTANTS?

So, maybe you get it now. You understand that you write your story but you may be wondering how this applies to life-changing instants. Because it all comes down to this... Life is made up of four action points: Desires, Choices, Decisions, and Consequences.

Decisions are a staple of life. Most of them are simple and the decision making process is so seamless that we're usually unaware of it. The process flows effortlessly into what we want and what we do. Many of those decisions have no long-lasting consequences while others can have a colossal impact on the direction of our journey.

Your destiny is designed every time you make a decision – every time you write a new page of your life. Acknowledging your ability to plan your future comes in the form of choices and consequences. Choices play a significant role in outlining and casting your life.

In a single moment, an unwise choice can upset your most comprehensive plan and alter the course of your path.

So how can you make sure you are making good decisions? Consider what you want from your life. Just like an architect needs a blueprint to create buildings, writers need the plotline to write the outcome you desire. Decide how you want your story to end and then work backwards. That way, every decision along the twisting and winding path will be easier if you know the end destination and what you are working to accomplish.

The key to making wise decisions is understanding the consequences. Every decision has consequences. Once you learn to evaluate your decisions based on consequences, all the other considerations fall into place. When you ask yourself what the likely result will be before you make the choice, decisions are easier. The story you lead today is a result of past decisions you've made.

It's that simple.

It all starts with our desires – something that we want. However, life will not change until you know – beyond the shadow of a doubt – that your greatest power is your power to choose and your power to act. If you are not serious about change, nothing new will ever happen.

When you take control, you are the victor and not a victim.

Let's look at a couple of common examples to illustrate the how decisions affect your future. Many people say they want to have a healthy lifestyle. Let's see what that might look like in terms of wants, choices, decisions, and consequences.

Desire: Have a healthy lifestyle by losing 20 pounds by eating better and exercising daily.

» **Choice:** Get up at 6:00 a.m. and exercise or hit the snooze alarm and miss out on your exercise time.

» **Decision:** Hit the snooze button and sleep

- **Consequences:** No weight loss or maybe even weight gain
- Or
- **Choice:** Eat a sugar filled donut or eat fresh fruit for breakfast
- **Decision:** Eat the doughnut
- **Consequences:** Bad health, risk of diabetes, weight gain, no weight loss, etc.
- Desire: Get a promotion, have a better job, better salary, and more financial freedom.
- **Choice:** Volunteer to lead the next project at work to showcase your skills or stay in the background as a bit player on the team.
- **Decision:** Stay in the background and not give any extra effort.
- **Consequences:** Your boss doesn't notice you. No promotion, no increase in salary, same debt.

When *you chose* poorly, *you live* life poorly.

Exercise and proper eating make you healthier, so if you make the choice to not do it, you'll sacrifice total fitness and you'll never lose weight. Additionally, putting in little effort at work doesn't get you noticed. If you want promotions, you'll have to do the things that get you noticed. It's the stand-outs who get the rewards.

But, let's reverse those choices. Great decisions result in life altering behaviors that transform your life. When you choose to eat the right foods and to exercise, your life changes. Acting responsibly means you make wise choices that lead to positive outcomes. The common denominator is you. You make choices. You chose what you write in your book.

THAT'S JUST THE BEGINNING

While life changes the instant you decide it changes, transformation takes time. That beautiful butterfly you see on your bushes in the summer, didn't start out that way. It started as a caterpillar and it was only through a process of metamorphosis that it transformed into something new.

Transformation is not an overnight process but continues by your daily actions and behaviors. The character in the beginning of your book rarely mirrors the character in the end of the book, but the type of transformation that is seen depends largely on you and what you choose and how you choose to live.

LIKE A PHOENIX RISING

Think about the symbolism of a new you like the Phoenix rising from the ashes. The Phoenix rising represents a time of growth, renewal and rebirth. If you aren't familiar with the story of the Phoenix, it's a mythical bird that's described as having a colorful plumage with a tail of gold and scarlet feathers. When the Phoenix nears the end of life it builds a nest of twigs made from sweet-smelling wood and resins. The Phoenix then exposes itself and its nest to the full force of the sun's rays until a spark ignites it into a burning rage of flames. Both the bird and the nest burn ferociously until they are reduced to ashes. But it is at this point that a young phoenix rises, reborn to spread its new wings and fly again.

Talk about a vivid image! And, what a way to think of your renewal. We all have personal downturns, but you can choose to soar instead of settle.

Desires. Choices. Decisions. Consequences. It's up to you. This is your life and your legacy. Your personal legacy is being established with every word you write. Write your story the way you want to live it by acknowledging the power you possess by the choices you make.

Jan Johnston Osburn is a Career Coach and Talent Acquisition Executive who owns Johnston Group International LLC, a boutique recruiting firm and career consultancy. Her first book, Dream Big or Go Home: Today's Dream is Tomorrow's Reality, is scheduled for release by Motivational Press in Spring 2016.

Scallop, Shrimp and Vegetable Stir Fry
Serves 4

Ingredients

2 tablespoons canola oil
1 tablespoon toasted sesame oil
8 large scallops, muscle removed, patted dry
12 large shrimp, peeled and deveined, tail left on
2 tablespoons ground coriander
1 large yellow onion, peeled, cut in half and sliced thin
5 large cloves garlic, peeled and sliced very thin
8-ounces sliced crimini mushrooms
2 large carrots, scraped and sliced into 1/4-inch thick coins
9-12 baby bell peppers in assorted colors, stems cut off, seeded and cut into large dice
2 cups broccoli florets
kosher salt and freshly ground black pepper
1/2 cup mirin
1/2 cup hoisin sauce
2 tablespoons Asian fish sauce
1 tablespoon soy sauce
1 tablespoons honey
2 tablespoon sriracha

Instructions

Heat the canola and sesame oil in a large skillet over medium high heat until shimmering. Season the scallops and shrimp on both sides liberally with coriander, salt and pepper. Sear the scallops about 90 seconds each side. Remove to a plate and tent with foil to keep warm. Cook the shrimp until opaque, about 1-2 minutes per side. Remove to the plate with the scallops and keep warm. Add the onion to the pan and cook until soft but not colored, about 3-5 minutes. Add the mushrooms and stir fry until browned, about 3 minutes. Add the carrots, broccoli, peppers and garlic and stir fry until crisp tender. Deglaze the pan with the mirin.

In a small bowl mix together the hoisin sauce, fish sauce, soy sauce, honey and sriracha. Return the seafood to the pan and pour the sauce mixture in. Stir to combine and heat through. Serve immediately. Delicious over steamed white or brown rice.

HAPPY ON PURPOSE: 30 DAYS TO MAKING A REAL DIFFERENCE

Janet Desautels

THE CASE FOR HAPPINESS:

Imagine a new world. Where everyone, including you, was happy. Imagine if happiness was actively, consciously cultivated, and seen as the most powerful means for not only giving to ourselves, but to others. Imagine a new you: satisfied in knowing you are giving your best to yourself and the world – not through effort and struggle, but in giving the love that you are through your happiness alone. Imagine knowing you have that power, and that you *are* that power. We all want to be happy, and we all want a better world, but often think we have no power to change anything. But we can actually do something individually which is very powerful: we can be happy on purpose. We can be *within* what we want to see in the world *out there*. With the energy of happiness, or love, at your back you can be a powerful agent of change. Being happy – on purpose – no matter what is the real key to helping others and making a difference in the world.

Somehow we got the idea that being happy is a bad thing. We are taught that when everyone around us is miserable, it's inconsiderate to be happy. It's insensitive. We should match their feelings, and "be with" them in their misery, complaint, or sorrow. That makes them feel better, of course, because misery loves company – but the relief they get is short-lived, and you end up feeling worse. You have added, through your commiseration, more negativity to an already negative situation. In actuality, your happiness serves the world far better than commiseration does. We reap collectively what we sow. This is not to say we don't care about others – but our caring need not take the form of added negativity.

People say, "HOW can you be happy when (select one): the weather`s miserable, the economy has tanked, children are starving, the climate is warming" etc. The world is a veritable cornucopia of people, events and things both wonderful and awful and everything in between. There are opposites within every person, thing, particle, and situation in this universe. You have the power and freedom to choose what to focus on, and your perspective about it. You are probably not accustomed to the idea that you can choose how you feel about things. But you can, and it`s quite a simple thing. In 30 days you can create a new habit of happiness which will transform your life completely – and the world you live in. You will see for yourself how powerful your happiness is to effect change and make a difference to others.

First, I`ll make the case for happiness, in other words why you should choose it, and then I`ll tell you how to do it.

It`s easy to love, be generous, give of ourselves, forgive, and look for the best in others when we`re happy. When we`re happy, we feel good. And when we feel good, we do good things. Happiness is a state of feeling good, and having a general sense of well-being. And in that expansive frame of mind, we give without strings attached, and without expecting something back. We give simply because it feels good. We give unconditionally. Reflect on your own experience, when you bought a present for someone you love and couldn`t wait till they opened it, or maybe you helped a stranger change a tire, or you stopped at an accident to help someone injured. Have you noticed that when you feel happy, you always have the impulse to DO something with it? It wants to get out into the world, and you are the agent it operates through. That is the love in you, and the love that you are. You might not have thought about it this way before – but recall how naturally the kindness flowed from you. Happiness feels like falling in love; it's a very expansive and open feeling. Now reflect on times you feel anxious, angry, or fearful. I'm willing to bet you don't feel generous, and if you do give anything, you resent it.

When you feel good, you love. And when you love, you feel good. Each feeds the other. Studies demonstrate that when we give, we feel wonderful. Giving might take the form of caring for a pet, a child, or plants, or even preparing a meal. When we know we are helping, we feel valuable, and we feel like we are contributing. When our actions come from our happiness, they fuel our well being and that of others. But there's more: our brains secrete feel-good chemicals. Feeling happy is actually good for us! It promotes health, immune function, and decreases stress. You may also have noticed that when you feel happy, things work out better for you. Opportunities show up, connections are made, and things go more smoothly than usual.

So in light of all the good things that your happiness brings...why are we not consciously cultivating it? The only barriers to happiness are our habitual resistance to life – and our sloppy thinking. That's all it is, and it is very simple to change it. The great news is you can create a new habit of thought in a very short time.

All things have qualities which we identify as good and bad inherent in them. And it is your choice as to which qualities you focus on. We have collectively developed the habit of seeing primarily the negative, but everything is in fact inherently neutral. Nothing makes an event bad but my perspective on it. As Shakespeare stated, "Nothing is either good or bad but thinking makes it so." You have heard stories about people who say their car accident, divorce, or illness, was the best thing that ever happened to them. If the weather is cold and rainy, you might hear friends say, "What a miserable day!" But of course the *day* is not miserable, it is simply cold and rainy. You have free choice, your choice is exercised with your focus, and your focus is powerful because it grows whatever it is placed on. It is true that some circumstances and people more easily lend themselves to positives than others. Still, you are the one with the freedom and power to decide what you will look for and what your perspective will be. Further, whatever you focus on grows; this applies to positive or negative qualities, solutions or problems. Look into your own daily life and past experience, and you will find that this is so.

So how do you become truly happy? Notice how your thoughts feel, then simply cultivate and follow the ones that feel good. Consciously direct your thoughts and attention toward things you prefer and regard as positive. Use that powerful energy of yours to focus on, and thus grow, all things that feel good to you. You must focus on your feeling state and make that your primary priority. Every thought has a physical effect in your body. If you pay close attention, you will be able to feel what thoughts feel good and what ones don't. There are 2 advantages to this: when you are able to identify the thought patterns that feel good and focus on them, you get to feel good individually, and when you feel good, you naturally extend this to others. Even better, your external circumstances will organize themselves around your state of being, and multiple positive events will be orchestrated at the same time.

You might say, "How do I know this will happen? Prove it!" I spent many years in university and by the time I was finished, I had little respect for anything that could not be explained or proven rationally, at least for a time. But the living of life softened my reverence for mental constructs and analysis, and this was due in no small measure to my experience of many magical moments (which were inexplicable through rational means).

We tend to discount all things that don't look linear, that things the mind cannot explain, and explicable in terms of physical cause and effect. If we can see and touch and feel it, it is "real" to us. But tell me this - have you ever seen a thought? Have you ever seen an emotion? And yet you would not deny they exist. You have seen evidence of them: evidence of anger might be a frown, a red face, throwing something, etc. Thoughts and emotions are real – and they influence our external reality.

We connect well to the Newtonian idea of physical reality: an apple falls from a tree and hits the ground. But there is another layer, or layers, to reality that cannot be explained by our physical senses. But even though it flies in the face of what we think is real, we must be open enough to consider the possibility of a connection between your thoughts and the reality you live in. Just be willing to contemplate the possibility. Then start looking around at your life. Can you identify recurrent themes?

I began to consciously pay attention to the physical sensation my thoughts generated in my body, and the correspondence between my state of being, driven by my thoughts, and what was happening in my life including: money, relationships, roadblocks and inconveniences, accidents and coincidences. Anxious thoughts would beget more anxious thoughts, and things would happen that created even more anxiety! An anxious person will find in their everyday life many situations cause more and more anxiety. A friend gets sick, the babysitter cancels, job security looks increasingly precarious, etc. Your state of mind generates more of itself internally and externally. I do not personally believe our minds have the capacity to perceive precisely how thoughts are translated into physical manifestations, but *that* they are. I don't think we can comprehend the infinite array of possibilities or how they are related. Fortunately, it doesn't matter. What matters is that you are able to recognize patterns and correlations, between how you feel and what you are living. You won't be able to trace a straight line between any of the events in your life anyway – pull one thread and we find it unravels the whole carpet. Everything is connected to everything else.

But you WILL see that the themes playing out in your life are reflections of your thoughts. You probably haven't noticed it before because you weren't taught to observe it, so you didn't pick up the habit. It is really that simple. This is new to most of us because we develop habits of thought so deep that we don't even know what we are thinking most the time. You needn't believe anyone about anything. Just try it and see for yourself. What you focus on expands. Look to your own life experience and you will see this is true.

Once you begin to notice the correlation between what you are thinking, and then feeling, and the people and events around you, you are in a perfect position to consciously guide your thinking in ways that bring you happiness. How will you know? You will feel expanded and open. It is not selfish to reach for this, because what we think of as selfish implies taking, clutching, hoarding, and grabbing. It implies negativity. But happiness is positive, giving, and oriented to life – it benefits the self that generates it, and all others that self connects with.

In the next 30 days, beginning today, take up this challenge:

In the words of Joseph Campbell, "follow your bliss". In every moment of every day, follow what feels good to you. Make feeling good your first priority. Think thoughts that feel good, say words that feel good to say, and do what feels good to do. You can trust your own feelings on this. If you are able to recognize when you feel good, then you know when you are happy. And when you are happy, you bring the best of yourself to every person you meet, and every situation you encounter. When you are happy, you forgive and forget easily, help others, and give of yourself in ways you cannot when you are miserable. The more you do this, the happier you will be, as happiness and giving reinforce each other.

Reach for happiness for the sake of being happy, unconditionally. This frees you from needing things to be a particular way, and makes you a very powerful agent of change. We think particular things will make us happy, and they do, but only for a short time. The seeds of duality, seeds of opposites, are in all things. When you feel happy because you have a new girlfriend, you will feel unhappy if she leaves you. When you feel happy because it`s sunny, you have given the power over how you feel to the weather! Take your power back, and decide for yourself what your state of mind will be.

Exercise the choice you have in every moment to look for the best in others – it is there, like a seed, waiting for you to water it. What you pay attention to will grow and take root. You will find people rise to your positive expectation of them more often than not.

Claim your power to be happy, choose it on purpose, and know by doing so you are not only feeling good yourself, you are uplifting others. You are being what you know the world needs most, and giving to the world what it needs the most. Be happy for yourself, and for the world in which you live -for your family, your friends, your community, and the world. Do your part for the world and take care of your own happiness. You cannot make a better world by adding more judgement and anger – you do it by adding more happiness. In a mere 30 days, if you consistently reach for happiness by paying attention to how you feel, make feeling good your priority, and always look for the best, it will be yours to have and share.

Janet Desautels, B.A., B.A., LL.B, is author of Dancing with Differences, a teacher, mother of 4, and lover of life. Her mission is simply to awaken us to our own inner wisdom, and achieve personal power and well-being independent of our circumstances. Inspired by timeless and universal spiritual principles and a love of humanity, she encourages us to expand our sense of who and what we are, and find ways to transcend mind patterns which limit us, make us unhappy, and perpetuate conflict in the world.

OPTION A OR OPTION B: THE LENS YOU CHOOSE DETERMINES YOUR SUCCESS

Dafna Michaelson Jenet

Have I got a story for you: It was a good day, and I was flying to a speaking engagement. I had planned for this keynote for many months. I had worked with the organization to build the audience. I spent time on social media promoting it and when the day came to leave I was excited and ready to roll.

As an avid traveler, with a TSA pre-check on board, I sometimes like to cut it pretty close to boarding time before arriving at the airport. This week was no different. I whipped open my mobile app, checked in to my flight and loaded my boarding pass on my screen. I threw a change of clothes and my make-up in an oversized purse and headed to the airport.

Security was a 90 second affair as expected. I checked in on Swarm and Facebook to let the world know I was on the move and to see what other road warrior friends I might connect with on my path.

I felt a special kind of power as I moved swiftly and confidently through the airport. I know there are people, my parents for instance, who hate to travel and consider it the greatest hassle but I love it and generally have flawless travel experiences.

I took my seat at the gate next to another seemingly seasoned traveler and began responding to the comments on my Facebook check-in. I was in the Facebook vortex for what seemed like a few moments before I caught a glimpse of the time and realized we should have been boarding. Then the announcement came:

"Ladies and gentlemen of flight 6222 to Austin, we are getting ready to board but it seems we are missing the flight crew and there may be a problem with the plane. I'll let you know more as I learn it."

This was the moment that I had the opportunity to choose a lens.

Option A: The lens of panic. I could have launched head first into the panic surrounding a now possibly delayed flight. What events would I miss? How bad was this going to be?

Option B: The lens of positive thinking. This was the lens I picked, I was positive that my good travel karma would save the day for me and my fellow passengers.

Two announcements later and there was still no flight crew although we had learned that our aircraft was in fine working order. As our gate agent finished his announcement I received the text message from my airline:

"Your 2:06pm flight to Austin is delayed due to air traffic control. UA6222 now departs Denver 7:00pm and arrives 10:12pm."

Once again I had that opportunity to choose my lens as a collective groan emanated from the waiting room and we alerted the gate agent to the flight delay.

A 5 hour delay meant that I would miss out on dinner with the VIP's and organizing committee for the event I was keynoting. Although I was getting in late I'd still be just fine for the keynote the following morning.

Option A: The lens of panic would have had me pacing the airport, bemoaning my fate, sweating through my nice suit and filled with anger at the incompetence that causes a flight crew to not be scheduled for a flight. I could have found an uncomfortable chair next to a plug to keep my devices charged while I tried to focus enough to do work while I waited for the 5 long hours to pass.

Option B: The lens of positivity gave me the opportunity to take a deep breath and realize that the 5 hour delay gave me just enough time to pick up my kids from school, catch an early dinner with my family at the airport and then catch my delayed flight. While I may not have been able to hob nob with the VIP set, I could still snuggle with my favorite VIP crew, my family.

I called my husband and had him swing by the airport to put Option B plan into place. No sweat, no panic.

Picking up my kids was a blast. They were surprised to see me and only believed for about 5 minutes that I had already gone and returned from Austin. It was an unexpected afternoon of togetherness and we were having a great time.

And then I got another text: "Your flight to Austin (UA6222) is canceled due to air traffic control."

In the interest of authenticity, when I read that text I went straight into option A. Panic. My kids and husband immediately started responding to my stress response, so I took a deep breath and tried to maintain the calm and positivity of Option B as I repeated over and over to the automated attendant "representative" barely concealing the absolute frustration in the possibility that I was not getting to Austin.

When a representative was finally on the other end of the line, I calmly explained that my flight had been cancelled and that I needed to get to Austin tonight.

And then he said the words that made me feel that positive thinking was ... OK I will not use an expletive here but I think you will quickly figure out what I was thinking.

"I'm sorry ma'am, there are no more flights to Austin today. We can get you into Austin by 1:00pm tomorrow."

At this point my eyes are closed and am doing Lamaze breathing from previous pregnancies. I needed to keep it together so I could think of a plan. I was not going to miss my keynote and leave my client in a lurch.

Before this I was regaling my family with about my college roommate who now lives in Houston exploding all over my Facebook airport check-in earlier. She insisted that if I was so close to Houston I should visit her. I had joked that she should call in sick and come down to Austin to hear me speak. My husband, the genius of the moment says to me "tell them to fly you to Houston."

Feeling the positivity of Option B starting to calm my breathing (as it turns out Lamaze does nothing for you when you are not in labor), I calmly asked the representative if he could get me to Houston tonight. He could.

I quickly got on the phone with my college roommate who was game for the plan.

In an instant the story shifted again. I woke up planning to go to Austin for a fancy dinner. By the time I got on my flight I was headed to Houston for a midnight road-trip with my college roommate.

Every single day we are faced with challenges that take us off guard or off track from our daily tasks. When this happens we have an opportunity to choose Option A or Option B. When we are tired, run down, or over stressed Option A, the stress response is quickly at hand. I challenge you to pay attention the next time you choose Option A, or better yet, watch someone else choosing Option A. In my airport story by the time that text message rippled through the seating area at our gate there was a long line of very disgruntled flyers standing at the gate agent's stand. They released their frustration and anger at the unwitting gate agent who was working very hard to maintain a calm demeanor.

Sure, that release feels good and doesn't take much effort to produce. Yet, once you've let that option take hold a trajectory of negative experiences follow. You may choose to post on Facebook about how incompetent the airline is and how awful it is to travel today and certainly you will find in your friends those who would love to jump on this band wagon of anger and frustration. Together you will work each other up until you are in a frenzy. Then when the flight was finally cancelled and you were fully entrenched in an Option A mentality it may be easier to call your client and blame the failure of the program and your inability to arrive on the mess you've found yourself in.

Option B takes forethought and an ability to utilize calming skills. It takes practice and intentionality. I'm not saying that it is easy.

As I was sitting in the gate area for my new flight to Houston I noticed that I had been placed in the back row of the plane – IN A MIDDLE SEAT. I stopped for a minute, took one of my deep breaths, forced a smile on to my face and approached the gate agent. As you know, I'd been working on the Option B lens for many hours at this point and I was tired. The gate agent looked up and acknowledged my presence even as he was in the middle of typing. I smiled at him and gave him my story of flight delay and cancellation and asked if there was any way he might be able to move me closer to the front of the aircraft and perhaps, into an aisle seat. He looked at my boarding pass on my phone and started to type. As he did so the pilot stepped out of the breezeway and asked the agent if he needed anything as he did a "walk-about" before the flight. He said "no" and I said, "I'll take a scoop of ice-cream, chocolate." The gate agent laughed as the pilot walked away.

I sat down with my new seat assignment, in premium seating, and sent a text message to my friend to let her know what time I'd be landing in Houston. I was all set. I knew there was a flight crew and a plane and I had a plan. Sure, it was a lot of hard work and I had a long night ahead of me but I was going to make it to my client and I was feeling relatively calm.

As people began to lineup for boarding the pilot returned to the plane, a scoop of chocolate ice cream in his hand for me. Option B allowed me to retain my sense of humor and make a connection with the pilot and gate agent. He felt good, I felt good and as I enjoyed my ice-cream a bit of excitement for a midnight road trip started to fill my mind.

Option A would not have given me the space and ability to crack that ice-cream joke. Riddled with anger and bemoaning my fate of a 3 hour drive in the middle of the night when I was so tired to begin with, all I would have gotten out of the day so far would have been deep wrinkles where my frown lines would have been deeply etched from a day of anxiety.

The flight to Houston was smooth and a very intriguing man across the aisle, who had seen the entire ice-cream incident, taught me tricks of his successful consulting business that will no doubt help my business. As I landed, I prepared to greet my friend who I hadn't seen in five years.

We traveled across Texas catching up on kids, spouses, and business and before I knew it we pulled into our hotel.

As the plans of the day began to twist and turn I was keeping my client updated via text. In this moment it was critically important that they understood that I was following Plan B as I did not want to disrupt their day by causing a full on stress response throughout Austin. Were I in panic mode, they too would have entered panic mode. With each new update I followed it up with the Plan B in action.

Message one: flight delayed, no worries but I may miss dinner.

Message two: flight cancelled, no worries I will fly in to Houston and drive

They were alerted and felt taken care of. The next morning I walked into the event and the organizers were overwhelmed with gratitude that I was there and my roommate was the savior of the day. Sure, I could have rented a car and driven myself with the same result but I would have missed out on the conversation and friendship, and the story surely would have lost some luster!

Finally it was time to take the stage. I stood up, a huge smile on my face and started my talk, "Have I got a story for you."

Here's how to choose Option B in 5 steps:

1. Step back, physically if you need to, and take a deep breath. Everything always seems more manageable with oxygen in your

system. Taking a deep breath is actually an art form. Place a closed fist about an inch below your belly button. As you slowly breathe in through your nose feel your diaphragm expand and push your fist out. Your shoulders should not rise. If your shoulders rise you are breathing into your chest which actually can cause anxiety to increase. Slowly blow the breath out of your mouth. Repeat.

2. Play out the best possible scenario in your head. Your plans were just changed, no time to waste complaining about the cause. What action can you take to keep moving forward?
3. Be very clear about the end result. My end result was to get to the speaking engagement. With a clear outcome goal in mind you can see the different pathways to success. Think about it like a maze, if you've hit a wall turn around and seek the next path.
4. Communicate. Don't experience your shift in a vacuum. Play out the scenario with a trusted colleague or spouse. It was my husband who put the pieces together for me to be able to see that I had a way to Austin through Houston.
5. Find a way to have fun, seek out the humor in the situation. We all know that life is too short so live like you want to enjoy it.
6. BONUS: Share your story. When you put the positive spin you will hear from friends and colleagues near and far that you've inspired them to seek out Option B too.

When opportunities for stress appear, step back and be intentional. Option A or Option B. Wrinkles and frustrated client, or ice-cream and a successful event? You decide.

> *Dafna Michaelson Jenet, author of the International Book Award winning "It Takes a Little Crazy to Make a Difference," is President of the Journey Institute.*

TOTAL BRAIN REWIRE

Corey Jahnke

"We cannot fix are problems with the same level of thinking we were at when we created them."

Albert Einstein

If you could live your life over again, do you think you could accomplish more than you've accomplished so far?

What would you be, do, or have if you had another chance?

How much would you be worth?

How much would you weigh?

What would your retirement plan look like?

These are the first questions I ask all of my new coaching clients and every single time, without exception, the answers paint a picture of an amazingly successful life.

Yet, when I ask them how they would achieve those incredible results, or why they think that their 'new life" would be infinitely better than their current situation, not one person can give me an answer that uses new or different strategies and techniques that would guarantee their success if they were given a "do over".

Most people think they simply wouldn't make the same dumb mistakes over again.

Successful thinkers, on the other hand, believe that good fortune is won or lost by the designing and executing of a solid action plan and the creation a strategic blueprint that virtually guarantees positive outcomes.

To them, everything else is merely commentary and wishful thinking.

Success is not an accident.

Success leaves clues.

For more than 40 years I have been studying and testing those clues and the results have been truly phenomenal. When I ask my clients, family members, and friends to describe their situation and circumstances, most people overestimate their position, and many aren't even close to an accurate perception of their reality.

Very few people know exactly who and how much they owe. The vast majority of adults cannot accurately share their ideal bodyweight or how far they are from it. And almost no one has a concrete understanding of how well they are positioned for retirement.

"I'm doing pretty well I guess" they tell me. "Especially compared to John Doe who lives across the street" they will add in an attempt to fool themselves into believing that everything is "okay".

It appears then that reality is largely based on our ability to rationalize away the mistakes we continue to make.

The worse our situation is, the harder we will work to make ourselves feel better about it.

This kind of thinking is not for you! What is for you is a hard look at where you are, a where you want to be, and the development of a rock solid plan designed to get you there.

A REALITY CHECK

As a community pharmacist in a small town for more than 25 years,

I've watched people go from 20-45, from 45-70, and from 70 to the great beyond, and what I've learned is that you never see misfortune coming until it is too late.

"I never thought something like this would happen to me!" Dave told me.

He had to retire early and leave his electrician business due to diabetes and congestive heart failure.

"I never took the time to plan for retirement because I always thought it was forever away, now what little money I had saved up is going towards medical bills. It feels like a jab in the ribs" he went on to say. "The worst part is, my doctor warned me years ago that I needed to eat less, work out more, and get my weight under control, but I was just too busy to listen" he confided in me.

I'll never forget the tears in his eyes when this hulk of a man asked me for a tissue. "I just don't know what I'm going to do" he mumbled as he walked away.

Dave is not alone. Millions of people are diagnosed with preventable health issues every year. Some take immediate action to turn their health around, most do not. Financial, spiritual, and relationship health all follow a similar progression.

The most important thing you can ever do if you want to IMAGINE the amazing future that you truly deserve is to take an honest inventory of your life and measure your "success vitals" carefully.

Successful Thinkers know their vital metrics. Vital metrics are the indicators and statistics that give an accurate and objective measure of how we are actually doing.

Your cholesterol level is what it is. It is unaffected by subjective measures like "Well, I feel pretty good!"

Author Brian Tracy says it this way: "Successful people study the situation carefully and then ask themselves 'What could possibly go wrong?' and then whatever it is, they do everything in their power to keep that from happening."

The late personal development guru Earl Nightingale said it this way: "All of us are self-made, but only the successful will admit it."

First and foremost, I urge you to take stock of your situation and really assess the good and bad for what they are and not for what you wish them to be. Information is power. Once we know where we are starting from, all we have to do is pick a direction, decide on the best possible plans, strategies, and tactics.

A TOTAL BRAIN REWIRE

You are not your current situation and circumstances!

Your current situation and circumstances are simply a measure of who you WERE.

Who you ARE will be determined by what you do going forward.

In the short run, hiding from our credit card balance, misplacing the scale, or having one last "well deserved " dessert before we begin a new diet comforts us in the moment, but can really set us up for future disaster.

This is called "Ostrich Syndrome" and the longer we stand around with our heads buried in the sand, the more life takes away from us. The universe has a built in reward system.

"If you don't use it you lose it!" the personal trainer tells his clients.

"If you don't mind the garden, the weeds will take it over." the financial specialist tells his followers.

Which gardens are YOU leaving unattended? Perhaps now would be a good time to take inventory!

"The problem" my friend tells me "is that every time I try to change my habits, it works for a little while, then I bounce right back to my old unhealthy ways. It is so frustrating!"

Isn't that always the case?

"Here's the solution" I tell him, "Don't try to change your habits!"

"Wait! What? Oh you're a lot of help! Not!!"

"It's not your habits that need to change, it's your THINKING!" I counter back with a smile. He stares at me unamused! I smile again and explain that even though we think we are a product of our habits, we are not. In actuality, we are a product of our thoughts. It's actually our thoughts that drive our habits, so trying to change our habits using willpower is a losing venture.

It's much like trying to stop a runaway train by standing in front of it with our arms outstretched.

Think about it. If our habits are the train, then our thoughts are the coal that gives the train power.

"Change your thoughts and you change your world!"

Norman Vincent Peale

So what choice do we have? We can either let our thoughts run wild and allow them to take our habits with them, or we can actually rewire our brain and program our minds for success in any area of life we choose.

"No way!" my friend argues with disgust. "My thoughts have a mind of their own! The little man inside of my head runs the show and all I can do is to try to do battle with him as best I can. Some days I'm just too tired to stay strong enough to win."

The truth is that I used to think that as well. Then I learned something that changed my life: MAN BECOMES WHAT HE THINKS ABOUT.

It's really that simple.

What you focus your mind on most often is what shows up in your life!

If you want to be strong, thin, and healthy you have to train your brain to think like a strong and healthy person who is building a health conscious future.

If you want to be wealthy, you have to train your mind to focus on wealth creation the way wealthy people do.

If you want strong and secure relationships, you have to train your thoughts and emotions to be loving, caring, and respectful towards others.

Do you want to be what others might call disgustingly happy? Then you guessed it, you have to constantly think happy thoughts! It's what they call The Law of Attraction and it means that what you think about, you bring about.

ACTION STEPS

Believe it or not, everything and every person that has come into your life have been attracted by the things you think about, the feelings that you use to execute your thoughts, and by the corresponding actions that you take on a regular basis.

You absolutely positively can control your thoughts and the things you focus on.

Is it difficult? Sometimes it feels near impossible.

Does it take a lot of work? Of course! But just like anything beneficial, it's worth the effort.

The client tells me to forget it. She doesn't believe in all that "Secret" nonsense and she wouldn't even know where to start.

I don't blame her.

So far, her thoughts have betrayed her and the life she is currently living what she signed up for.

Isn't that the case for most of us?

Before I truly understood the Law of Attraction, I remember thinking: "Man this is so unfair. This is NOT the life I deserve to be living!"

But, looking back, it was. Only, I really deserved to have it worse. I had chosen all of the wrong friends, the wrong foods, and the wrong purchases. My brain had me thinking that I was doing the best I could do! I wasn't.

"Sherry" I tell her, "I want to help you, but I need you to trust my belief in you, and I need you to believe that what worked for me will work for you."

She was hesitant, but I continued.

"Before I learned my 7 step plan for creating and controlling the kinds of thoughts that have brought me peace, happiness, and prosperity, my life was a mess. My weight, my finances, and my relationships were all a disaster. At that time, no one could have convinced me that I could get to where I've gotten to today. But someone whom I admire believed in me, just like I believe in you, and gave me the secret to living an incredible life and now I'm going to share that secret with you."

She was skeptical but intrigued, so I explained to her that my entire life changed the day that I decided to start living on PURPOSE.

P-Prioritizing! Successful people stay calm, quiet, and still until they understand and become crystal clear on exactly what they want to achieve and why they want to achieve it.

U-Understanding! There were reasons why I had failed over and over again in my life and I needed to understand exactly what those reasons were, what I did to cause them, and what I could learn from my failures.

R-Recognizing! It quickly became apparent that my own thinking was my biggest obstacle in life. I committed to challenging my negative thoughts and creating a visual image in my mind of the life that I truly wanted to manifest for myself. I practiced and practiced until I learned to keep my thoughts focused on what mattered most to me and the successful completion of my goals.

P-Positioning! I often said I wanted to accomplish a given goal and then refused to set myself up for success. If my goal was weight loss, why was I still buying ice cream? If I wanted to save money, why was I surfing the electronic store's website. It wasn't until I learned to position myself for success that momentum began to swing in a positive direction.

O-Organizing! Life is messy! It is easy to get lost in life's clutter and allow them overwhelm and cause us to procrastinate or quit altogether. The key is to organize your thoughts and your life around your goals and to figure out what you can do to stay on course. Making your lunch the night before work can keep you from eating out and spending money you don't have, on calories you don't need.

S-Strategizing! Wishing is not a strategy! I found that writing out my goals, reading them to myself, and saying them over and over is the best way to stay on target. When I stopped wishing *things* were better and started wishing that *I* was better, I immediately went to work determined to make it so. The better I got, the better my life got.

E-Eliminating! Even the best laid plans and intentions are a waste of time and energy unless we are committed to eliminating the obstacles, distractions, and excuses that hold us back. Asking yourself: "What can I eliminate?" is the most powerful success gadget in your toolbox and its importance should not be underestimated.

My challenge to you is to create an image in your mind of a goal that you would really like to accomplish. Think about how your life would change if you attained that goal. How would your life be better? What opportunities might now be available for you? Who could you meet as a result of achieving that goal?

Create a strong vision in your mind and hold onto that image as if it were your last dollar.

Practice repeating to yourself everything you can about that goal and resolve to never ever let go of that image until you reach it. Once you reach it, your life will never be the same!

Here's to you and your brilliant future!

Corey Jahnke is a full time hospital pharmacist, high-performance coach, and best-selling author. Corey has devoted his life to the study of the principles of success and the role that the brain plays in achieving our goals and dreams. Connect with Corey at www.CoreyJahnke.com and receive the free gifts he offers to everyone who visits his website.

MAKING WORK-LIFE BALANCE REDUNDANT – DON'T WAIT TO LEAD YOUR IDEAL LIFE – DESIGN IT NOW

Elise Sullivan

Ann had worked in the same large government department for nearly ten years. She started working there for a secure source of income, and jumped at the first job that came up. Previously, she had been working in higher-level positions, running her own business, even doing a term in the local government. She loved this work. She was able to fully express her passions for developing the community and engaging with people, and for coming up with the big, audacious, strategic visions and plans. Even though she took a bit of a backward step in her new job, she was recruited on the basis of her evident expertise and qualifications in Organizational Development (OD) and Psychology. Initially, she drew on this knowledge to perform her role. For a while her need for security was satisfied, but within a short time this stopped being the case. People came and went, as they do. The department was restructured, as happens with the introduction of every new Department Head or government.

One day Ann realized that only one of her needs was being met: security.

She was no longer called on for her expertise. People stopped seeing her expert in OD and Organizational Psychology, and started to see her as a Public Servant Level Five ("VPS 5"). That that meant to them: managing contracts, writing briefs, "ministerials" (letters that public servants write for the minister to sign), arranging and attending meetings. She started hating her job. Meanwhile, her need for a secure income had increased with the addition of a new mortgage, so she stayed. Over the years, she started doubting herself, her ability to do her job well, and even the work she was highly qualified to do.

Then there was another organizational restructure, and this time her job was no longer needed by the organization. The illusion of security went with it, and all she was left with was a mortgage. It was around this time that I started working with her to help her make sense of a bad situation and make the transition out of the department.

Ann's view of herself had shifted over the years. She now only saw herself as a VPS 5—and not even a good one. The only place where this makes sense is in a government department, which is no longer the safe haven it once was. Government is now as temporary and vicarious as any private organization. Your fate is defined by the whims of, and your relationships with, the people you work with. If they don't like you, for whatever reason, then they will make it impossible for you to stay. Ironically, it makes very little difference how skilled you are in areas of which they have no understanding.

Our work together was to shift her identity from being a VPS 5 to an individual who is an expert in the areas about which she is passionate. It was about distilling her essential self, her skills, and her expertise. In a world of change, the only things that you can count on are yourself, what you know, and what you love—nobody can take that away from you.

IMAGINE IF YOU COULD NEVER RETIRE?

That was the question posed by Tim Ferris in his best seller "The four hour work week". It is a powerful question because it puts work into perspective. Many people are working towards their retirement with a view that once they reach that Holy Grail they can really start living the life they want. They just need to survive the next 5, 10, 20 years, and build up a big enough nest egg to support them.

And like Ann, they eventually reach a point when they look back and wonder what happened to their life. What difference did it make? What difference did they make?

I am from Australia and we have a reputation for being pretty laid back. Picture sun burnt country, lolling around on a beach with prawns on the 'barbie' (BBQ), 'downing a tinny' (can of beer) and 'chucking a sickie' as soon as the sun comes out (taking a mental health day!). The reality is quite different and much more like that experienced by your average American. In 2013, according to the OECD, 14 per cent of Australian workers worked more than 50 hours per week, which is well above the average of 9% across the OECD countries. Australians are working the longest hours in the developed world at an average of 1,855 hours each year, 200 more than workers in other countries (Australian Institute). Eleven percent of Australian workers did not take any leave at all in 2014. Australia, America and Japan are ranked as the most stressed out countries in the world.

NO REALLY – WHAT IF YOU CAN'T RETIRE?

The idea of never being able to retire is becoming a reality for many people. The Baby Boomer's in particular have watched their superannuation go down the drain during the GFC. Rising housing prices has left people with a mortgage that is likely to extend well into their 60s, the. Their parents are living longer diminishing any inheritance that could have contributed to a retirement fund.

"We were retiring earlier and earlier until about 10 years ago, and then things started to roll backwards," Michael Rafferty of University of Sydney says. "While people used to look forward to retirement as a time to hook up the caravan, now it's something they worry about. Fluctuating (superannuation) balances mean you can't make solid plans anymore."

In 2012, an Australian Bureau of Statistics study into retirement intentions found that the average age of retirement for those who'd left work in the previous five years was 61. More telling, is that 13% of people 45 years and over believed they would never retire which Rafferty describes as "a significant social change inside a generation". The generation of Baby Boomer retirees "will probably be one of the first facing the very real possibility of actually outliving their funds because of increased longevity," said John Dani (Ipac Securities national manager for advice development). Unfortunately for some, the Australian Government will, for the first time in 100 years, raise the age that people can access a government-funded pension from the current 55 years to 67 year by 2023.

SO WHAT TO DO: KEEP WORKING TO ACCUMULATE MORE SUPERANNUATION?

There is a rule of thumb that for every year of work beyond 55, you can extend your retirement funds by about three years. That's because of the double whammy of not drawing on the funds that you have accumulated, while adding more. But staying in the one job is no longer guaranteed with business and even the public sector undergoing major contraction. Besides, the idea of staying for another 20 years in the same job may well feel like a death sentence to some.

To add to the dilemma, there still seems to be an age bias in most industries. People looking for work at 50 years are finding it increasingly difficult to compete with younger applicants. In March 2014, ServiceNow, a large Santa Clara–based IT services company, proudly declared on its careers page, "We Want People Who Have Their Best Work Ahead of Them, Not Behind Them." In 2007, one of our industry leaders, Facebook CEO Mark Zuckerberg, told an audience at Stanford, "Young people are just smarter." Mind you, I am sure he thinks the older he gets, the smarter he gets too.

OUR ATTACHMENTS ANCHOR US

I remember the first mobile phone my work gave me. I felt enormously valued and then I was given a computer to set up at home, and the technical ability to log on from home, anytime – Wow, they must have really loved me! And to repay this deep trust that they obviously had in me, I started working when I came home, late into the night, and over weekends. It became a bit of a competition between us at work: who could send an email the latest during the night (and still make sense!!). Oh yeah, those were the days.

But, now I see it for what it is. The mobile phone was their first down payment to owning me outright. Another down payment is giving me a title – 'Director'. The next is a corner office. Then the car. With each privilege we become attached to our position and it becomes harder and harder to give up. Until we have so much to lose that we are willing to do whatever it takes to keep it - even give up our health, relationships and life. And if you don't think you have given up your lives, then check your diaries. For those who are still working for the man, it is entirely possible that we are living the organization's life - not ours.

ARE YOU ACTUALIZING OR DESPAIRING?

Throughout my own careers and working with others to fulfill their professional dreams, I have found that 3 in 4 people are either stagnating, hoping things will get better, or worse, they are despairing that this is all there is (refer to the table below). Their sense of fulfillment vacillates somewhere between 0% and 60%. Three out of four of the remaining people are actually leading a life that is satisfying. They are quite content, motivated and managing pretty well; either because they are doing what they want, or because they have resigned themselves completely to what they have - and this is not necessarily a bad thing - especially if you feel fulfilled 60%- 80% of the time.

The ideal of course is to feel fulfilled 80%-100% of the time, to be actualizing your purpose and leading your best life by being your best self. You know you are **self-actualizing** when you feel positively energized and you energize those around you to a higher level. People like being with you because you make them feel good. In this space you become an empowering leader. You are totally solid in yourself, your situation and those around you. You have more choices because you stop being beholden to external resources and people - things that are tenuous and impermanent. You can let go and walk away.

How you feel	How you are	Level of fulfillment
Positively energized	Actualizing	80%-100%
Content	Satisfying	60%-80%
Worried	Hoping	40%-60%
Stressed out	Stagnating	5%-40%
Burned out	Despairing	0%-5%

The alternatives are:

Hoping - You are a bit worried most of the time and see this as pretty normal; it's hard but looking forward to things settling down and getting on top of it. You vacillate between feeling fulfilled most of the time and not feeling fulfilled at all. It is a tenuous and fragile state often determined by external factors that you bring into your life to give you a little dopamine hit. Your sense of fulfillment is not usually linked to your work, which is unfortunate because that is where you spend most of your life at the moment. At this point we form the habit of working too much because we are driven by a false hope that we can finish our work and everything will be better. We are looking forward when we should be present to what we are doing or not doing it at all.

Stagnating - But the worries never do settle down until you take control. If you don't, then nothing changes - you set a new normal - you start stagnating and find yourself on the same tread mill day in day out. You get so caught up in this that you stop being able to imagine a life worth living, and start stressing out.

Despairing – But the real issue is that many people get so caught up in the terror of losing their security and their identity, that when a career transition comes they plummet down the slope into despair and cannot imagine how to climb out to create an even better life. They are attached to external things, which are tenuous at best. You have a revelation that nothing can change. You feel helpless to the change your life and feel like you are drowning. Something major needs to happen to pull you out of this malaise and it is usually a physical or mental break down, what we often see as burn out.

Your greatest hope for security, ironically, is within. Build yourself up so that you can weather the storms. Like a palm tree that has the strength and flexibility to bend in hurricanes instead of a Blackwood Wattle tree, which grows fast but blows over with the first strong wind.

WORK-LIFE INTEGRATION – THE KEYS TO A FULFILLED, ACTUALIZED LIFE

At the very depths of the recession in 2009 I chose to leave the comfort and security of the public service. Many people still say they thought I was terribly 'brave'. And yes it was a bit scary but also exciting - I love change and transitions and the idea of working for myself, working on things I loved, with people I like and the way I wanted- which absolutely outweighed the risk and fear. And I have never looked back. One of my friends, who recently found out that her position was made redundant, made a very poignant observation. She said, "You worry so much about doing the right thing. Try so hard to keep your job; fall into line; do things that you don't really like to do, only to find that none of that will matter if they want to reduce their budgets." Paradoxically, I am now more secure than I ever was in the public service. By leaving the public service, I essentially spread my risk from one employer to many.

So my challenge to you is: What would you do if you could never retire? Keep working, but at something that you love doing for the rest of your life. What do you need to do now is to realize your dreams. Take the plunge into a life that is worth living NOW - don't wait!

The whole work-life balance concept becomes redundant. If work is not life, then is it worth doing? What we are after is work-life integration – where the work you do contributes to a purposeful, fulfilling life. The way I see it, balance is a state of mind, a statement of values and a product of focus.

MINDSET

Change your mind and you can change your world. Work-life balance is as much a state of mind as it is a state of being. Start with your mindset because there is nothing more powerful than your beliefs, assumptions and thought patterns to create the life you want, or to undermine it. This is about understanding why we say yes when we really need to say no. It takes belief in yourself and others, and practice.

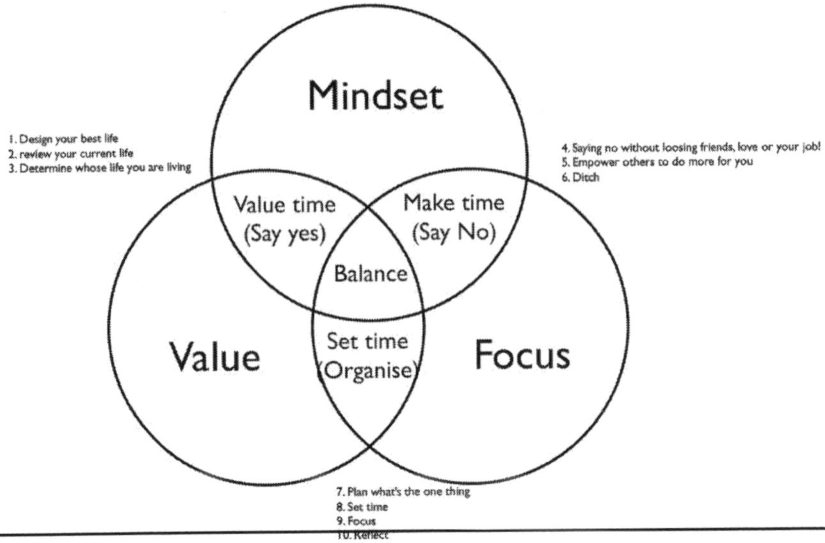

VALUE

What we value is written in our diaries. Where we spend our time tells us how we value our time, so check out your diary. Fulfilled lives are a result of living purposefully and achieving the things you believe are your purpose. This is the ultimate value of life in my view. So check out your diary and ask yourself, am I living a purposeful or pointless life? Whose life am I living?

FOCUS

Are you dithering on doing what matters? Devotion to the cause will get you further than spinning plates. How you spend your time will have a direct impact on the quality of the outcomes you achieve and how fast you achieve them. Multi-tasking is out, and laser focused, presence is in. If you are finding yourself being distracted by too much to do, ask yourself: "What am I trying to avoid here?" Is it achievement or failure? Focus is about devoting the time you need to the things you value, which will deliver the life you want on purpose - all the time. It takes discipline.

To achieve life balance, you need to take action and the change happens in the intersections. Value your time, make time and set time.

Here are 10 steps toward a more balanced life, where work becomes the center piece – not the counter point of your life:

Value time - and work out what to say yes to:

1. Design your best life: Describe what a fully lived life looks like to you. Consider your passions, your expertise and what people will pay for. At the intersection of these three is a career that will allow you to do the things you love, with people you like and the way you want to do them. It will allow you to work on purpose.
2. Reflect on how you are currently spending your life. What are you saying yes to? Look at your diary and add up the time you spend on the various areas of your life (work, home, health, relationships, spiritual pursuits, etc).
3. Whose life are you currently living? Identify who is defining your life. Is it you? Or is it someone else? Consider why this might be. What are you attached to? Their regard for you, material possessions, status? This will tell you what currency you are using to pay for the life you have.

   Make time to spend on the things that matter, you need to say 'no' to the things that are not contributing directly to a more fulfilled life:

4. Say no: Steven Covey famously said that "a purpose, a mission...a clear sense of direction and value, a burning "yes!" inside...makes it possible to say "no" to other (less important) things." (p.149, 7 Habits of Highly Effective People). When you are coming from this place, a considered 'no' to a request is possible without losing friends, family or your job. Saying 'yes' only to please others will eventually turn into a 'no' that is laced with contempt. Try saying 'no' to requests that are not in line with your purpose or that divert you from what is important to you right now. When said

with good intention, great respect and a suggestion as to what else they could do, a 'no' is easier to swallow.

5. Empower others to do more for you – delegate. One of our greatest motivators is autonomy, the ability to make decisions over what we do. The irony is that many if not most managers and parents, have a tendency to do too much for others! Accept that others also want autonomy; make your mission to empower and enable others to achieve more in their lives through delegation and coaching. Remember the old adage: fish and you can feed a man a meal. Teach him to fish and you can feed him for a lifetime.
6. Identify what can be ditched. Many who live in Western societies are so acquisitive that they tend fill every space with stuff, including their spare-time. Seriously weigh up what's on your plate by asking yourself "why am I doing this?" If the answer is: "I don't know", or for reasons unrelated to your purpose, then ditch it. Assess the risks and experiment to find out the consequences of doing nothing.

   Set time - get organized.
7. Plan – What are the three things that you need to do this year, this month, or this week that will have the greatest impact on your purpose and contribute to your ideal life?
8. Set time – Each week, set time in your diary to work on these mission critical things. Make your purpose your boss.
9. Focus – Give up multi-tasking and focus on what matters. Think about how and when you can devote focused attention to these mission critical things. I find that my focus, energy and creativity are at their highest early in the morning, so I block out 2 to 3 hours early each morning to do my exercise (health is important to me) and then focused thinking and writing on subjects that are contributing to my three mission critical activities.

10. Reflect: At the end of each week, set a time to sit in a place where you can reflect on your week and consider what you achieved, what you learned, and what you would do differently. The danger of not stopping to reflect is that you reach a point in your life when you realize that you have been running around in circles or climbing ladders that are or have been leaning up against the wrong walls. It might be here that you realize that you are focusing on the wrong things and need to adjust your sails for a new adventure.

Elise works with people who want to advance their careers, their roles and their lives – to ramp up their impact and make a bigger imprint in their worlds. She helps individuals to find the courage to do whatever it takes to lead a purposeful life and make a difference.

Elise Sullivan has a doctorate, which focused on empowering nurses to practice more autonomously. Her research uncovered the key conditions needed to operate as an empowered, autonomous contributor to powerful collaborations. She has further developed her research and has translated it into potent strategies to build collaborative cultures that foster individual autonomy and empowerment. She believes that the future of organizations rests in the capacity of every individual to operate at their highest level, all the time, in dynamic collaborations.

Elise believes deeply that to get the most out of life and the people around you, you must first find your own source of power - be self-empowered. Her book "Laying bare the power of you" is soon to be released by Motivational Press.

This paper forms the basis of Elise's Work-life Integration Program. If you would like to know more about this, contact her at elise@elisesullivan.com)

Chicken Cacciatore

Serves 4

Ingredients

2 boneless skinless chicken breasts, cut in half crosswise

4 bone in chicken thighs

1/2 cup all purpose flour

3 tablespoons extra virgin olive oil

1 large yellow onion, peeled and cut into large dice

8-ounces mixed mushrooms (such as crimini, shiitake, oyster, button), sliced

1 red bell pepper, stemmed, seeded and cut into large dice

1 yellow bell pepper, stemmed, seeded and cut into large dice

5 large cloves garlic, peeled and minced

3/4 cup dry white wine

1 (14.5-ounce) can diced tomatoes with juice

3/4 cup low sodium chicken stock

1/4 cup capers, drained

1/2 cup sliced pimento stuffed olives

1-3 teaspoons hot red pepper flakes, depending on how hot you like

1 tablespoon dried Italian herb blend

kosher salt and freshly ground black pepper

Instructions

Season the chicken liberally on both sides with salt and pepper. In a shallow dish combine the flour with a teaspoon each of kosher salt and pepper. Heat the olive oil in a large skillet on medium high until shimmering. Dredge the chicken in the seasoned flour and shake off the excess. Place the chicken pieces in the hot oil and allow to brown, about 5 minutes per side. Transfer the chicken to a dish and set aside. Add the onion to the pan and sauté until soft, but not colored, about 5 minutes. Add the mushrooms and season with salt and pepper. Cook the mushrooms until browned, about 3-5 minutes. Add the peppers and garlic and cook, stirring until peppers are softened slightly, about 2 minutes. Pour in the wine and cook until the wine is reduced by half. Add the remaining ingredients, stir and nestle the chicken into the vegetable mixture so it is coated. Reduce the heat to medium low and simmer for 20 to 30 minutes until the chicken is completely cooked. Remove the chicken and tent with foil to keep warm. Raise heat to medium high and cook until sauce thickens. To serve place the chicken on a large platter and spoon the vegetables and sauce over the chicken. Serve immediately.

YOUR PERSONAL TOOLBOX- A SEVEN STAGE GUIDE TO EFFECTIVELY USE ALL OF YOUR GIFTS AND TALENTS FOR THE GREATER GOOD

Fay Maureen Butler

We are all born with gifts and talents. This seven stage guide is for those who want to open and effectively use all of the tools- our gifts and talents- in their toolbox. What is in your toolbox?

My proposed definition of the toolbox: Unique gifts and talents within us waiting to be used or sharpened. We should use these tools to improve our quality of life so that we can influence the environments we interact with daily and positively impact future generations. Opening the toolbox is just the beginning. To successfully and effectively use all of our personal tools, one must move through 7 proposed stages: realization, investigation, visualization, practical, service, wisdom and sustainability.

What is in your toolbox: Lets open the toolbox.

THE SEVEN STAGES

The First Stage, Realization requires that one Know their family history regarding natural talents and skills. Realization means acceptance of that special family talent and gift. Some never stir up or awaken their gifts because they are blinded to what is in their hands. It may not always be easily recognizable. Because of this, the realization stage demands the ability to see beyond the regular interactions with family. It also demands close scrutiny of similar interests and tastes in families that bring individual or group satisfaction.

The Second Stage-Investigation is the investing of time and resources in learning about the family skills and talents. This stage introduces the person to the actual talents or gifts up close. The investigative stage centers on exploring what is needed to be successful. This stage also includes a dimension of choosing how to use the gift or talent.

The Third Stage- Visualization is all about Seeing... That is, seeing yourself effectively using, or mastering the gift or talents. This stage is the critical stage to the process. Why is this the tuning point? After investigating the gift or talent is, one must have the confidence to SEE a future of success. The learner has to distinguish what he or she needs to look for in the toolbox when they open it. What tools do they see themselves using effectively? They will have to SEE their choices. Seeing will allow for the transition to the next stage which involves stirring up or the beginning use of the gifts and talents.

The Fourth Stage- the Practical Stage requires that one serve as an apprentice with another experienced family member or a subject matter expert in the field. If one reaches this stage, the toolbox is open and the learner has selected the appropriate tools and has a desire to learn to use the tools effectively. Distractions, doubt and discouragement are the challenges during this stage and the time of apprenticeship depends on the learners' aptitude for that special skill, his or her attitude and approach. Family members may have an equal amount of talent and potential, but time and dedication will determine the outcomes. Sometimes distractions or indecisiveness will hinder the progress through this stage, but if the learner overcomes this and learns to appreciate small wins, the next stage will be extremely gratifying.

The Fifth Stage-is the service stage is total commitment to the gift or talent. The toolbox has been opened, the proper tools selected, and time has been spent learning how to use the gifts and talents for the greater good. The mastery of the tools coupled with positive daily interactions as it relates to the use of the tools bring rewards, satisfaction and enjoyment. The tools remain sharp because of constant use and stand ready.

The Sixth Stage-Do No Harm- the Wisdom Stage this stage, is all about ethics and morality. That is, don't use your expertise to harm, to disrespect others, or misappropriate your gift. You should possess the wisdom, willingness and maturity to offer yourself for service without compensation. This stage demonstrates the effectiveness of using the tools for the greater good.

The Seventh and Final Stage- Sustainability-Generation to Generation ... One of the ways in which our tools remain sharp and relevant/sustainable is that we teach the next generation. By teaching we are practicing, staying ready and using our tools as well as educating the next generation.

Let me use my family as an example. My maternal grandmother and her sisters were cooks, bakers and organizers of social events. They hosted and entertained people of faith frequently. My mother and her sisters were likewise involved. My mother taught her children, so the unique tool of the love of cooking/ entertaining, organizing social events and hosting people of faith is alive and well in my generation. I, my brothers and sisters all exhibit some degree of this family talent, and yes the next generation is being taught.

WHAT IS IN YOUR TOOLBOX?

It is never too late to open the toolbox and to begin the journey of discovery with these seven stages.

The Toolbox Seven Stages to Effective Use of Skills and Talents

STAGE ONE Realization	Know your Family History regarding natural talents and skills.
STAGE TWO Investigative	Investing of time and resources in learning about the skills and talents.
STAGE THREE Visualization	Seeing yourself effectively using, or mastering the gift or talents.
STAGE FOUR Practical Stage	Requires that one serve as an apprentice with another experienced family member or a subject matter expert in the field
STAGE FIVE The Service Stage	Total commitment to the gift or talent
STAGE SIX Do No Harm- The Wisdom Stage	Don't use your expertise to harm, to disrespect others and don't misappropriate your gift
STAGE SEVEN Sustainability-Generation to Generation	One of the ways in which our tools remain sharp and relevant/ sustainability is that we teach the next generation.

Dr. Fay Maureen Butler, Life Coach, Social Media Strategist for Ministries, Pastor, Author, Ministry President and Web Radio Hostess. She is a graduate of William Smith College, and has received two Masters Degrees and a Doctorate, all from Columbia University. DrFayMaureen is known for excellence. Her brand, coaching and media products are respected by her many followers. Find out more at http://drfaymaureen.me/

GET UNSTUCK: TWO LITTLE-KNOWN SHIFTS WITH BIG IMPACT

Laura van den Berg - Sekac

'The Biggest Mistake You're Doing Is Not Loving Yourself'

Many people spend their lives feeling stuck and disconnected – from themselves, and from others. In fact, hardly anyone hasn't experienced this at one point or another. Being stuck can be very frustrating. It often affects other areas of our life and undermines our confidence and decisiveness, which are exactly the vital qualities to get back in flow again.

In this chapter, I like to teach you about 2 little-known essential shifts that will help you get unstuck and regain the sense of control, joy, and fulfillment. You'll discover what's going on beneath the surface of being stuck, and what causes you to get stuck in the first place. You cannot make an effective change without understanding this:

» The real cause of getting stuck and disconnected
» The biggest mistake you don't know you're making
» The 2 essential shifts with big consequences you must make to get unstuck
» And a quick highly effective tool to help you to reconnect with yourself

How is it possible to get stuck and lose control? This happens when you let what doesn't belong to you to take possession of what's yours. You allow wrong goals and false beliefs to chase away your own truth, like living up to other people's demands and expectations, taking on too many responsibilities, or flood yourself with feelings of shame and guilt.

On the surface, everything may look fine. However, something different is going on. In reality each time you deny your own needs, cross your boundaries, neglect your heart's dreams, and make yourself small, some inner part of you leaves your true life path, turns off, and enters a new, restricting road.

Walking such a road restricts you as well. You lapse into limiting thoughts, emotions, actions, and you forget your own truth. Each time you don't support your own dreams, values and priorities, you stray further away from the pathway.

The more you go astray, the more a part of your heart gets lost in the gone, and the lesser the bond with your heart and soul becomes. Your trust slowly disappears, and your passion and motivation sneak away from you, too. You and your heart separate which draws you apart from the person you truly are.

An inner conflict develops then because your authentic nature cannot express itself fully anymore. Also stress comes up because *you can express yourself fully only if you follow your own life path.* It's because you, your heart and your life path are all really the same. When one of them falls apart, your life breaks up. You get stuck and stop to live. All you can is to survive.

'No big deal', you may say, 'that's life'. But it IS a big deal. Survival equals stress and triggers negative emotions –who only cause more distress.

And the worst is, by betraying yourself and not respecting your own magnificent nature, you put yourself in distress.

Stress causes narrow-mindedness, lack of clarity, and makes you feel overwhelmed. It also affects the way you run your life and the way you perceive the world. It often leads to bad choices. Your relationships suffer as well when you don't communicate. You may think you do. In truth, you're in the fight or flight state, and your ego is involved.

And again, on the surface everything looks fine. In reality, you stand there, your inner fists up, ready for the all-out-battle or to scurry away as quickly as possible. You don't listen because your mind is too busy with how you'll reply. Your ego frenetically calculates the consequences of a defeat, and the humiliation it might bring. You feel angry, scared or defensive. Or you do the opposite. You freeze and are unable to say a word. You don't hear what others truly say. All you perceive is 'danger'.

In truth, what your life may need, is you to be assertive or wise. Yet you don't dare to be assertive or express your needs. When it would be better for you to leave, you keep at the arguments. You stay too long in bad jobs and wrong relationships, but leave challenges unsolved. The conflict between who you truly are and your own betrayal shuts your heart down. It's hard then to meet others with an open mind.

This damages your bond with other people. When you're in survival mode, everything becomes all about *your* needs, *your* position and *your* (right) point of view. But when you make it all about you, others may feel as if they're not important, not respected, nor heard.

They instinctively know what you're up to, and they'll avoid you. You then wonder why your relationships go so bad, why people don't do business with you or why they withdraw. In the end, you may even conclude something must be wrong with you.

But it isn't about the struggle with other people; it's about the fight between your true nature and your 'lost' self that got involved with the wrong activity.

1. THE 1ST SHIFT

The first shift you must make so you can get unstuck is to understand that it happened because you didn't follow your own life path and your own nature. We all do it from time to time. First, be honest with yourself:

» Acknowledge where you aren't honest with yourself. Where are you doing things you deep down know you shouldn't be doing? Where are you fooling yourself? Don't judge yourself, just acknowledge it. You're human.

» Acknowledge that betraying yourself puts you in distress and that getting stuck is the consequence of it.

» Acknowledge that it's yourself who puts you in distress. Therefore you have the power to undo it - even if you may not have the strength right now.

Can you decide to do everything it takes to get back on track? Even if you don't know how? If not, it doesn't mean you're week. It only tells you have more work to do. Are you ready for it? If you cannot commit to make a change, you cannot make this shift (yet).

When you get scared or angry it's never your adult-self who's angry or frightened. It's the child in you.

In times of stress, which occurs when you start to be untruthful to yourself and stray from your own path for a longer period of time, the Fight or Flight survival instinct takes your body over. Likewise, when you feel fear and confusion, a scared, confused little child hijacks your psyche and sets you back into your childhood.

He pulls you mentally and emotionally into his childish perspective, and you start to perceive the world as if you were that age. It may be hard then to see things objectively or to put yourself in another's shoes. The emotions that come up during stressful situations link you directly to the moments where you underwent them as a child. When you feel fear, anger, guilt, and so on. You, in fact feel the emotion you've experienced for the first time when you were a child.

Positive feelings like joy also connect you to your inner child. But those come from quite another source. They make part of your glorious essence – which is the essence of your child as well. You access your positive creative imagination trough this child, too, but only if he feels safe. When he feels afraid, your imagination will shut down. It will be difficult then for you to imagine a positive outcome or new possibilities for your life.

Your inner child feels only safe if your heart is open. Consequently YOU feel only safe and in peace when your heart is open towards yourself.

When your inner child feels his very existence in danger (this happens any time when you criticize yourself, or get angry about yourself) - his conclusions are black and white and a kind of dramatic. Recognize some of them? 'They don't like me. They will leave me. I have to provide for their happiness. I'm lost. I'm bad. I have to save my mum. It's all my fault. I'm no good. Nobody listens to me. Others hate me. Others are better. It's better to be better. It's better to make myself invisible. It's safer to play dead, and never take responsibility'.

When you catch yourself thinking this way, it may be a warning signal that you are in distress, and therefore, have landed in a childish reality where you see the world through a scared child's eyes. You become one with that child, and he'll confiscate your life. You're interconnected with this child. When he takes the lead, he thinks, feels, speaks, and acts through you and on your behalf. It's HIS mindset then that decides what YOU will do. If he's hit by fear and anger, his reactions will be based on it, and so will be yours. If he doesn't dare, you won't dare. If he feels guilty, you will. When he takes things personally, you'll feel attacked as well.

When you reject yourself, or don't take yourself seriously, you in reality reject your inner child.

This child also is a synonym for your relationships, work, prosperity, health and everything you do. They all are parts of you. When you judge yourself, your work or your relationships, you also judge your magnificent essence AND the child in you. It doesn't matter whether you criticize others or only yourself. When you're in the 'reject' mood, your child will sense it and he will take it personally. He then falls in distress, and pulls you with him there.

2. THE SECOND SHIFT

The 2nd shift you need to make is to stop upsetting your inner child. Here are some steps:

- » Stop criticizing yourself and others.
- » Stop talking in a negative way about yourself, others, your work or relationships.
- » Never doubt your value.
- » Never be angry about yourself.
- » Never tell your body it isn't okay. It will take it personally.

Acknowledge again where you do things that aren't honoring your true magnificent nature. Don't judge yourself, but feel compassion with yourself –actually with your little inner child that longs so much for your love.

If you feel ashamed, guilty and so on, feel compassion again. Remember that you only experience an old shame or guilt, that has nothing to do with what happens here and now (and that even may not be yours. Actually my own experience is that 99 % of our negative emotions are not ours).

If you cannot feel your magnificence, it only means that you feel a lie. All children are born with a magnificent nature. You don't believe it because you denied it over and over and your inner child took it over. So HE doesn't believe it, and you take it to be true. From now on, start recognizing your inner beauty (and the inner beauty of other people even if you cannot see it) every day and every hour.

3. "LET'S IMAGINE IT" TOOL

This is a visualization exercise that I use every day. It's simple, powerful and effective. The more you practice it, the better it works. You don't actually need to 'see' something, just 'knowing' is fine. Think, for example, about a bicycle. Even if you don't 'see' it, you still know how a bicycle looks.

Focus also on your feelings and the sensations in your body.

Let's start:

'Think about something you'd like to achieve. Finishing a project, having a conversation, or just connecting to a wiser and more aware you.

Now take a deep breath, and relax. Close your eyes and imagine there's nothing to worry about. There's no fear, anger, guilt or whatever inside you. Everything is quiet and serene. Feel your breath and relax even more.

Imagine now that you look in front of you. It's YOU sitting there, somewhere in the future. A week, month, a year, whatever you want. You, having a larger perspective. Send your future self all your love, light, and blessings. Send more love, and then, when you feel a kind of connection, switch the position. Move to his or her place, and become one with your future self.

Feel how your body feels. Larger, bigger, calmer? Is there joy, freedom? Whatever you feel, feel it in your whole body.

Look then through the eyes of your future self at yourself back in the present time. What would you like to say to yourself about the situation?

And then harmonize your both selves with each other so that you both feel the same.

Enjoy it, and then get back to yourself in the present situation, but with the feeling of the future you.

Focus now about the situation. How does it feel?'

This exercise is very important because it helps you feel what kind of energy there can be in the future. When you can imagine a joyful future, future steps may cause less stress then when you are unprepared. It also helps you to focus more clearly on what you want.

SUMMARIZING THIS ALL:

- **When you stop being true to yourself and to your heart's dreams, your life becomes a lie. You get stuck – which is a way to get you back on track.**
- **When You Reject Yourself You Also Reject Your Relationships, Work, Prosperity, Health, and everything you do.**
- **The world shows you how you treat yourself so you know if you're on the right path or whether you need to make a shift.**

Both shifts in this chapter are in fact the same. It's about loving, respecting and honoring yourself.

It brings you the most profit. Only an egoist doesn't love herself.

It's that simple.

P.S.

If you cannot make the shift, it means you may need more awareness. Or perhaps you have some questions. Please feel free to send me an email at imagineShift@gmail.com or visit www. Essenticals.com

Laura van den Berg- Sekac, M.A. is a best-selling author and improvement strategist with more than two decades of coaching and consulting practice. She also is the author of the forthcoming book 'Be Authentic: 24 Secrets To Unlock the Real You'.

Her knack for digging to the root of things and seeing the patterns between underlying behaviors and events helped thousands of men and women to gain clarity, larger perspective and deep understanding of themselves and their life, in order to unpack their inner power, joy and creativity, and achieve greater personal and professional happiness.

Laura now lives in France, and works from there internationally.

HEALTH

FIND YOUR WHO

Brian Campkin

The Heart and Stroke Foundation of Canada states that every seven minutes in Canada someone dies from heart and stroke disease. That means by the time you finish reading this chapter two or three more Canadians will have succumb to this dreadful disease. In fact, eight years ago I was one clogged artery away from joining that group myself. But thanks to a lifesaving emergency triple by-pass surgery I was able to avoid becoming a part of this statistic.

Every time I share my story with someone I always get the response, "but Brian you don't look like the typical candidate for heart disease!" And they're right, I did not. In fact I was 46 years old and in the best shape of my life, or so I thought. What I came to learn is that an illness like heart disease does not discriminate against age, gender or religion. It just chooses you as it did with me. In fact heart disease can strike anyone, young or old. The Heart and Stroke Foundation reports that 90% of Canadians are living with one symptom for heart disease. That's the bad news, the good news is they also report that 80% of this is preventable by diet and exercise. What this tells me is we know what to do but we're not doing it.

To sum it up we are in denial, and the facts indicate that we as a society think we are healthier than we really are. I truly believe we are all walking around with the, "it won't happen to me syndrome." I whole heartedly disagree as I am living proof that it can and does happen to anyone, even healthy people like me. I say this because I did not have any of the typical symptoms for heart disease, like high blood pressure, high cholesterol, diabetes and I was not over weight nor had I ever smoked. I was a weekend warrior when it came to exercise, whether it was playing hockey or tennis, I was always kept myself active. But still out of nowhere came the diagnosis that of my four main arteries three were clogged at 100%, 99% and 86%. Wow, I was barely firing on one cylinder.

Now when something goes wrong with your body it's not like you calling up your car dealership for a tune-up. Your body is not like a car with lots of replacement parts, when they operate on you, you are the car. With that in mind let me give you a brief description of how open heart surgery works.

1. The area of skin to be cut will be washed with an antiseptic solution to get rid of germs, then shaved where necessary.
2. You'll be given an intravenous line and anesthesia to make you comfortable, ensure you don't feel any pain, and make you fall into a deep sleep for the surgery.
3. A tube connected to a respirator will be placed through your mouth and into your windpipe to help you breathe during the surgery.
4. Another tube will be placed inside your nose, which will run down your throat and into your stomach to prevent air and fluids from building up in your stomach.
5. Medical personnel will also place a catheter (a thin tube) in your bladder to collect urine that is produced while you are in surgery.
6. You'll be given an anticoagulant or blood-thinning medicine to prevent blood clots.
7. You will be hooked up to a heart-lung machine so that your surgeon can operate without your heart beating during the surgery.

8. Your heart will be stopped and kept cool during the surgery when the heart-lung machine is used.
9. The doctor will harvest a piece of vein or artery from somewhere else in your body – often the leg, arm, or sometimes an artery from the chest wall when it is open.
10. This process may be repeated several times if there are several blockages.
11. The total time of the surgery is from two to six hours, based on how many grafts are needed to be performed.
12. When completed they wire your chest shut and staple your skin back in place.

Let me tell you, it really is no fun getting cracked open like a lobster. This surgery is very evasive and no one prepares you for that first sneeze, which is a memory that lasts a lifetime. Now ask yourself is this enough of a wake-up call for all of us? My guess would be a disappointed no, otherwise the previous statistics I shared would be different wouldn't they?

With that in mind what can you do to prevent yourself from landing on treatment trail with heart disease or worse yet dying from it? The answer is really quite simple, you need to find your who. What exactly is that you may be asking? Well, most of our population know why they should exercise and eat right and they know how to exercise and eat right. But we still choose not to. Therefore, if we can't get in better shape and healthy for ourselves then who can we do this for?

Quite often when I share this idea with others the first question they have is, "Brian what was your who?" And I have the same response. When I was diagnosed with heart disease one of the first things I learned from the Heart and Stroke Foundation of Canada was, that 50% of the people who are first diagnosed with heart disease the first symptom is death. I realized just how fortunate I was to be alive after my diagnosis, so I chose to take on my second chance at life. And the one thing I was going to do was not to leave my kids without a father prematurely like

I was. I was going to do everything I could to have the opportunity to walk my 3 daughters down the aisle on their wedding day. They were and still are my WHO! They are the reason that I:

- » Exercise 30 minutes a day – 5 days a week.
- » I don't smoke.
- » I Follow the Canada Food Guide and eat right.
- » I Go for my annual check up

Let me give you another reason why my daughters are my WHO. For a year after my surgery I wrote a column for the Heart and Stroke Foundation about my journey, from my symptoms and diagnosis right up to recovery road and beyond. My three daughters have been an inspiration to me because they were so wonderful during my diagnosis, surgery and rehabilitation.

I thought it best to have them tell you what they were going through during this ordeal. At the time of my diagnosis my eldest, Megan, was 19 and just finishing up her first year of university. Julie, my middle child, actually turned 17 on the day we found out the results of my angiogram, and Kelly, my youngest, was getting herself prepared for high school as she finished up Grade 8. I was truly touched and moved that they were willing to share their personal feelings. Here are their stories.

MY ELDEST, MEGAN

I remember the day that I found out my dad needed to have triple bypass surgery. It was winter and the whole family had been sick with colds. So when he was tired and out of breath from playing tennis, we thought he was still fighting off his cold. However the cold just wouldn't go away and he knew there was something more, so he went to his doctor. They ran tests and saw nothing wrong, yet he was still tiring out easily. He was persistent, however, and wanted to find out what was causing this. I am very glad my dad was determined to find an answer because there is no way he would have been walking around with three clogged arteries for very long.

When my mom told me, after a long day of tests, that my dad had three clogged arteries I was shocked. He didn't smoke, wasn't overweight, exercised, and ate pretty well so I didn't understand how this came out of nowhere. I was upset and scared because any surgery has risks, but heart surgery is definitely not something to be taken lightly. As a family we came to terms with the diagnosis and got ready for dad to go for surgery.

I think the hardest part was the wait. It felt like, at any point, something could happen, like a heart attack. At this point, his heart was not damaged at all, which was very good news, but that did not mean that damage could not be done. His surgery was pushed three weeks and then they called to push it again. This was very frustrating; we all just wanted it to be over so he could be back home recovering. Finally the day came; it was my last exam for my first year at university and my dad's surgery all at the same time.

Luckily, the hospital was a five-minute walk from my school, so I joined my mom and dad on our early trip to the hospital. It felt like a long time waiting. I had mixed feelings because I wanted it to be over, but I also didn't want to see him being rolled away. The actual waiting during his surgery was not as long as I thought it would have been. I had to leave and write my exam at one point, which probably helped to break up the wait. I made it back in time to hear that it had gone really well and dad was in recovery. I was very, very happy and relieved.

I know that bypass surgery is very routine and common, but when it is being done on someone you are very close to, whom you love, then it doesn't feel so common and routine. I am glad my dad was given a second chance and that he took full advantage of it. He has recovered and followed his rehab religiously. I am very proud of him.

MY SECOND CHILD, JULIE

I'll never forget the day I found out that my dad had heart disease: it was my 17th birthday. I didn't understand why God gave me a sick dad for a birthday gift.

My family had never been faced with a tragedy like this before. However, I soon realized why God gave us, as a family, an obstacle to overcome. It is because I have a loving family who is strong and very close; there was no way we were going to let this bring us down. Through hope and support, my dad had a very successful surgery. His heart is still going strong today to prove it. Throughout this whole ordeal, I never lost faith in my family, in God and especially in my dad.

He is a very strong and determined man who had the right mindset and never let his sickness bring him down. Instead it made him an even healthier, happier person.

I am thankful to this day that my family is stronger than ever and sometimes all it takes is a little faith.

MY YOUNGEST, KELLY

The moment I found out my dad had to go in for bypass surgery I really did not understand what was going on. My Aunt Debbie and family were in our living room a few days after finding out the news and busy preparing a list of family and friends to call and tell them about this sad news. It was at this point I turned to my sister, Megan, and asked her, "Why is this such a big deal?" My sister turned to me and said, "Dad's going to have surgery that can be very dangerous Kelly that is why this is such a big deal!"

After that moment, every day I learned a bit more and started to understand what was going on. My sisters took it more seriously than I did the first month or so because I never fully wrapped my head around the fact that my dad would be getting cut open and moving all sorts of things around in his body to try to fix him.

My family and I started watching the T.V. show Grey's Anatomy a few months before the surgery, everyone except my dad. It seemed in every episode at least one person would die or barely survive. As I got into this show and saw more loved one's dying, I started to thinking, "What if I lose the man who has always been there for me?" He was there to motivate me at 6 a.m. for hockey practice, coached me as only a good father can, and always gave me the confidence to sing or perform in front of family and friends.

What if I lost my dad, the person who made me who I am today? Where would I be now? All this was answered the day my mom and sister Megan took my dad to the hospital for his surgery. When they called to say his surgery was over and he was okay, all my worries and fears lifted from my heart and mind as the person I thought was going to be lost was given a second chance at life.

As you can see I have some very special young ladies that gave me a very special reason to have them as my reason. For many people in society their main goal in life is to simply make it to the next weekend and live life by the rallying cry, T.G.I.F. "Thank goodness it's Friday". I think all we need to do is adjust the sails on this acronym a degree or two and change it to, "Thank goodness I'm fit!"

Since I had my surgery in the Spring of 2008 I have had the awesome pleasure of reaching the following milestones:

» Celebrated my 25th wedding anniversary one year after my surgery.

» Walked my eldest daughter down the aisle and witness my first grandchild being born.

» Watched my middle daughter graduate from high school and be on the honour roll four years in a row and now chasing her dream of nuclear medicine.

» Saw my youngest daughter graduate college and get a degree in early childhood education where she now enjoys a blossoming career.
» Plus many, many more!

As your turn this last page I encourage you to find your who to get healthy for and pursue it with undying trust. Become the C.E.O. of your health, become your own personal chief, exercise officer, and you might just change your life and share many life milestones like I did.

AT 46, Brian Campkin was diagnosed with heart disease and required an emergency triple by-pass surgery. From the minute he began his recovery, he knew he wanted to make a difference. As a survivor, he volunteered for the Heart and Stroke Foundation of Canada, speaking to audiences about his struggle to regain his health. Brian has been featured in the Toronto Star, The Globe and Mail, Maclean's Magazine and on television and radio. In 2012 Brian won the Heart and Stroke Foundations Heart of Gold Award.

Linguine with White Clam Sauce

Serves 4

Ingredients

3 tablespoons extra virgin olive oil

5 large cloves garlic, peeled and minced

3 (6-ounce) cans chopped clams, drained with liquid reserved

kosher salt and freshly ground black pepper

1 pound linguine, cooked al dente according to package directions

1/2 cup pasta cooking water

1 tablespoon chopped fresh flat leaf parsley leaves

1 tablespoon chopped fresh oregano leaves

1 tablespoon chopped fresh basil leaves

1/2 cup freshly grated Parmesano Reggiano + more for serving

Instructions

Heat the oil in a large skillet over medium heat until shimmering. Add the garlic and cook until fragrant, about 1 minute. Add the clams and sauté for 1-2 minutes. Add the clam juice, salt and pepper and simmer until thickened slightly. Add the cooked linguine to the pan along with 1/4-1/2 cup pasta cooking water and toss until the sauce is creamy and the linguine is coated. In a large serving bowl place the Parmesano Reggiano, the linguine with the clam sauce, and the herbs and toss to combine. Serve immediately, offering extra grated Parmesano Reggiano at the table.

IMAGINE HEALTH

Sarah Piper

As I sit here contemplating the meaning of "health", I'm having a hard time connecting what I thought was health to what I think now. Growing up, I was a very strong, athletic individual who was always fit, free of spirit, loved life, and lived each day to the maximum possible. That has changed in the recent past, and has made me more introspective and attuned to others struggling with any type of disease. This morning I woke up to the fact that I was going in for another 3 day stint at steroid infusions in the hospital. I would have to walk into the hospital knowing I was a patient and not a volunteer, that I had a three hour procedure in front of me, and that I'd have a port in my arm for the three day duration of the process. But here's what I realized....I am lucky. I have the ability to pay for my services, to get the services I need, and have the support group and surroundings that allow me to receive the best care I can get.

I came into the infusion center this morning feeling downtrodden and upset that this was happening yet again, but by the time I left, I felt so very lucky that I could walk out on my own two legs, that the infusion was helping, and I was lucky that I was who was born into the age where there actually was something that could be done about it. This is not something I've been dealing with for long, but this is my story.

Two years ago I was having problems with balance, with writing, with speaking, and it was scaring the heck out of me. But I didn't have insurance at the time, and the ER could only do so much. My wonderful boyfriend at the time put me on his insurance as a "domestic partner", and got engaged soon after. I spent a few days in the hospital being evaluated and learned, very quickly, that I had Multiple Sclerosis. In case you haven't heard of it, MS is a degenerative disease that basically eats away at the surroundings of your nerves and disconnects the impulses your brain or spine are giving to the rest of your body. It's scary and there is no cure, but thankfully there are therapies and medications that can help the symptoms. It's a disease that they still don't know much about, like the realm of brain and neurological issues like ALS. There is a lot of cross-discovery being done between diseases, which is very exciting.

So I found out I had MS and had no idea what to do with that. As I said, I've always been healthy and athletic – dancing most of my life, cheerleading, running, rowing, hiking, and working out. Pretty much anything you put in front of me, I was ready to go. Now I had this diagnosis that was perhaps sentencing me to a life in a wheelchair, or worse. I wasn't ready for that, nor will I ever be. So many of the people I met in the month or two after being diagnosed were in much worse shape than I. They had been diagnosed years earlier when there weren't many therapies or aides to help with symptom control. They were already in wheelchairs or using walkers. I'm sure you've heard the term "drop foot", but that's something that happens with people who have MS.

I fell into a very deep depression. These people who also had the disease were either chair bound or bedridden. They had caregivers, who were often their spouses, and there's no way in the world I could imagine my husband being a caregiver. Not because he's not a wonderfully loving and caring man, but because I can't imagine having to be cared for. So my depression deepened, I almost lost myself two or three times, stopped exercising, stopped writing, stopped doing anything that was important to me or made me happy in any way. I was, in a phrase, awful to live with and be around.

I would like to say I was able to bring myself out of the depression quickly and get back to my life, but that's not true in the slightest. The basic core of who I was and who I had known for 40 years had been changed, and that wasn't an easy thing to get around. I get change, I get grief. My mom died when I was 21 years old in a car accident two weeks before my first wedding. My Aunt wasted away from ovarian cancer and I was right outside the room when she died. I get grief. It's horrible, and heart wrenching, and so incredibly hard to get past. In fact, I don't think you ever get past it, you just learn to live with the new normal. So I understood what I was going through...I just wasn't able to get over or around it. This was hard to compartmentalize because it was happening to me – inside my body, not to me outside my body. This was all about me, there was no way I was getting around that.

Here I was, 40 years old, on the precipice of a brand new life with a wonderful husband, amazing family and friends, and the desire to use my schooling and experience to do good things in the world. But I was still struggling with the niggling worm in the back of my mind asking me if I was up to it...if I had enough energy...if I was still the person I was when I was "healthy". It was a hard thing to deal with – I'd never before had even the slightest thought that I couldn't do anything I wanted to do. Climb Mount Hood? Of course!!! Back pack into Eagle Cap? No problem! Hike the PCT? Sign me up!!!

The depression persisted for two years. And truthfully, I'm still learning to come out of it. Because I'm a fairly private person, so I've tackled this mostly on my own. I have an amazing support group, but I rarely call on them because I know they all have their own issues and demons to deal with, and don't want to add to that. But here I am, sitting in the infusion room by myself because I didn't want to bother any of my friends or family to come and spend time with me.

I'm in the infusion center today because they found a new lesion on my brain. Apparently I have 40-50 smaller lesions on my brain as well as several in my spine that give me relapsing-remitting symptoms. I didn't want to hear they found a new lesion, I didn't want to go back in for more steroids, but I feel so fortunate and lucky that I have these therapies available to me. And please don't get me wrong – I was in no way, shape, or form, happy about the new lesion. Thank God for Xanax! So here I sit, listening to the others around me who are having chemotherapy infusions, who are in pain, and clearly hurting from whatever disease has inhabited their body, and I thank my lucky stars that I am one of the ones who doesn't have to have a wheel-chair. I can walk out by myself, I don't need a caregiver, and am still strong.

MS is an interesting disease because you often can't see the physical symptoms. I have balance issues (people sometimes think I'm drunk), occasional speech and writing issues (I tend to type more than I hand-write anymore), and anything else that may crop up. It's kind of a silent disease because people can't detect it automatically. I haven't lost my hair, I don't have a port in my body on a regular basis, I have no casts or outward appearing apparatus's that would help determine what's "wrong" with me. I have a hard time with this, because people have thought I was faking it before. But sometimes I get sick, really sick, and just need to be left alone to relax in the comfort of my own home. Every person with MS experiences it differently. I have friends who have had no symptoms for 10 years and are still on the same medication. I also have a friend who has opted for a more naturopathic remedy and isn't taking any of the pharmaceutical options on the market. Both are doing fine, especially for themselves and what they want to accomplish.

For me, I want to harness everything I can to insure I'm not in a wheelchair, depending on my husband for feeding, or bathroom issues, etc. The medication I was on for two years worked well, shrinking one of the larger lesions in my brain, but now it's not being as cooperative as it once was. So, this morning, I started a new regimen of getting off my old anti-depressant (doesn't deal well with the new medication), and starting a new one. I also had an EKG and am wearing a holter for 24 hours to make sure my heart rate is stable. Tomorrow morning I have a complete eye exam to make sure there's no macular degeneration. Tomorrow afternoon I have a teeth cleaning (which really has nothing to do with MS...just like to keep my teeth clean). The next day I have a test for the JC Virus (no idea what it is, but it coincides with the new meds), and then a chicken pox vaccination. It's not an easy process, and it's fairly time consuming, but well worth it in the end.

When I started this process, I had no idea what to expect. I was new to the disease, new to the world of hospitals, new to all of it. I was scared beyond belief, and I didn't know what the future would hold. I was ready to fight as hard as I had to. So I've been fighting, I've been snapping up every opportunity. I've made friends with people going through the same thing, I've realized I already had friends with the disease. I've created a community where I can safely bring my concerns and worries and feel nothing but support and care. It's still very, very, very scary. I still worry on a daily basis that I'm not doing all that I can to insure my health and well-being are the best they can be. But I'm so fortunate to have the medical and personal support surrounding me that have kept me safe.

It is definitely a process. You are never told you have a disease, whatever type it might be, without repercussions. You don't walk away from that conversation saying, "ok...I'm ok...it's all going to be ok". You walk away thinking you have no idea what's going on inside or outside of your body and worried you'll never figure it out. It's a scary process that is best done with at least one other person close to you. My dad, for example, went with me to my original neurology appointments to make sure we both heard and retained everything we needed to. Without him, I would have lost more than half of what the neurologist was telling me. It's too fragile a state of mind when you're being told news that is less than optimal, and relying on memory or recall isn't the best way to go.

But the process continues. Some people go through the 5 stages of grief: denial, anger, bargaining, depression, and acceptance. Some of us go through the stages in a different order, and still more of us go through the stages leaving out one or two. For me, I went through it all except acceptance. I still haven't accepted that this is something that will define me for the rest of my life. Have I accepted that I have it? Of course – how can you not? I give myself shots three times a week and am monitored constantly for how my body is accepting the medication. But have I accepted that this should be what defines me and makes me who I am? No, absolutely not. Only my very close friends and family know about the disease, and that's how I want it. I don't want people to look at me like I'm a sad person who shouldn't be given the same opportunities and options in life as everyone else. I tell my employers only because I occasionally have to take a day off for tests or treatments, but besides that, it's my own struggle.

Many may disagree with that, and that's fine. This is how I've chosen to live my life with MS. I don't want people to know because I don't want to be treated differently, to be pitied or looked down upon. Because no matter what disease might "inflict" me, I'm still me, I still have a fighting spirit, and I am still a beneficial and positive addition to this world. So as I walk out of the infusion treatment center today, I am buoyed by the fact that I am still fighting, that I still have control over what I need and want to, and that I am still a strong and independent woman. MS may have taken a lot from me, but it has not, and will not, take my freedom, my personality, and my will to be.

> *Dr. Hall is an accomplished expert on women and mentoring, is coming out with her first book soon, and owns 8 Trees Consulting, which helps organizations establish successful and sustainable mentoring programs for women.*

FREE THE CASTLE: BREAK THE HABIT OF NOT BREAKING HABITS

Lynette Louise

I found myself in a woman's shelter surrounded by my six children. How had I gotten there? How had this happened? The schedule on the wall said that we had to be in bed by ten. I was lucky if my adopted, handicapped autistic sons slept for twenty minutes, how was I to get them all corralled by ten? The chart also called a housekeeping meeting for ten the next morning.

"I guess they like the number ten." I thought. Then I cried.

I cried because my newly bathed children were donning brand new pajamas. This was their first pair. I had never been able to afford *new*. Was I on the precipice of something special? Something freeing? Something happy? I resolved to follow this woman's shelter journey as far as it would take me. I would learn what was being shared so that I could change our story. My children deserved that.

But how, how could I do it?

I was terrified to be living in such a public setting where others could observe me and call me a bad mother. How do you stick to a resolution and enjoy the process? The more important the resolution, the easier it is to stick to. But how do you enjoy the process? I mean, think about it. We have all done it, especially on New Year's Eve.

It's easy to make that list of things to change on New Year's Eve with a glass of champagne guiding your belief in the future, but how do you keep the momentum of a habit changing choice? After all, habits are entrenched in us and cued by our people and places. Our environment literally holds them in place.

Because, as they say: "What fires together wires together."

And that is not just a saying. It's true. That is exactly what happens in the brain. Habits are hardwired for easy repetition. It takes a great deal of effort to not follow the path of least resistance. Even electricity has never figured that one out. An electric storm with all the lightning bolts following the easiest path to the ground is only intending to find the ground. You, as a habit changer, are intending something more sophisticated. You intend to rewrite your nature and recreate your style. That is a taller order than we give credit to while drinking and dancing our way through the New Year's resolution list.

Understand this, when you have a habit you are repeatedly responding to in a particular way to a particular stimulus (even boredom is a stimulus). Every time you respond this same way you create a path of easy to follow neuronal behavior.

Think of it like this: You're a child on the beach. You're building a sandcastle far enough from the waves to not be destroyed by the swooshing attack of the water. You dig a moat around your castle but need a water source. You know the waves will wipe out your work so instead you create a path within which the water can travel less aggressively. You call that a river and dig it with methodical patience, performing the same task over and over again.

So you dig a trench to the water. The water laps in and peters out as it gets absorbed by the dirt and sand before reaching the moat. So you dig deeper. It goes a little farther this time. You dig deeper. A little farther, deeper, farther, deeper, farther. Eventually, you have a well- worn river feeding your moat. You have done it! You have made a "habit moat" that encircles the castle and has no other purpose. It just holds the castle in a state of separation from any land creatures that cannot swim.

Like your habits, the moat is a way of controlling the environment and not always worthy of all the effort you put into making them. A moat imprisons the castle and your habits imprison you. But it took so much effort to make the moat that it's hard to just wash it away and start again. Instead we admire the moat and close our eyes to the negative aspects of separation. We shore up the commitment to our 'habit moat' by making a case for all the good reasons one has, all the benefits to being separate and safe from others.

That is how I ended up in the shelter.

I had been doing this exact maladaptive "habit moat" separation exercise for several years.

I had been married to an abusive husband. And during that time I kept thinking about how safe the kids and I were if anyone climbed in our window and tried to attack us. I believed that he was definitely a moat of deterrent to this type of person. So strong and forceful. We lived in our prison, in danger from within and safe from without. Eventually I deemed the cost too high and stepped outside without him. Apparently there were no land monsters waiting to attack us because the air was fresh, clean and friendly.

Divorce washed him away like a tsunami – leaving rubble and redirected tributaries and an opportunity for new growth. I learned to live without my moat. But it was hard. Even though it was better.

This is what it is to have a habit. Habits are more than the route you drive to work. A habit can be formed in how you choose relationships, bite your nails or how much you drink. Habits are everywhere and permeate everything.

A habit feels easier because a habit becomes automatic through repetition. It is the act of doing something without thinking because you have done it so much that it feels perfect and totally right. All habits begin for a reason. At some point every habit has a purpose, but any habit tightly adhered to eventually becomes a moat. Habits, like moats, separate you from the freedom of choice and alternative action. Habits are good things to break!

In fact, they are even good things to make. As long as you make them weak enough to easily break. You can learn from habit formation, but when they have been well worn they are harder to eradicate and make us more likely to fail at living with purpose and clarity.

Unless you use my tool. It has changed my life, my children's lives and the lives of my clients. It has made habit breaking as easy as twenty sessions of video games done over thirty days.

How awesome is that?

It's called biofeedback for the brain or EEG feedback or neurofeedback. I call it neurofeedback because this name seems the most applicable especially given that neurofeedback reeducates the very neurons of your brain.

How? Let me explain.

Your brain wave activity is listened to through sensors on your head. This information is then fed into a computer via an amplifier that makes the electrical activity in your brain big enough to read and display. This display is shown to you in real time, on a graph similar to watching your heart beat via the screen on a hospital monitor. The main difference between the two is that your brain has many more "beats" than your heart. Of course, they are not really beats like the heart's noises as it pumps in and pumps out. They are waves of electrical activity with many frequencies and locations to look at.

So you look at your brain wave activity. Understand: Who you are aware of being is essentially created by your brain. So, when you look at your brain's behavior, you and your brain are automatically being taught about itself. And the brain loves to learn.

With neurofeedback you can send messages directly to the source of your habits in order to rewrite your desires and options according to your own design.

As you fire in that hardwired loop, similar to the river built to feed the moat, the neurofeedback screen speaks to your neurons by having you manipulate a game via brain wave amplitude changes.

It's okay that you have no idea how to do that. Your brain will figure it out via trial and error. After all, you have no idea how you play a game using your hands either. You simply want to play and so your brain communicates with your hands. Then, through trial and error, you learn how to use the game controller and coordinate it with your auditory and visual processing system. You don't know what neurons you have to fire or not fire in order to make this happen. You only know that you will make it happen. Eventually, through practice.

Practice forms habits. It also dissolves them.

This is an example of why you want to make a habit, to replace the undesirable one. Nature does not function in a void. To stop a habit you have to make a new one. But make it weak. You may change your mind as you cascade upward into sophistication and maturity.

So neurofeedback makes this habit exchange easier. This is because when you do "make it happen" aka "get the game to work" every time you fire in that new loop your brain says: "Eureka! That's how it's done." Trial and error, guided by technology and science.

And because this is happening in milliseconds it only takes a small amount of time for your brain to get a large amount of practice with the new loop. Very quickly it begins to do that "new habit thing" more than the "old habit thing" that it used to be used to because old habit doesn't work anymore.

That old loop is no longer a hardwired event.

Let me reiterate and explain for clarity.

Every time your brain fires in the old way inside that feedback loop, to that old river and the undesirable moat, the game refuses to work. This refusal is a clear *no* to the brain. It's a clear communication of, "Stop doing that. That's just a habit that we don't want for this purpose," to your neurons.

Brains love to learn, to be in control, to be the boss of you while still doing what you want. So the brain seeks to run the game, to learn how to be the boss, and give you what you want. And as it succeeds it gets the supporting message of, *"Yes, that's a better choice. Fire like that instead!"*

This is what you do when you learn anything. However, with neurofeedback your neurons learn faster than your old negativity and reinforce new habitual beliefs. So it's easier.

Imagine being able to speak to your neurons without a science degree. All you need is the desire and intent to change. You choose your focus and play a video game to wash away your rivers of hardwired habits. In fact, it's so easy it's hard to believe. It's hard to choose to believe in this ease because having habits can be hard to break.

Most people don't want to believe it's this easy, but it is. All you need is the desire and an intention for change. And some neurofeedback professionals to hook you up, of course.

Not breaking habits really is a habit.

It's a habit I had when it came to mates. I chose my husbands and stayed, come what may. Until they raised the ante. One molested my daughter. At that point I knew I had to change the handsome husband hurts me habit but – *it was still hard!*

I had spent so much time building that river of belief based on how safe his nasty temperament was keeping us, that seeing him as the habit to break required breaking all the reinforcing habits I had built around him. If he hadn't upped the ante to such an unacceptable degree, if he had only ever taken his anger out on me so that I could fool myself into believing he was keeping us safe while I was keeping the kids safe, I may never have broken that husband habit.

He was my hero. My carefully constructed through mental gymnastics hero. My man. I would not have left.

I did not have neurofeedback when I broke this habit. I reached for experts and chose a shelter. They taught about mind loops and the habit forming cycle of abuse. I went on a tangent of learning about this cycle and the many ways it recreated itself in my mind. I learned about life changing and habit breaking. Everything from smoking to organic food to the people I let into my children's lives was assessed and redesigned. I was a force to behold. But I was in a constant health challenging state of habit breaking stress.

The thing about life is every new discovery or epiphany simply leads to a new trajectory for learning. And so I learned. I became an expert in habit changing (among other things) and learned how to reframe and recreate myself the hard way. I ended up ill and in the hospital after having lung surgery. By this point, I had tried on two more husbands. And "tried on" is the right phrase because I broke those ill chosen habits so quickly we only lived together for a few weeks.

I was in the hospital thinking over my life; the life I had almost lost. I was trying to see where this habit breaking trajectory would take me. I was loaded with morphine and floating around in my mind. The only thing I knew at that point was that decisions are hard to make when you can't focus or gain clarity of thought. And that was it, the epiphany!

I have never liked to use drugs or alcohol, and now I knew why. I – like my brain- want to be in charge of my life while learning how to choose with care. I come from a childhood of abuse. That had set me up with many habits of thought that I have wanted to disassemble ever since I can remember.

I had been learning the *why* of abuse and of habit formation. I had even been finding ways to break them, but I had not learned how to break them with ease. I wanted to, though.

I took a few courses in hypnotherapy. Chanted, meditated and trained in The Option Process which is a Socratic method of questioning one's beliefs aimed at self-recreation via epigenetics. But still, my brain stayed fuzzy and easily overwhelmed, which sent me running back to habitual thoughts and behaviors.

Until neurofeedback.

Within a month I was a different person. Less dependent on coffee but happy to enjoy its flavor. Less stressed by self-analysis while able see the changes needed to grow stronger and clearer. Less dependent on men and more dependent on myself. Less volatile, more patient. Less unhappy and lighter in my step. Everything I chose to be I became. All by playing a simple video game with my brain.

Neurofeedback has changed my life and the lives of my children and clients. If you give it a chance it will change yours. Thirty days to a new you is not only real, it's really easy. How cool is that?

Neurofeedback is truly freedom giving.

For most problems twenty half-hour sessions (five a week for four weeks) will recreate your river of neuronal firing. Think of it like the tide coming in and washing that old river away. Once the sand smooths out you can remake the same old moat with the help of memory but not out of habit. In fact, going back to the old habit will take almost as much effort as it did to build it in the first place. But you likely won't want to anyway, because this time you don't have the commitment to the old goal or the naivety that says it's good to separate yourself from others.

Once change has been made you will likely decide to try a new game with a more liberating end result. And since there is no undertow pulling you back into river building, the choices are not only easier, but also more abundant.

You are free to build yourself according to your own design.

I designed myself to be independent of the need for a mate. Though I'm happy to have one as long as he makes my life better in every respect.

Who you become is up to you, not the habits entrenched by your childhood or life traumas. Who you become is up to you, now, more completely than it ever was because you let me share.

Thank you! And that is how easy it is. Now go and use my tool. It really is only thirty days to a new you. Just imagine, no more panic on the freeway, or day dreamy focusing, or anxiety scheduling. All because you stopped playing that hard wired game with your brain and played instead a habit breaking life giving neurofeedback video game that supported your brand new wishes and desires *with your brain.*

Mind games are inevitable. Choose the right ones.

Lynette Louise MS BCN BCN-T is known as The Brain Broad. She is an international mental health expert, mom, speaker, and show host. Her international docu-series FIX IT IN FIVE with LYNETTE LOUISE aka THE BRAIN BROAD is changing the way families around the world connect, play, and grow healthy together.

Sicilian Shrimp with Penne

Serves 4

Ingredients

1 pound large shrimp, peeled, deveined, tail left on
3 tablespoons extra virgin olive oil
1 large sweet onion such as Vidalia or Maui, peeled, cut in half and sliced thin
6 large cloves garlic, peeled and minced
1 small fennel bulb, cored, top cut off, thinly sliced
1 (14.5-ounce) can diced tomatoes with juice
3/4 cup raisins
3/4 cup chopped kalamata olives
1/4 cup Sambuca or other anise flavored liqueur
kosher salt and freshly ground black pepper
1 pound penne, cooked al dente according to package directions
1/2 cup pasta cooking water
1 tablespoon each chopped fresh basil, parsley and tarragon leaves

Instructions

Season the shrimp liberally on both sides with salt and pepper. Heat oil in a large skillet over medium high heat until shimmering. Sauté the shrimp until opaque, about 1-2 minutes per side. Remove shrimp to a plate and reserve. Add the onion to the pan and reduce the heat to medium. Sauté until soft but not colored, about 5 minutes. Add the garlic and cook until fragrant, about 1 minute. Add the fennel, season with salt and pepper and sauté until slightly browned. Add the tomatoes with juice, raisins and Sambuca and simmer on medium low for about 5 minutes until sauce is slightly thickened. Add the penne to the pan along with the shrimp and cook until heated through. Toss to completely coat the pasta adding 1/4-1/2 cup pasta cooking water to create a creamy sauce. Transfer to a serving bowl, add the herbs and toss thoroughly. Serve immediately.

RELATIONSHIPS

BABY BOOMERS AND RELATIONSHIPS

Rick Bava

This chapter is a commentary on Baby Boomers and their relationships. Baby Boomers are defined as people born between 1946 and 1964. As I traveled the country interviewing Baby Boomers for my book, "In Search of the Baby Boomer Generation," there was a topic that kept coming up and was clearly paramount to Baby Boomers: Baby Boomers' views of relationships. I am pleased to have the opportunity to share the thoughts of Baby Boomers on their relationships in this prestigious book, IMAGINE.

I recall my father saying that a person needs many relationships in life to make them whole. Thus this concept is the framework of this chapter, Baby Boomers see wisdom in my father's words. Most Baby Boomers are influenced by the family life of their childhood. Those relationships formed with their parents, siblings, and extended family continue to carry them forward; they remain an important part of the Baby Boomer for the rest of their lives. At this stage of life, most have an even greater appreciation for their parents than they did while growing up. Sometimes this is because they are in now in a care-giving role; in other cases it may be because they have lost the parents who were once the rocks of the family, and now the memory of those parents is pronounced.

In their youth, Baby Boomers went to parents for advice and council, but the role is reversed as they attempt to care for elderly parents while giving those respected parents the good quality of life they deserve in their remaining years. Take a couple from Ohio: two Baby Boomers who are educated, professional people with a family. They face the tricky balance of worrying about their own children and grandchildren, while at the same time being the key caregivers for their elderly parents. This couple now know a great deal about the Medicare system, rehab facilities, and the decision making involved with trying to keep their parents in the family home. These are decisions that Baby Boomers across America are dealing with. They are helping make decisions on where their parents should live out their lives and trying to balance their dedication for their parents with keeping an eye on their own lives. This balance is difficult, but also one that a Baby Boomer freely embraces. Those parents did so much for them, and now it is the Baby Boomer who seeks to step up and be there for their parents.

This couple described is a great example for this chapter, for they are truly a couple who love and support one another. They approach each day of their lives with teamwork in mind. They are a couple who believe in the institution of marriage. They have worked hard all of their lives, exceeded expectations in their professional life, and are proud of the family that they have raised. They put three children through college, and now those children have gone out in the world to seek success of their own. This couple is an example of what many Baby Boomers seek: a partner in life. Baby Boomers will share with you that the greatest gift that life can give to you is finding the person who you want to spend the rest of your life with and finding happiness together. While all Baby Boomers don't fit the model of our Ohio couple, there are many aspects that apply to other Baby Boomers. For example, this couple is based on the love that a man finds in a woman and the life they want to share together, which is a goal for many Baby Boomers. So in a chapter about Baby Boomers and relationships, two key identifiers have already played out - Baby Boomers' respect for their parents, and the love they find in a partner for life.

This couple from Ohio also spends time with friends. They like to have brunch with other couples and seek interaction with friends. This couple, like many others, know the importance friends can add to one's life. So many Baby Boomers recall the days when they were college students and their days in the dorm, when walking to class with a friend was an easy exercise. But later in life the focus became paying the mortgage, going to work, and watching their daughter in the school play. They will tell you that as life became more complex, keeping up with friends was sometimes difficult. But this couple from Ohio somehow always found time for friends. They felt friends were important and added to the quality of their lives. It is the mantra of many Baby Boomers that friends enrich our lives. A friend can be a sounding board, a part of your support system, or just be a good listener when you need to talk. Many have found renewal in the richness of friendships. Some have sought through social media to find friends from their past, to recapture what once was and can be again.

What can be admired about this couple from Ohio is the attention that this Baby Boomer couple give to their siblings. The wife, a respected health care professional, cherishes her relationship with her sister and no matter how busy she is, she always finds time to call her and offer support or encouragement when her sister needs it. She loves her dear sister and she reminds her frequently with both her words and her actions. The husband of this couple never hesitates to help his brother, whose daughter has struggled with major health issues since she was very young. Being a supportive arm for his brother and his brother's family is more than just a responsibility to this honorable him – it is an act of love. What this couple demonstrates is that attention to siblings does not have an age barrier. The sister who you saw grow up and graduate from college, is still the one you care about as she gets married. The brother that you watched football with when you were both just children, is still the person you want to go to a game with as adults. So is the phase of life, siblings and family.

So as we look at Baby Boomers and relationships, we see a thread, multiple facets of the Baby Boomer life, and the people that make that life count. Parents that provide the foundation, a spouse that gives your life meaning, siblings that provide context, and the friends that are simply there for you. Not all Baby Boomers are as fortunate as our couple in Ohio, who seem to have it all, including relationships with extended family. This couple would describe themselves as fortunate. They have the gift of life, family, friends, and most of all, that special person in life. If they could speak to you, they would share that keeping up these relationships takes work, but it is an endeavor that has the wonderful benefit of making your life whole.

So as we bring this chapter to a close we come back to the premise that Baby Boomers think multiple different relationships are important, and every day they seek to improve those relationships. Relationships to Baby Boomers do not have a score card, or a bank balance, but rather they bring about satisfaction of living life to the fullest with the people who count most.

This chapter was written by Rick Bava, a national leader on the Baby Boomer Generation and the Author of "In Search of the Baby Boomer Generation," published by Motivational Press. "In Search of the Baby Boomer Generation" is a book for Baby Boomers, written by a Baby Boomer. The book details the input of hundreds of Baby Boomers. It is a book that many feel speaks to and for the Baby Boomer

Generation.

Rick Bava is a national leader on the Baby Boomer Generation and the Author of -- "In Search of the Baby Boomer Generation".

FATHERS & SONS

Carl David

Fatherhood is second only to motherhood in its importance as a life role. It is the highest honor a man can have. It is a privilege, a gift, and a challenge that comes with a forever responsibility.

When you sign on to become a father, it's a lifelong commitment, not just a day job or night job. There is no contract dispute, no changing the job description; it is simply your responsibility, period!

Your child didn't ask to be born, you chose to bring them into this world so you owe them the very best you can give. Aside from the basics of food, shelter and clothing; love, warmth, joy, comfort, protection and security are most important and are absolute prerequisites. You have the infinite power of shaping a life and that is a huge job with basic ground rules. Sure, there are proven methods and rules to follow but they are not hard and fast. There are so many variables that come into play and you are in uncharted territory. You have basically opted for the Life Coach occupation and have plunged head first into the sea of child rearing and life shaping. There is no turning back.

The upside is the experience of fulfillment and the achievement of success in this indefinite pass fail system because you grow with your child, learning along the way as you make choices or mistakes (no one is perfect).

Children need to be loved and know they are loved, unconditionally. And that they get that from their parents, first & foremost. If they don't, or if you falter along the path as they grow, then you have failed at the easiest pleasure in the world. Loving your children is a gift, not a chore. It should come as naturally as the sun rises.

How can you not indulge your children with forever love and affection? That is unconscionable; it is against the very law of nature. Parents who hold back their love from their children, or use it as a vehicle to bribe them or sabotage them should not be parents. They cause serious emotional disturbance and sometimes irreparable harm to children who unwittingly absorb their parent's negativity and selfishness.

It really upsets me when I see or hear about fathers in particular who are angry, resentful or take the job with too cavalier an attitude.

I was very blessed to have been born into a family where love and affection and warmth were ever present, it was unconditional love. That's not to say that we could run roughshod and do whatever we wanted and that there were no consequences. True love teaches privileges but with commensurate responsibility.

I can speak only on Fatherhood, as I am a father. I had the greatest father in the world. "Sure", you say, "but my father was the best Dad in the world." Well, I sincerely hope you feel that way, for if you do, count yourself lucky. We are far out-numbered by those who had a less than satisfactory childhood or worse yet, an abusive one. Some of you never knew your fathers; others wish you had never known them.

Realizing that I am in the minority, it is important to me that I share my happiness and with someone who knows only a negative aspect of fatherhood and let them see that there is a better way, and that they must not take out on their children what was done to them. This destructive chain must be broken so that when they are a father, they will do good, not evil. Anger and resentment should be worked out in therapy and not taken out on one's children, for that is criminal in every respect. Sorry, no excuses; you're out.

Never raise a hand to your children or threaten them, intimidate them or make them shiver in fear of you, for it is wrong in every way for every reason. They should respect, honor, and love you because you have earned their love, not stolen it from them.

My father was the greatest human being I have ever known. He was loving, kind, warm, affectionate, caring, exciting, brilliantly funny, dedicated and always there for me. His love was permeating, be it a hug, a kiss, holding my hand or just a smile of approval from his sparkling blue eyes. For him life was a celebration to be shared with his family. We were his universe and aside from having to work to make a living to provide for us, he was always there.

I remember him teaching me how to throw and catch a ball, how to rider a two-wheeler as he ran behind me holding on until I was finally able to balance on my own. A real picture of fatherhood! We built go karts in the garage from scratch, without plans using Briggs & Stratton lawn mower motors, kitchen chairs cut down and aircraft tubing- giving all the kids in the neighborhood rides when it was finished.

We went flying in small airplanes which he piloted, went fishing, played ball, shared road trips, played the piano together, built snowmen, played chess, shot pool, went to museums, took family vacations, read books, watched television together, sat in front of the fireplace in the dead of winter, roasting pieces of salami on a stick and tossing in orange seeds to hear them puff and they blew up while our faces blushed red from the searing heat of the flaming logs as we stoked the fire for hours on end until we'd fall asleep from the intense driven heat.

The memories are thick and rich, although too brief for my Dad passed suddenly at the young age of 58. But he had in that eclipsed time raised the bar to extraordinary heights and clearly set the example for me to follow. He gave me all of the tools fundamental to survive. With the help of my older brother Alan, I was able to learn enough in that first year after losing pop, to run our family art business. It was 1974 now and the economy was in the midst of a raging recession so we had to work hard and fast to re-tool and reinvent ourselves. I employed the knowledge, tactics and techniques I had so vigilantly watched my father use in his business and knew we would survive. I identified with Michael Corleone from the movie "The Godfather" as he too came out of the shadows full force after his father died. Like he, I took control of the reigns of our family business with stiffened resolve, but without the violence, and fought my way to certain victory. I had to carry on the legacy my father had built; I owed that to him. I could not let his efforts and endless work, come to an end. I was his son, which was an honor and a privilege, and I would make him proud.

I carried him within my heart and soul everywhere, honoring the years of life lessons and steadfast devotion he so generously imparted to me. I vowed to pass his greatness on to my children when they would enter the world several years later. They needed to know how incredible their grandfather was. They would only grasp at his presence by proxy though me and through the passage of his traits and characteristics to them. It was a current of goodness and love that would bridge the generations willingly, as that would have been my father's ultimate dream. His spirit and soul would live on through me and through them with more than an occasional visit, and only for those whom the message was intended.

My father was a master of spirit communication. At the cemetery after his funeral, there was a Piper Aztec circling above with its unmistakable sound. My mother, Alan, Arlyn (my wife) and I all looked up in unison and then looked at one another and nodded in contented acknowledgment. We knew he had moved to the next realm of existence; that he was free from the bonds of earthly restraint and was still able to fly, his first passion after his family.

Pop had been a pilot for years after taking his first flight at age 15. He had the bug and pursued it until he got his private pilot's license, glider's license, instrument rating and then his commercial rating. He clawed his way up from a series of single engine airplanes to a twin engine Piper Aztec, his baby.

I started flying with him when I was six years old at a private grass field airstrip. I was petrified but after several humiliating aborted attempts to lift off and "go around" I mustered the nerve. He was ever so patient and sympathetic to my fears of the airspace between us and the ground below. I clutched that airframe seat for dear life. It got easier every time with his gentle reassurance and guidance to overcome my fears until we were fast sky partners on a regular basis.

After he died, I lost my partner and wondered if I would ever fly again. Later that month, I called my father's old instructor and took him up on the offer to go flying one last time. We had a beautiful clear day flight for an hour with me flying left seat. After we landed and taxied back to the hanger I called the line crew to put her back and left the airport.

Torn, I went back a couple of weeks later and had the line crew take her out. After a walk around and a complete pre-flight check I climbed in to the intoxicating smell of the red leather, started her up and taxied out to the end of the runway. I debated whether or not to go up. I had no license as I never logged my hundreds of hours, but I could do this. Those twin Lycomings were ready, but it turned out that I was not. It just wasn't the same. There was a wide void and I was disabled by it. I was restrained with an emptiness that enveloped me. I turned back, set her up by the hanger and leaned out the mixtures till her propellers sputtered to a halt. I knew this would be the last time; I got out, gave her a kiss and a loving pat farewell. Later I made that dreaded call to a pilot friend of my Dad for the name of a broker who would find a good home for her. I knew he'd have wanted it that way, knowing full well how painful it would be for me. I know that he'd have done the same thing.

In a symbolic gesture and with great emotional conflict, I sold her, giving someone else the opportunity to experience the love and goodness my father had shared with me, his son. It was my way of moving forward, which is just what Pop would have wanted. He spent his life paying forward to his sons, and so we would do the same. You can see how the chain of time, either positive or negative can be passed forward to the next generation of fathers and sons.

I have spent my life giving to my own two sons, whom I love dearly. I have tried to live up to my Dad's standards and make him proud. I work tirelessly to maintain the same levels of excellence and integrity in my personal life and in our business. I am made of the same moral fiber as my father, and my sons are as well. We all have the goodness and stand up attitude he possessed. These are traits that we have been gifted and taught to practice sometimes by direct instruction but mostly by imitation and have continued to keep them alive through the generations. Hence the everlasting connection.

I began to write a book several years after Pop's passing because my children, not yet born, would never really know him except through my recounting and stories. I had to paint a portrait with words which would create an indelible vision. It was a painful venture which I shelved sometimes for months at a time. The loss was persistent but so was my goal, so I continued digging my way through the tunnel of darkness until I began to see light again. Nearly three decades later, "Bader Field" was born. "Bader Field" was a small airport just outside of Atlantic City where we used to fly in and out of on a regular basis. It was the last place I saw my father in the summer of 1973. That is where the story begins as it flashes back to earlier days and traverses through our family's life. It is truly a journey of love, forgiveness and acceptance. Pop was immortalized for all to know him and feel his loving embrace. Our sons would now have a living record of my father and his larger than life presence and his positive influence on myself and them.

It is my hope that the book will show how good life can be and the need for more fathers like mine. That someone reading it will relinquish their anger and resentment for not having had that idyllic father and turn it around and give his son what he never had. The emotional richness of such a positive transference fills that void and supplants it with new found love, enabling the next generation with a positive, fulfilling love. Hopefully they will show this to their next generation.

Life lessons of this kind are precious and can only be fully appreciated by the application of this good deed. In life, we get what we give, good, bad or indifferent. It does not cost anything to be nice and loving especially to our sons, but the price of nastiness and disdain toward them is something no one of us can afford. It is unjust, immoral and just plain wrong. Logic, good sense and physics dictate that the best way to counter negative space is to fill it with positive space. Like a base solution mixing with an acid and diffusing it as it infiltrates it, disabling its harmful and disfiguring effects.

My father was a great art dealer, legendary even. He once staged a Baroque painting exhibition while coordinating an evening with the Baroque Quartet he purchased from a public television charity auction. The gallery was packed; standing room only. He bought my mother a drill press for her birthday once so he could finish building a go kart in the garage. He was an accomplished musician (piano & harmonica), a practical joker, story teller, teacher, mentor, master chess player, pool shooter, crackerjack pilot, totally devoted husband, son, brother and so much more. But he was to me first and always, the greatest father of all time. He was my best friend....

Born in Philadelphia, Carl David is the third descendant of a four-generation art dealer family (David David Gallery) specializing in American and European nineteenth and twentieth-century paintings, watercolors, and drawings.

He is the author of "Collecting & Care Of Fine Art" (Crown, NY 1981 & Revised Edition Skyhorse Publishing February 2016) and "Bader Field; How My Family Survived Suicide" (Nightengale Press) as well as many published articles. His newest book, "Waking Dreams; The Subtle Reality" became available Summer 2015 (Motivational Press).

Carl is also a suicide prevention advocate, professional photographer, accomplished musician/songwriter and passionate animal healer.

IMAGINE THE POWER OF CONNECTION!

Meridith Elliott Powell

STRATEGIES TO BUILD YOUR NETWORK & CHANGE YOUR LIFE

Imagine and visualize the last time you gathered with a room full of people. Think about where you sat, who you sat next to and who else was in that room. What did you see in the faces around you? You probably noticed a great smile, a stylish outfit, a bald head – the physical characteristics of the crowd. But let me ask you, did you see the hidden potential of all of those people, the hidden potential they have to help you get whatever it is you want? You probably didn't, but the truth is someone in that room had the power, the knowledge, the connection, or the information to help you get whatever it is that you want. That is the power of relationships.

Now imagine what it is that you want? Perhaps you are looking for a new job, or need to know how to solve a problem at work. Maybe you are in search of a challenging opportunity. Maybe your kid needs a summer job or maybe you want to travel around the world and meet fascinating people. The fact is, it doesn't matter what it is that you want, building relationships and connecting with other people is the best way to ensure you get it.

Imagine, at any given time, you are just one connection away from the help you need to move closer towards whatever it is you want in life. Fortunately for you (and for all of us), most people we connect with are happy to be a resource or source of helpful information. The basic human need and desire is to help other people.

Isn't that amazing? To get what you want, all you have to do is connect with the right person, and connecting is easy. Connecting is just networking, and networking is easy...right?

Unfortunately, I think networking is one of the most dreaded words a in the world of business. It ranks right up there with public speaking, cold calling, and the 360 review. Many people go so far as to say they even hate networking. Few people get excited by the prospect of walking into a room full of people they don't know and making conversation about topics in which they may or may not have the slightest interest.

If you happen to know one of the few people who actually love to network, it would be worth your while to watch them in action and treat it as a lesson in success. Research and statistics prove that effective networkers are the lucky ones; they enjoy more opportunities, experience less stress, and have more fun at work and play than those who hate to network. A master networker is proven to make more money, get promoted more often, and receive more opportunities in their personal life than an individual of equal experience, education, and skills. The return on investment for learning to network is high, and few other skills you develop and practice will do more for your career, your life, your family, and your long-term happiness.

So if networking (connecting and building relationships) is so good for us and produces such a strong return on investment, then why do so few like to network? My theory is it is because we were either never taught to network or we were taught to network all wrong. Truly, when were you ever taught or encouraged to talk and connect with people you did not know? Never right? In fact, you were taught the opposite. You were taught not to talk to strangers.

Then when you finally did learn that networking had value, or you were "forced' by a boss or supervisor to network, you were given skills that made the process at best uncomfortable. Being the over achiever that you are, you took a class or attended a seminar on networking, and a well-meaning business associate or trainer taught you that the purpose of networking is to get ahead or to get business, and right at that moment you started to dislike networking. That was the moment you were taught (incorrectly) that networking is selfish, focused on you, and impersonal. You might have learned skills that felt pushy and awkward. For instance, many so-called networking "experts" recommend that you repeat a person's name three times when meeting them so that you remember it. How awkward is that? Talking with someone you don't know already takes you out of your comfort zone, and the last thing you want is to sound like a robot.

"Hello Dick Smith, what brought you to this networking event, Dick Smith? Dick Smith, what do you do for a living?"

Then you may have even been taught to prepare and practice a 30-second elevator speech. Not many of us have hopped into an elevator to have someone ask us what we do for a living. It's probable that people avoid that kind of question to explicitly dodge the elevator speech.

With tools and skills like that, no wonder we do not like to network and at best it is an unnatural and uncomfortable. So if it is uncomfortable, why do some people love to network?

Because there is something that those people know, that the rest of us need to learn. Networking and building relationships is natural, and when done correctly is actually a mutually beneficial and fun thing to do. And to do "it" naturally, there are just three things you need to know.

3 STEPS TO BECOMING A NATURAL NETWORKER

Step 1: Serve.

Step one gets you out of the gate and takes the stress out of networking. To effectively network, you must take a genuine interest in other people. This means approaching others with a servant's heart and following Steven Covey's advice to seek first to understand.

Serving is about putting others' needs ahead of your own and taking a genuine interest in discovering the value of others – their talents, skills, and accomplishments. Just by being willing to understand another person's unique skills and talents you are serving them. You also serve yourself by using that understanding to build a network of people with a broad range of talents and skills that complement yours. This enables you to see how you can connect, relate, and work with others. We are all stronger when others are available and willing to help us reach our goals, accomplish more, and have more fun.

To seek first to understand others, we must be willing to invest in them, before we ask them to invest in us. Imagine walking into a networking event and feeling no stress and no fear. Well that can happen if and when you lead with a servant's heart, and give with no expectation of return. Instead of focusing your time and energy on yourself and your fear, you instead focus your time and energy on other people, thinking about how you can connect with them, learn about them, and serve them in a way that first helps them achieve their goals.

When we lead with a servant's heart it takes the stress and pressure of worrying about achieving our goals, and instead focus' on ensuring we help others achieve theirs. As another great leader told us, Zig Ziglas, the fastest way to get what you want is to first help others get what they want.

Through networking, and serving first, you have the opportunity to discover the unique skills and talents of others and how those talents and skills can combine with yours to make life more fun, easy and effective. When pressed with a challenge or a problem, we often ask, "How am I ever going to do that?" When you learn to serve, the question becomes a more effective and far less daunting one:

"Who do I know can help?"

Step 2: Engage

We know that networking is connecting with others through service. We recognize that the value of different people is in the unique talents and skills they have to offer. I find that one of the biggest objections people have to networking is the fear they have talking about themselves. The fear that they do not know what to say, talk about, or fear that they will feel like it is bragging.

But that is the wonderful thing about networking, is not about you. To network naturally, you must really engage the other person, and learn about them. You invest your time and energy in discovering their unique gifts and talents. You already know all about you. The intrinsic value of networking lies in learning about the other person.

You can best engage others by keeping the conversation focused on them. You may still play a large part of the conversation, and in fact keep the conversation moving, but the content of the conversation should focus on them. How? It's as easy as asking questions. If you ask a question, they will answer it. If they think you are interested in them, people will answer as many questions as you offer up. People love to talk about themselves.

In this scenario, you both win. You find out who the other person is, what is important to them, and maybe learn a little about their background and what you have in common. They feel important because you are expressing an interest in their life, and they may even feel a certain kinship to you because of what you have in common, if you work to find it. You can practice engaging others very easily. Here is a list of questions that might help you get started:

Connecting Questions

Where are you from?

What brought you to this event?

What do you do when you are not working?

What is the best vacation you have ever taken?

What do you do for a living and how did you get started?

What is your favorite food to eat?

If you hit the lottery, what would you do?

What is the best piece of advice you've ever received?

What are you most proud of?

Once you ask a few questions you should pat yourself on the back. You are networking! In showing an interest in someone else, you effectively served another person and engaged them. You discovered interesting facts, amusing stories, previously unknown commonalities, and likely have an idea how you can help one another. You connected, and you networked. By simply engaging, you established a strong base upon which you can continue to build. You no longer have to imagine, it really is that easy.

Step 3: Expand your network.

With a foundation of serving and engaging others built, you will now be ready to take enough anxiety out of networking that you'll feel comfortable expanding your network. First, congratulate yourself for pushing the boundaries of your comfort zone, leading with a servant's heart, and respecting the value of others. By engaging others in conversation and learning who they are, you've tackled the hardest part of connecting - and it is time to take your networking to a whole new level.

You must recognize each and every opportunity to expand your network, and make effective use of your time in any situation that offers the opportunity to meet new people. Networking should become a lifestyle, not a task. The more routine it becomes, like brushing your teeth or washing your face, the easier and more valuable it will become. If you set a goal of meeting one new person a week, that would total 52 people every year. The average person has 250 connections -people you can tap to help you, professionally or personally, get whatever you want.

Now you move into the driver's seat. When you expand your network, you become the relationship builder, rather than the person waiting for others to get to know you. You become the person who has access to the knowledge and information you want and need rather than the person who is waiting for it to trickle down to you.

You are the person who takes responsibility for the relationships you want, the person who sees the possibility in any social situation. You have gained an empowering sense of control! The steps you practiced to serve and engage others may have been uncomfortable at first, but they were also relatively easy in the scheme of things. Think about taking your skills to another level by visualizing the job site you are currently working on or some upcoming time you expect to spend with a group you are going to have to engage to get to know. What actions could you take to expand your network?

Use your natural instincts and what you have read here to ensure you build relationships that can help you in work and in life. You do not need to build it into a to-do list, or try to drum up business through an awkward conversation. Just choose three ideas you want to pursue and are actually willing to do to expand your network. Do not make these goals for the distant future – these should be things you can do immediately and continue to do to make networking part of your lifestyle.

The power of networking is so obvious. The success of the companies that make it a priority is so real. The happiness level of employees who choose to embrace it is so unmistakable. The balance and decreased stress of those who take it into their personal lives is unmatched. It is bar none the most powerful and impactful skill you can have. So take a moment and commit to yourself. Name and write down three simple actions you can take that will make networking fun, easy, and incredibly effective.

Networking can be fun, effective and is as easy as:

» serving – learning to lead with a servant's heart and understanding that there is real value in the talents and skills others bring to the table;

» engaging – investing in others first – taking the time to ask questions and get to know them; and

» expanding – taking responsibility to go after the relationships you want and continue to build your network.

Just remember these three little steps to SEE the opportunities that arise due to the power of connecting with others.

Challenge yourself to build your network and by doing so change your life. Understand that at any given time you are just one connection away from someone who can help you find the answers, the solutions, or the opportunities that ensure you will get everything you want. Networking can become the most fulfilling part of your life.

When you leave a job, it is not the work you did that you or other people remember; it is the relationships you built that both parties will find most enduring. When you leave a conference or event, it is not your title or position that people remember; it is how you made them feel and how much fun you had together. And when we are all sitting back in our rocking chairs living off the memories of our lives, it won't be the system we upgraded or the new technology we installed that will fill our minds. It will be the people we met, the stories we created, and the relationships we built that keep us going.

It is just networking, just building relationships and that is easy!

Meridith Elliott Powell, Business Growth Expert, is the CEO of Motion-First a speaking and business strategy company working with today's leaders to decrease stress, increase profits by creating cultures of employee innovation.

Garlic Shrimp with Eggplant, Spinach and Feta

Serves 4

Ingredients

1 pound large shrimp, peeled, deveined, tail left on
3 tablespoons extra virgin olive oil
1 large yellow onion, peeled, cut in half and sliced thin
6 large cloves garlic, peeled and very thinly sliced
1 medium eggplant, stem cut off, sliced in 1/2-inch thick rounds, then into 1/2-inch dice
2 large Roma tomatoes, chopped
1 pound baby spinach leaves, thick stems removed
3/4 cup chopped kalamata olives
1/2 cup dry white wine
2 lemons, zest and juice
kosher salt and freshly ground black pepper
1 pound rotini, cooked al dente according to package directions
1/2 cup pasta cooking water
3/4 cup crumbled feta cheese
2 tablespoons toasted pine nuts

Instructions

Season the shrimp liberally on both sides with salt and pepper. Heat oil in a large skillet over medium high heat until shimmering. Sauté the shrimp until opaque, about 1-2 minutes per side. Remove shrimp to a plate and reserve. Add the onion to the pan and reduce the heat to medium. Sauté until soft but not colored, about 5 minutes. Add the garlic and cook until fragrant, about 1 minute. Add the eggplant, season with salt and pepper and cook until browned and softened. Add the spinach, tomatoes and black olives and cook until spinach is wilted. Pour in the wine and simmer until the wine is reduce by half. Add the lemon juice and zest and continue cooking for 5 minutes longer. Add the shrimp, pasta, feta and 1/4-1/2 cup pasta cooking water and toss to coat completely and heat through. Transfer to a serving bowl and toss in the pine nuts. Serve immediately.

YOU HAVE ONE UNREAD MESSAGE

Anita Narayan

A MESSAGE FROM THE HEART

The following inner conversation took place between my heart and mind on a life and death matter. It turned out to be a defining point in the relationship with myself and my life. Up until that point it was luke warm at best. It took me out of what felt like a 'train station' of questioning my existence, despite my apparent success, and set me on a definite journey of continuous adventure and abundance. I come across so many people and professionals who are struggling with feelings of futility, disillusionment, depression and suicidal feelings. They are too ashamed to acknowledge it.

May this shared experience impact the relationship you have with yourself in a new and fresh way, a way which will save you and enable you to thrive now with powerful purpose and great joy. I will return after the conversation

THE CONVERSATION

HEART: I want to have a chat with you about you. I know you're busy and this may seem a luxury item but let's step outside and go for a walk and talk in nature. I promise it will be worth your time.

MIND: This feels a bit self-indulgent. Do I have a choice?

HEART: Always, though it would be preferable if you said yes.

MIND: I get the feeling you won't go away if I say no, and I am too tired to resist. My head hurts and I have this brain fog right now.

HEART: Sorry, I was behind that. I found that trying to reason with you wasn't working so I had to find another way to get your attention, because this is too important.

MIND: I had a feeling this was coming. OK the platform is yours, let's walk, you talk, I am all ears!

MESSAGE FROM THE HEART

By the way, isn't nature wonderful? Have you noticed how it can act like a tuning fork, enabling you to feel its contrasting energy, helping you to shed stuff and regain balance as you engage with it in deep appreciation? You should spend more time with nature. On that relaxing note, back to you.

I know your mind has been ignoring me because you have 'stuff' to do that will supposedly help you accomplish things. Yet, everything I have been observing tells me that you are spinning your wheels, and not progressing or accomplishing your ideal life as you once dreamt.

Yes you once had a stunning dream of a life that was rewarding and fulfilling, with a vibrant loving you that awakened to her true creative power. I remember it well because I was involved in that dream.

Yet slowly and somewhat ironically you derailed and chose to go it alone. You detached from me and reduced your journey to a series of tasks and skills that needed execution in order to achieve the dream. Your energy became more labored and flat.

You were unable to feel good about yourself unless you were achieving something work related. You also disengaged from the creative source that formed those dreams within you. In separating from me you disconnected from yourself.

I watched the disconnection play out, slowly, and systematically. Your lack of trust in others resulted in your withdrawal into self-sufficiency. I also noticed that you didn't seem to know, like, or trust yourself that much. I watched you burn out from the unresolved conflict.

I feel your weak objection to this. I know you did your best to look after yourself and give yourself a good life, but I am not referring to the duty and responsibility to look after yourself. I am referring to the deeper bond of love that is nurturing, and appreciative of who you are.

The irony is that if you could form that intimate bond with yourself you would achieve so much more, because the way you relate to yourself affects the way you express yourself. Right now you lack authenticity and power because you are trying to fit in with the rest of the world, while dragging yourself along.

I understand why you doubled your efforts when working, to compensate and bridge this gap. Intimacy has been an awkward subject for you, but your approach has only served to widen the gap. You have suffered great losses and you are not one to seriously entertain suicide, but I heard you when you said to yourself, 'death would be a sweet release'.

You have regrouped of course, but you can't quite shake off the gnawing sense of futility and disillusionment that is like a thorn your side. You know deep down that you can't keep doing this vicious cycle. None of what I am saying surprises you because I know you had this message in a dream one night.

At the time it was hard to embrace the message because your mind could not handle it, and you were caught up with immediate survival issues. Nevertheless it was part of an awakening that has come round full circle.

Now it's time to wake up and embrace the message because I can't bear to watch you continue to suffer like this. I know a rich inheritance awaits you and your life truly depends on taking this message on board.

I have been patiently waiting to impart great gems of wisdom which will change your life dramatically towards fulfillment and success. Will you work in partnership with me? Will you go on a short journey with me? This is something you need to experience beyond a verbal explanation, in order to realize its true power.

I can see weary resignation in your eyes, but all that is going to change. I feel you are hungry for more yet extremely tired, that's why I asked if you would go on a short journey. All you need is honesty and the decision to reconcile with yourself.

You have that inquiring look on your face. Let me expand. Honesty is the start of true freedom. It is difficult to move from a place you pretend to be in, when you are truly somewhere else. Denial can take you to that place and before you know it you feel lost.

Honesty is that awakening moment of looking at yourself with transparency, and acknowledging the true status of your own relationship without beating yourself up.

Secondly, this journey cannot begin without a decision based on that honesty. So many people think you need to have the 'know how' or 'how to' before you can make a decision, but it's the other way round. There is something about making a decision that unlocks the resources needed en route.

Remember the time when you made the decision to break free from your depression after severe trauma? You had no idea how you were going to bring about the change. You just knew you were going to find the solution. There was a certainty and a commitment that unlocked unknown resources along the way. You broke free within a short time, which was great!

But now you have gotten stuck in survival mode, which is why you are feeling the way you are. What you are silently communicating is your desire to feel alive again. And so you should, after all life is your true inheritance.

I can see the light coming on for you now. Your body language has changed.

You have lost your way, and with your permission I would love to help you restore your vision, purpose and direction. The destination of this short journey is self-reconciliation. Once you reach that point other things will naturally open up and expand in ways you cannot predict right now.

As we embark on this journey I want to give you a new lens through which to experience yourself and the world around you. The good news is that although it will be a profound journey, it does not have to take long.

Do you recall your recent adventure of walking across hot coals and breaking a plank of wood? Apart from the important discovery that you could successfully complete something you thought was impossible for you, there were two other discoveries.

You completed these challenging feats with less than two hours training and discovered that the brain can learn faster than you thought. You also learned that when you integrate your inner resources towards an outcome, your experience of the process feels lighter and you achieve your outcome quicker and more effortlessly.

We will use that on this journey, and you will not notice the time.

MIND: Something tells me to continue with you. My head says I don't have time, yet at the same time you have read me so well, even voiced hidden things. Something needs to change, you are right, and I feel the urgency of the moment now. Your message is compelling me to journey with you. Let's go!

THE POWER OF A JOURNEY

MIND: ok so what is the awakening and inspiration I need to reconcile with myself to feel alive again?

HEART: That's a great empowering question. You should ask more questions like that! Your mind has become used to complexity due to the severe challenges you have gone through. This is simple and streamlined in comparison. The answer is that you need to become a best friend to yourself. The way to do that is through imagination and empathy. Imagine a close friend and experience yourself through their eyes.

This won't be easy at first because you are not used to flexing those inner muscles toward yourself. It won't take too much time though, because you are great at building friendships. Short, frequent appointments with yourself, along with proper engagement will get you there quickly.

If you practice this first it will also help you adjust your thinking away from the rigid thinking that limits the possibilities for your life. I address your thinking last because reflecting with accuracy is more than just a mental process. It's a process that requires you to be on side with yourself.

The new relationship with you is like a new lens. When you reflect through that lens without criticism, you open yourself up to more insights instead of filtering them out. You can build more accurate reflection by simply asking empowering questions, being open to receive the answers, and making decisions accordingly.

If you treat any outcome to your decisions as mirrors through which you can reflect and adjust your path accordingly you will become more accomplished because you won't get caught up in the failure dialogue that has often caused anxiety for you. That's right you are developing an open heart and an explorer's mentality.

MIND: I can already sense the expansion and simplicity of this process, and feel so much lighter already. Why did I not see this before? Thank you so much

HEART: Things tend to happen when you are inwardly ready. Your empowering questioning about awakening and inspiration is a great one for developing inner readiness.

MESSAGE RECEIVED: END OF MESSAGE

I am grateful and thrilled to say that I took the above message on board and did the journey with profound results. I write more fully about the circumstances and the journey in my book and song called "Breaking Free".

I had been shown the power to unlock resources that previously laid hidden from view. The inspiration was more powerful than any education I had received alone, including educational training received during my nursing days in psychiatry.

It is a journey that has taken me beyond the business that my gifts and talents bring, to a place where I can impart new life to those for whom the light has gone out in their lives. Without this journey it would not be possible to do that.

ANY GIVEN MOMENT

In any given moment you have the opportunity to change your life and the relationship with yourself for the better. I discovered that many of the clues for creating that change lie in the unread messages that we have superficially engaged with. I have shared one such personal message from the heart. Often the message has a familiar ring to it. What becomes new and powerful is when you engage with the message via a personal journey.

You can break free from past memories and their erroneous messages that hold you back from feeling alive. They are simply conditioned responses. The good news about conditioning is that once you know how it works you can also recondition yourself toward a new direction with relative speed. You can create new memories and empowering messages that will reignite your life starting with you.

Your honest appraisal of the relationship with yourself and the decision to change it for a new and more intimate bond is all you need to start. The rest of the resources will unfold on the journey itself.

FUEL FOR THE JOURNEY

Allow me to throw in some added fuel for your journey in the form of some powerful tips. Sprinkle your journey frequently with these tips so you can enjoy the journey and make a great adventure of it.

Imagine ....

I – Ignite your journey by surrounding yourself with things and people that inspire you

M – Make peace with yourself through becoming your best friend, and forgive yourself too

A – Appreciate yourself and your gifts, and ask more empowering questions of your life

G – Give to others, because you can choose to not for what you will get back.

I – Inject fun and humor into your life now

N – Never give up on your dream, playing big is better than playing not to lose

E – Explore life and express yourself with love and authenticity

This short journey it will make you want to go the distance. That is the power of an inspirational journey. I invite you to empower yourself with the gift of an inspired new you.

I love to gather and share truly inspirational journeys and I would love to hear about how you fare on this journey. I imagine a community of truly alive and inspired people from all over the world, igniting others from the new message they have created with their lives. I look forward to celebrating your journey with you.

Anita specializes in helping people eliminate the self-sabotaging behaviors that block fulfillment and success, and is author of the forthcoming book and song Breaking Free. http://www.breaking-free.co

LISTENING MINDFULLY: ABSORBING OURSELVES INTO THE MOMENT

Josh Misner

Whether we call them epiphanies, moments of clarity, there are moments in our lives when we are awestruck by a sense of profound self-realization. For me, those moments occur in the most peculiar settings. One of these events happened to me on a sweltering summer day while fueling the minivan outside a local convenience store. My wife had stepped inside to purchase drinks for us and our children, but what she emerged with commanded my attention: a comically large caffeine-enriched energy drink, a beverage I see my many of my students consuming in classes after pulling all-nighters during finals week. Considering my wife had never cared much for such canned rocket fuel, I asked her why she purchased it. When she informed me it was a "special treat" for my 12-year-old daughter, I had to retrieve my jaw from the pavement. My emotions blasted off, and I immediately interrogated her in my typically self-righteous, know-it-all demeanor, a tone she has often referred to as "lecture mode."

"Don't you know how bad that junk is for a 12-year-old?" The deafening silence as she then peered at me over the top of her glasses should have warned me I was treading on dangerous ground, but my indignation blinded me. "Did you ever think to ask me what *I* thought about giving her that much caffeine?" A quiet inner voice futilely whispered to the rational part of my brain, "Josh, what the hell are you doing?"

The argument that ensued may rank among the top 10 most volatile disputes in our relationship's history, but the most curious aspect was that throughout the argument, our respective points were comprised of two distinctly *different* arguments. From her viewpoint, it was my condescending, know-it-all tone, but from my vantage, it was what I perceived to be a flagrant disregard for my concerns regarding adolescent caffeine consumption. Looking back, the best solution would probably have been for both of us to walk away and allow our tempers to cool. However, at the time, all-out war seemed the more attractive option. Hours later, as I calmed down, clarity replaced adrenaline, and I finally realized what ignited the dispute. Unintentional and unrealized as it may have been, it was *my* presumptive and incessant need to be right. The imperious attack I launched on my wife's apparent lack of knowledge of the effects of caffeine on adolescents, in comparison to my pompous expertise (regarding a subject I should never attempt to debate with a real expert), caused me to react defensively. After all, my fragile ego was at stake.

Undoubtedly, there are people in this world who are capable of allowing others to be right, even when their truth is distorted. There may be people out there who can do so without having to think twice, but I have to wonder: why are people like myself not numbered among those more fortunate? More importantly, what can people in the same predicament as me do about this relentless need to be recognized as the most knowledgeable person in the room?

Before we can answer these questions, we must look into the nature of these situations, specifically at the interplay of ego, listening habits, and response mechanisms. For a possible solution to the effect of ego-defense on interpersonal dynamics, we may turn our attention to the East, to Buddhist writings that attempt to answer the problem of self-absorption, which predate the Freudian concept of ego by over two millennia (De Silva, 1994).

Buddhist wisdom traditions offer practical solutions for releasing oneself from the constraints imposed by excessive pride through the practice of mindfulness, which is the careful sense of consideration and awareness for the suffering of the other. When this concept of mindfulness is applied to a scenario such as the one mentioned above, a solution emerges for the inhibition of ego-defense through the cultivation and practice of mindful listening.

Contemporary psychoanalysis studies acknowledge the ego as the driving force behind individuals' behavior. Such studies have their roots in Freud's work, in which he stated that ego-defenses dictate instinctual drives and subsequent reactionary behavior. Such ego defenses are used to protect the fragile nature of the ego from painful or uncomfortable ideas and/or impulses. Nietzsche wrote of this nature in *The Will to Power*: "The 'ego' subdues and kills: it operates like an organic cell: it is a robber and it is violent. It wants to regenerate itself--pregnancy. It wants to give birth to its god and see all mankind at his feet."

Narcissism takes the concept of ego-defense a step further, defined by the American Psychiatric Association as "a pattern of grandiosity used to bolster and enhance a fragile sense of self-esteem." Although not all ego-defensive reactions are the result of clinically defined narcissism, low levels of narcissistic behavior are evident. In a 1960s study, Reich made a connection between narcissistic self-inflation of the ego and the regulation of self-esteem, in addition to linking feelings of competitiveness and contempt for others during interaction. In the case of the previous scenario, there was no conscious self-evaluation taking place within the heat of the moment, but rather, the use of defensive pride, self-centeredness, and high self-regard painted the tone for my reaction.

The connection between self-esteem and ego-defense is furthered by a set of nonverbal communication cues that reveal the intent of one's underlying defensive reaction. By conservative estimates, about 80% of all messages we send are nonverbal. Usually if what is being said does not match what is being displayed, then nonverbal cues are far more likely to be taken as the intent behind the message itself. Nonverbal behaviors contributing to an ego-defensive reaction are often described as demonstrating low confidence through uncertainty and aloofness, which is then compensated by an air of dominance and detachment. As the conversation continues, ego-defensive behavior results in frequent interruption, demonstrating the listener's lack of concern for the other person's ideas. Through these interruptions, the person engaging in ego-defensive behavior seems to move toward an end not shared by the other person.

Contemporary views on humility perceive it as a weakness more so than a desirable characteristic, despite being a core component of multiple religious and secular traditions from all over the world. Humility and its partner, patience, are required for listening, especially in cases where the other person makes inaccurate or untruthful statements. Closely related and bound with patience, is the construct of mindfulness, which is an active and fluid process involving a heightened sensitivity to the present moment. Mindfulness operates on three basic principles:

1) The ability to recognize the uniqueness of the present moment through intentional awareness.
2) The questioning of automatic behavior (such as ego-defensive reactions).
3) The ability to carefully consider alternative points of view.

Mindful listening involves being present and aware of potential preconceptions while listening to another person and resisting both external and internal distractions. In contrast, *mindless* listening, may be what J. Krishnamurti described in *The Book of Life*:

Do you listen with your projections, through your projection, through your ambitions, desires, fears, anxieties, through hearing only what you want to hear, only what will be satisfactory, what will gratify, what will give comfort, what will for the moment alleviate your suffering.

The characteristics of mindless listening are remarkably similar to the ego-defense-initiated reaction from my earlier story. If mindful listening is the antithesis to mindless listening (which we know is a byproduct of ego-defensiveness), then there is a high probability that through practicing mindful listening behaviors, the likelihood of ego-defensive responses decreases.

Through the combination of mindfulness (intentional, present-focused awareness) and listening, we arrive at a solution to remedy defensiveness and to promote deeper listening. To test this theory, I presented a mindful listening exercise to my students. I gave them instructions in mindful listening, which involved having them breathe slowly and intentionally while listening, noticing their thought processes as they listened, and resisting the urge to latch onto those thoughts and instead remain focused on the speaker. The experiment showed extremely positive results in reducing interference of preconceptions while listening. With a success rate of nearly 100%, students consistently reported the following results from the exercise:

» Dramatic increases in their ability to listen freely and patiently

» Not feeling rushed to compose their responses to the listener

» Greater appreciation for what was being said, regardless of the topic.

Additionally, some students reported performing the exercise during arguments, and stated that it led to more efficient dispute resolution and greater understanding for the other person's perspectives – *even when they disagreed*!

After reviewing the results of the classroom exercise, the first question I posed to myself was this: When was the last time I listened to my spouse so fully that I felt enthralled by what she was saying, regardless of the topic? My memory took me back to when I first met her, when everything was new, fresh, and we were falling madly in love. Thich Nhat Hanh discussed an intriguing analogy in several of his presentations, suggesting that, in the springtime of our relationship, my wife was like a beautiful flower. As such, I cared for her vigilantly and mindfully. As time passed and settled, the health of my "flower" changed for the worse with ever-reducing attention and waning care, my attention focused elsewhere. By focusing on other aspects of our lives and taking our relationship for granted, my behavior turned mindless, not having practiced the three key elements of mindful behavior: recognizing the uniqueness of the moment, questioning my automatic behavior, and weighing differing points of view.

When our relationship was in its infancy, I *studied* her more rigorously than I might study to write a paper. The investment of time and mental energy in the beginning produced vast appreciation for unique experiences from one moment to the next, little-to-no automatic responses, and more attention to her perspectives than my own. As the years went by, however, I may have subconsciously felt as though I had learned everything I needed to know. At some point my previous habit of "studying" my wife fell prey to a reprioritizing my mental energies elsewhere. What I failed to recognize was the blindingly obvious fact that people change over time and to keep current on those changes, mindful attention for the other is required. I realized that to reframe my ego and listen more deeply, I must first learn how to study those whom I love, with the notion that I still have much to learn.

The next question I asked myself was this: Could I think of a time when the other person stated something I knew to be inaccurate, but resisted the urge to correct that person? Eventually, I recalled an instance that also involved my wife. The details of the conversation are irrelevant, but I can clearly recall her making a speculation that I knew to be completely inaccurate and as she spoke, I felt justified in disagreeing with her. However, I refrained from doing so. As time passed, she proved her own speculation wrong through a natural course of events, which prompted her to admit fault casually, calmly, and without hesitation. I could have easily felt vindicated and shouted, "Ha, I was right!" Instead, I remember feeling admiration for her admitting her fault openly and with humility.

The other possible outcome of the scenario may have seen me acting on my ego-defensive impulses and correcting her faulty speculation straightaway. This likely would have created resentment, as well as an epic argument, like the one at the beginning of this chapter. By noticing my defensive response internally and allowing it to pass without acting upon it and allowing my wife to discover the truth for herself, I nurtured her potential for learning and self-growth. In the end, she felt empowered for having reached a conclusion independently and I felt rewarded for having helped her reach such a state rather than condescendingly correcting her.

Coming back to the story from the beginning, in the end, I approached my wife and acknowledged my error. Humbly, I admitted to having succumbed to a defensive and automatic reaction for the umpteenth time and asked forgiveness. Her response was justifiably cautious, prompting her to ask why I often exhibit an incessant need to be right. This question required some vulnerability. I admitted to massaging my fragile male ego to perpetuate the delusion that I was somehow intellectually mightier than others. I also acknowledged that, despite all my academic knowledge of communication, my listening skills may not be as mindful and effective as they should be, since I frequently spend more time on crafting clever responses than mindfully contemplating what has been spoken before responding.

Following our conversation and her subsequent forgiveness for my prior actions, I spent additional time in self-reflection with one final question: What might I do to ensure my listening is mindful, empathetic, and supportive of others? The first step is to become aware of when the ugly ego-defense monster rears its head, which is easily recognized by an overwhelming urge to interrupt, correct the other, or disagree, all before the other has finished speaking. Once this impulse is recognized, then self-awareness must replace ego-defense and re-center the focus on breathing, as well as the words of the other person.

Mindful listening takes the place of harmful automatic reactions, which leads to deeper understanding and empathy, but also results in the other person perceiving us as considerably more authentic and sincere. Eastern philosophy, along with other traditions worldwide, has stated for two and a half millennia that being fully aware of the present moment is a critical prerequisite to becoming more enlightened. The practice of mindfulness has shown itself to have broad clinical applications in reducing anxiety and depression, but this specific application also reduces those mindless and automatic responses that often plague many of our most important relationships. Mindful listening can drastically transform those relationships through patient humility required to set aside our distractions and focus on the presence of the other. As Leo Buscaglia stated, "Too often we underestimate the power of a touch, a smile, a kind word, a listening ear, an honest compliment, or the smallest act of caring, all of which have the potential to turn a life around." Listening is not passive when combined with a mindful presence. Mindful listening possesses the power to change the world, one person, one relationship, and one moment at a time.

Josh Misner, PhD is a communication professor and mindfulness expert whose work has been featured in The Huffington Post, Time, and Good Men Project. He is the author of several books on mindfulness as applied to various contexts of interaction, including The Dadly Way: 10 Steps to More Active Fatherhood and Equal Parenting. As a devoted husband and father of four, Dr. Misner also founded MindfulDad.org in 2012 to bring about awareness of the impact of mindfulness with respect to father-child relationships.

33844226R00201

Made in the USA
Middletown, DE
30 July 2016